the official

theory test

for drivers of large vehicles

valid for theory tests taken from 16 July 2001

London: The Stationery Office

Written and compiled by the Publications Unit of the Driving Standards Agency (DSA)

Questions and answers are compiled by the Question Development Team of the DSA with support from the National Foundation for Educational Research

Published by The Stationery Office with the permission of the Controller of Her Majesty's Stationery Office on behalf of the Driving Standards Agency.

First published 1996
Second edition 2000

ISBN 0 11 552225 5

A CIP catalogue record for this book is available from the British Library

Other titles in the Driving Skills series
The Official Theory Test for Car Drivers and Motorcyclists
The Official Theory Test for Motorcyclists
Motorcycle Riding – The Essential Skills
Official Motorcycling – CBT, Theory and Practical Test
The Official Driving Manual
The Official DSA Guide for Driving Instructors
Driving PCVs – the Official DSA Syllabus
Driving LGVs – the Official DSA Syllabus
The Official Guide to Tractor and Specialist Vehicle Driving Tests
The Official Driving Test
The Official Theory Test CD-ROM - 'Your Licence to Drive'
The Official Goods Vehicle Driving Video
The Official Guide to Accompanying Learner Drivers

Acknowledgements

The Driving Standards Agency would like to thank their staff and the following organisations for their contribution to the production of this publication.
National Foundation for Educational Research
Transport Research Laboratory
Department of Environment, Transport and the Regions
Driver & Vehicle Testing Agency, Northern Ireland

Every effort has been made to ensure that the information contained in this publication is accurate at the time of going to press. The Stationery Office cannot be held responsible for any inaccuracies.

Information in this book is for guidance only.

All metric and imperial conversions in this book are approximate.

Information

Theory and Practical Tests
DSA Bookings and Enquiries: 0870 01 01 372
DVTA (Northern Ireland) Booking and Enquiries: 0845 6006700

Faxes: 0870 01 04 372
Minicom: 0870 01 06 372
Welsh speakers: 0870 01 00 372

Postal applications for theory tests to:
Driving Standards Agency or Driver and Vehicle Testing Agency
PO Box 148
Salford M5 3SY

Driving Standards Agency:
(Headquarters)
Stanley House
Talbot Street
Nottingham NG1 5GU

Tel: 0115 901 2500
Fax: 0115 901 2510

Driver & Vehicle Testing Agency
(Headquarters)
Balmoral Road
Belfast BT12 6QL

Tel: 02890 681831
Fax: 02890 665520

Driver Vehicle Licensing Agency
(GB Licence Enquiries)
Tel: 0870 240 0009
Fax: 01792 783071
Minicom: 01792 782787

Driver and Vehicle Licensing Northern Ireland
Customer Services
Tel: 02870 341469
02890 250 500 (24 hours)
Minicom: 02870 341 380

Website addresses:
DSA: www.driving-tests.co.uk
DVTA: www.doeni.gov.uk/dvta

The Driving Standards Agency (DSA) is an executive agency of the Department of Environment, Transport and the Regions (DETR).

You'll see its logo at test centres.

DSA aims to promote road safety through the advancement of driving standards, by

- establishing and developing high standards and best practice in driving and riding on the road; before people start to drive, as they learn, and after they pass their test
- ensuring high standards of instruction for different types of driver and rider
- conducting the statutory theory and practical tests efficiently, fairly and consistently across the country
- providing a centre of excellence for driver training and driving standards
- developing a range of publications and other publicity material designed to promote safe driving for life.

DVTA

The Driver & Vehicle Testing Agency (DVTA) is an executive agency within the Department of the Environment for Northern Ireland. Its primary aim is to promote and improve road safety through the advancement of driving standards and implementation of the Government's policies for improving the mechanical standards of vehicles.

DSA Website

www.driving-tests.co.uk

DVTA Website

www.doeni.gov.uk/dvta

CONTENTS

PART FOUR   Further Information

As the driver of a large goods vehicle (LGV) or passenger carrying vehicle (PCV) you must have a high degree of vehicle handling skill to be considered 'professional' in the true sense of the word. You must also have knowledge and a clear understanding of the principles of safe driving and how to apply them. Whether you're responsible for the safe transportation of goods or passengers, the need for comprehensive knowledge is recognised by the requirement for a separate theory test.

Passing the theory test is an important step in becoming a professional driver. When you drive a large vehicle you should demonstrate your ability to drive safely and set a good example to others on the road. Your attitude and approach should be courteous and considerate. The safety of the goods or passengers you carry could depend on it.

This book will help you to prepare for your theory test. It contains the questions, set out in an easy-to-read style with plenty of illustrations. To aid learning, it explains why the answers are correct and identifies good driving practice.

Robin Cummins

The Chief Driving Examiner
Driving Standards Agency

This book will help you to

- study for your theory test
- prepare and be successful.

Part One gives you information on how to get started.

Part Two tells you about the test itself.

Part Three shows you the questions that may be used on your test. Your test will have 35 questions.

To become a professional driver you must have a thorough knowledge of the regulations that apply to your work. The questions in the theory test will test you on this knowledge. Combined with a high level of driving skill, this will ensure that you carry out your work safely.

If you're driving a passenger carrying vehicle (PCV) you'll be providing a service to paying customers. These passengers have been entrusted to your care. You should be aware of this and the responsibility it carries.

If you're driving a large goods vehicle (LGV) you must ensure that your goods arrive at their destination safely. This will involve not only the safety of your load but also your attitude to others on the road.

From the start, you must be aware of the differences between driving smaller vehicles and driving large buses or lorries.

You must have a sound knowledge of *The Highway Code*, including the meaning of traffic signs and road markings. You must be especially aware of those that indicate a restriction for lorries or buses.

Books for study

To prepare properly for the theory test DSA strongly recommends that you study the books from which the questions are taken. These books, known as the source material, consist of: *The Highway Code, Know Your Traffic Signs, The Official Driving Manual, Driving LGVs – the Official DSA Syllabus* (formerly known as *The Official Goods Vehicle Driving Manual)* and *Driving PCVs – the Official DSA Syllabus* (formerly known as *The Official Bus and Coach Driving Manual).*

Other media

There is an Official CD ROM available which contains all the questions and allows you to practise mock theory tests.

The Official Goods Vehicle Driving Video will help you on the road to a successful driving career.

These books will help you to answer the questions correctly and will also guide you when studying for your practical test. Keep them so that you can refer to them throughout your driving life. You can find them in most booksellers, together with relevant books from other publishers. Information about these, and other DSA products, appears at the back of this book.

It's important that you study – not just to pass the test, but to become a safe driver.

To ensure that all candidates are tested fairly, questions used in the theory test are under continuous review. Some of the questions used will be changed periodically to reflect changes in legislation, or as a result of customer feedback. There may be questions in your test that don't appear in this book. The information needed to answer them is available in the series of Driving Skills products and *The Highway Code.*

Driving is a life skill; your driving tests are just the beginning. When you pass your theory test you will be given a certificate. **This has a life of two years from the date of your test.** You will have to take and pass your practical test within this two-year period.

If you don't, you will have to take and pass the theory test again before a booking for a practical test can be accepted.

If you want to drive a large goods vehicle (LGV)

You must apply to the Driver and Vehicle Licensing Agency (DVLA) in Swansea for the provisional entitlement to drive large goods vehicles. Application forms D1 and information sheets D100 are available from post offices. In Northern Ireland (NI) apply to Driver and Vehicle Licensing Northern Ireland (DVLNI).

In order to drive a lorry you must

- have a full driving licence for category B vehicles (cars)
- hold a provisional LGV driving licence
- meet the eyesight and medical requirements
- normally be over 21 years old.

Full details can be obtained from the DVLA enquiry line on 0870 240 0009. In Northern Ireland telephone the DVLNI on 02870 341469.

When you receive your provisional licence you must

- sign it
- only drive under the supervision of a person who holds a current licence for the category of vehicle being driven (Minimum licence requirements apply. Check with your trainer.)

- display L plates (or D plates if you wish when driving in Wales) at the front and rear of the vehicle
- display LGV plates to the front and rear of the vehicle when driving in Northern Ireland.

You'll have to be fully qualified in a lower category of entitlement before seeking to gain entitlement in a higher category or sub-category.

You'll have to

- pass a category C test before taking a category C+E test
- pass a category C or C1 test before taking a category C1+E test.

You won't have to gain category C1 before taking a test in category C.

Register of Large Goods Vehicle Instructors

DSA maintains a Register of LGV Instructors. In order to gain entry onto the register instructors have to pass theory and practical examinations of their own driving and their instructional ability. Both these tests have to be passed to a high standard before entry onto the register is granted.

For details of the LGV Register Tel 0115 901 2625. There is no comparable register in NI.

If you want to drive a bus or coach (PCV)

Buses and coaches are referred to as passenger carrying vehicles (PCVs).

You must apply to the DVLA for the provisional entitlement to drive a PCV. Application forms D1 and information sheets (D100) are available from post offices.

In Northern Ireland apply to Driver and Vehicle Licensing Northern Ireland (DVLNI).

In order to drive a bus you must

- have a full driving licence for category B vehicles (cars)
- hold a provisional bus licence
- meet the eyesight and medical requirements
- normally be over 21 years old
- satisfactorily complete a criminal records check (NI only).

Full details can be obtained from the DVLA enquiry line on 0870 240 0009. In Northern Ireland phone the DVLNI on 02870 341469.

When you have your provisional licence you must

- check all the details are correct
- only drive under the supervision of a person who holds a current licence for the category of vehicle being driven (Minimum licence requirements apply. Check with your trainer.)
- display L plates (or D plates if you wish when driving in Wales) at the front and rear of the vehicle
- display PCV plates to the front and rear of the vehicle when driving in Northern Ireland.

You'll have to be fully qualified in the lower category of entitlement before seeking to gain entitlement in a higher category. You'll have to

- pass a category D test before taking a category D+E test
- pass a category D or D1 test before taking a category D1+E test.

You won't have to pass a test for a D1 (minibus) category before taking a test in category D.

Medical requirements

You'll be responsible for goods or passengers, so it's vital that you meet exacting medical standards. The medical requirements apply for both LGV and PCV licences.

You can't hold an LGV or PCV licence unless your eyesight meets the high standard required.

You must be fit and free from any condition that affects your ability to retain control of a large vehicle. If you're disabled you may drive a vehicle that has been especially adapted for you.

If this is your first application for either an LGV or a PCV licence you must have a medical. This must be carried out by a doctor. The medical report form D4 (DLM1 in Northern Ireland) must be completed and submitted with your licence application form.

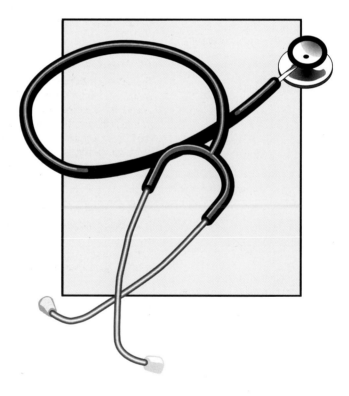

About the theory test

During your test questions will appear on a computer screen. You will select your answers by simply touching the screen.

This 'touch screen' system has been carefully designed to make it easy to use.

You can work through a practice session for up to 15 minutes to get used to the system before starting your test. Staff at the test centre will be on hand to help you if you have any difficulties.

The screens are easy to read. Only one question will appear on the screen at a time. You will be able to move backwards and forwards through the questions. You will also be able to 'flag' questions that you want to look at again. It is easy to change your answer.

Some questions ask you to select more than one answer option. The system will alert you if you have not completely answered a question.

Can I take my practical test first?

No. You have to take and pass your theory test before a booking for the practical test is accepted.

Does everyone have to take a theory test?

Normally those upgrading their licence within the same category will not have to sit the test. For instance, candidates upgrading from a rigid-bodied to an articulated lorry will not have to take the test. **However, anyone with sub-categories C1 and D1 entitlement, who obtained those categories when they passed their car test and wants to upgrade to a C or D licence will have to obtain the correct provisional entitlement and pass a theory test.**

If you have a full category C licence and wish to take a practical test for category D you will have to pass the appropriate theory test first, and vice versa.

How many questions are there?

There are 35 questions in the test. You should try to answer all of them. To pass you must answer at least 30 questions correctly.

How long do I have to complete the test?

Each test lasts for 40 minutes. You can take all this time if you need to. The time remaining for your test is displayed on screen.

Where do I have to go to take the test?

There are over 150 test centres throughout England, Scotland, Wales and Northern Ireland. Most people have a test centre within 20 miles of their home, but this will vary depending on the density of the population in your area. You can find a list of test centres at the back of this book.

When are the test centres open?

Sessions are provided on weekdays, evenings and on Saturdays. However, where demand is less than 100 tests per year test sessions may be less frequent.

Will I know the result straight away?

Not straight away but you should receive your result at the test centre within 30 minutes of completing the test.

If I don't pass, when can I take the theory test again?

You will have to wait a minimum of three clear working dáys before you take the theory test again. If you fail your test you've shown that you aren't fully prepared. Good preparation will save you time and money.

Can I bring a translator with me?

Yes. If you don't understand English you're allowed to bring a DSA or DVTA approved translator with you when you take your test. The Special Needs team at the booking office will tell you who is approved. When you have made arrangements with the translator you should tell the booking office who you intend to bring with you.

If you bring an approved translator with you the responsibility for the contractual arrangements, including the fee charged, is between you and the translator.

Are there any provisions for special needs?

Every effort has been made to ensure that the theory test can be taken by all candidates. It's important that you state your needs when booking so that the necessary arrangements can be made.

There is an English language voiceover, on a headset, to support candidates with dyslexia and other reading difficulties. You can also ask for up to double the normal time to take the test. As evidence of this requirement you will be asked to provide a letter from a teacher or educationalist, a psychologist or doctor (if appropriate). If it isn't possible to get this confirmation from a relevant professional, DSA, or DVTA, will consider a letter from an independent person who knows about your reading ability. This could be your employer, but if you are unsure about who to ask please telephone the Special Needs section on 0870 01 01 372 (Fax 0870 01 04 372) or on 0845 600 6700 in Northern Ireland.

DSA and DVTA are unable to take responsibility for the safe return of any original documentation sent, so it is advisable to send copies only.

If you require wheelchair access and your nearest test centre doesn't provide this, DSA or DVTA will arrange for you to take the test at a location suitable for you, such as a library or job centre, or take you to another test centre where the facilities are provided.

How do I book a test?

The easiest way to book a test is by telephone, using your credit or debit card. The person who books the test must be the card-holder.

If you book by this method you'll be given the date and time of your test immediately. You can do this by calling **0870 01 01 372** or **0845 600 6700** for Northern Ireland at any time between 8 am and 6 pm Monday to Friday. When you phone you should have ready your

- DVLA/DVLNI driving licence number
- credit or debit card details.

If you're deaf and need a minicom machine telephone **0870 01 06 372**.

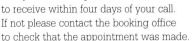

Welsh speakers can telephone **0870 01 00 372**.

You'll be given a booking number, and sent an appointment letter that you should expect to receive within four days of your call. If not please contact the booking office to check that the appointment was made.

Alternatively you can book a test by post.

Application forms are available from

- theory test centres
- driving test centres

Your driving instructor may also have one.

You should receive an appointment letter within 10 days of you posting your application form. If not, please telephone the booking office to check that your application was received and that a test appointment has been made.

DSA and DVTA cannot take responsibility for postal delays, If you miss your test appointment you will lose your fee.

How do I cancel or postpone a test?

To cancel or postpone a theory test appointment you should contact the booking office at least **three clear working days** before the test date otherwise you will lose your fee. Only in exceptional circumstances like documented ill-health or family bereavement can this rule be waived.

At the test centre

Make sure that you have all the necessary documents with you. All the documents must be original – DSA can't accept photocopies. You'll need

- **your signed driving licence and photo identity, or**
- **both parts of your signed photocard licence.**

The form of photographic identification acceptable at both theory and practical tests is as follows

- **your photocard driving licence**
- **your passport**, or document of like nature. Your passport doesn't have to be a British one.
- ***cheque guarantee card or credit card** bearing your photograph and signature
- **an employer's identity or workplace pass** bearing your photograph and name or signature or both
- **Trade Union Card** bearing your photograph and signature
- **Student Union Card** with reference to either the NUS or an education establishment/course reference number. The card must bear your photograph and name or signature or both
- **School Bus Pass** bearing the name of the issuing authority and your photograph and signature

- ***card issued in connection with sale and purchase of reduced-price railway tickets** bearing the name of the issuing authority and your photograph and signature. This is a card issued by a Railway Authority or other authorised body to purchase a reduced-price railway ticket (e.g. a Young Person's Railcard)
- ***Gun Licence**, including a Firearm or Shotgun Certificate, which bears your photograph and signature
- ***Proof of Age Card** issued by the Portman Group bearing your photograph and signature

*Not valid in Northern Ireland.

Remember...

No photo
No licence
No test

If you don't have any of these you can bring a signed photograph, together with a statement like the one shown below, that it's a true likeness of you. Both the statement, and the back of the photograph must be signed by the same person. This can be any of the following

- *Approved Driving Instructor, but not a trainee (pink licence) holder
- *DSA-certified motorcycle instructor
- Member of Parliament
- medical practitioner
- *local authority councillor
- teacher (qualified)
- Justice of the Peace
- civil servant (established)
- police officer
- bank official
- minister of religion
- barrister or solicitor
- *Commissioned Officer in Her Majesty's Forces
- *LGV Trainers on the DSA Voluntary Register of LGV Instructors.

*Not valid in Northern Ireland.

If you don't bring these documents on the day, you won't be able to take your test and you'll lose your fee. If you have any queries about what photographic evidence we will accept, contact the enquiry line on **0870 01 01 372** or **0845 600 6700** in Northern Ireland.

Arrive in plenty of time so that you aren't rushed. The test centre staff will check your documents and ensure that you receive the right category test. If you arrive after the session has started you may not be allowed to sit the test.

I (name of certifier), certify that this is a true likeness of , who has been known to me for (number) months / years in my capacity as

Signed

Dated

Daytime phone no.

LGV Trainer no.

11

Test Content

At the start of the test you'll have the opportunity to complete some practice questions. You can take up to 15 minutes on this practice session.

Most questions will ask you to mark ONE correct answer from four. Other questions will ask for TWO OR MORE correct answers from a selection. Some of the questions will show you a picture. This is to test your knowledge of traffic signs or your ability to spot a hazard. Look at the question carefully.

The questions will cover a variety of topics relating to road safety. Touch the box alongside the answers you think are correct.

Some questions will take longer to answer than others. There are no trick questions. If you're well prepared you won't find them difficult.

Take your time and read the questions carefully. You're given plenty of time, so relax and don't rush. Try to answer all 35 questions.

When you think you've finished, use the 'review' feature to check your answers before you end your test.

At the conclusion of the test you may be asked to complete trial questions for next years question bank. You may also be asked to complete a customer satisfaction survey. Both these help DSA and DVTA develop the test and the service provided.

this shows you which question you are seeing

your name and category of test here

this shows how much time you have remaining and will flash when you have 5 minutes left

this will flash to indicate how many answers are required for the question

question

touch the screen to indicate which answer(s) are correct. If you change your mind and you do not want that answer to be selected, touch it again. You can then choose another answer

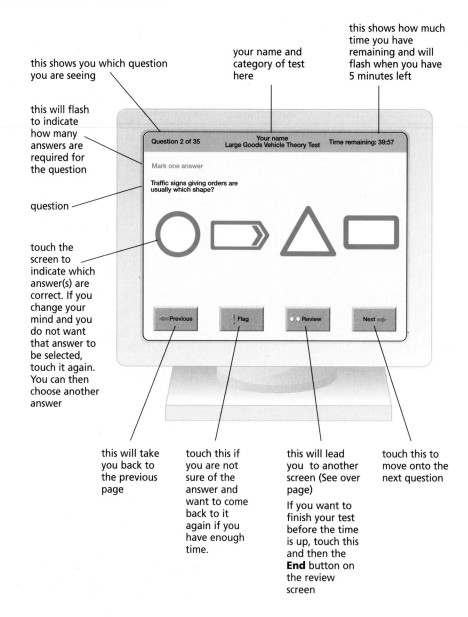

Question 2 of 35

Your name
Large Goods Vehicle Theory Test

Time remaining: 39:57

Mark one answer

Traffic signs giving orders are usually which shape?

Previous

Flag

Review

Next

this will take you back to the previous page

touch this if you are not sure of the answer and want to come back to it again if you have enough time.

this will lead you to another screen (See over page)

If you want to finish your test before the time is up, touch this and then the **End** button on the review screen

touch this to move onto the next question

Reviewing questions

When you press the review button you will see this screen.

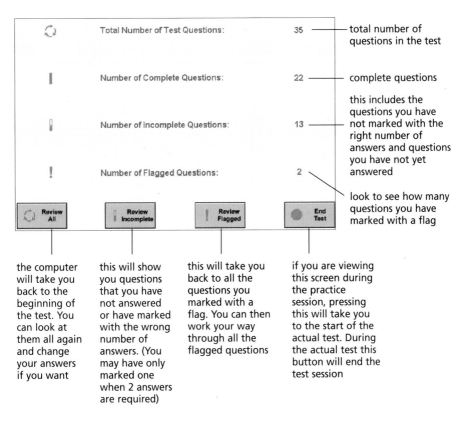

Total Number of Test Questions:	35	total number of questions in the test
Number of Complete Questions:	22	complete questions
Number of Incomplete Questions:	13	this includes the questions you have not marked with the right number of answers and questions you have not yet answered
Number of Flagged Questions:	2	look to see how many questions you have marked with a flag

Review All — the computer will take you back to the beginning of the test. You can look at them all again and change your answers if you want

Review Incomplete — this will show you questions that you have not answered or have marked with the wrong number of answers. (You may have only marked one when 2 answers are required)

Review Flagged — this will take you back to all the questions you marked with a flag. You can then work your way through all the flagged questions

End Test — if you are viewing this screen during the practice session, pressing this will take you to the start of the actual test. During the actual test this button will end the test session

When you have finished your test you will be shown some trial questions. These help us to see if we will use them in future theory tests. They **do not** count towards your final score.

We want to ensure that customers are completely satisfied with the level of service we provide. You will be shown some questions designed to give us some information about you and how satisfied you are with the service you have received from us. Your answers will be treated in strictest confidence. They are **not** part of the test and will not be used in determining your final score. You will be given a choice of whether you wish to complete the survey

About Part Three

In this part of the book you'll find questions that might be used in your theory test. The answers have been provided to help you to study.

For easy reference and to help you to study, the questions have been divided into topics and put into sections. Although this isn't how you'll find them in your test it's helpful if you want to refer to particular subjects.

The questions are in the left-hand column with a choice of answers beneath. On the right-hand side of the page you'll find the correct answers and a brief explanation of why they are correct. There will also be some advice on correct driving procedures.

DON'T JUST LEARN THE ANSWERS. It's important that you know **why** the answers are correct. This will help you with your practical skills and prepare you to become a safe and confident driver.

Taking exams or tests is rarely a pleasant experience, but you can make your test less stressful by being confident that you have the knowledge to answer the questions correctly.

Make studying more fun by involving friends and relations. Take part in a question-and-answer game. Test those 'experienced' drivers who've had their licence a while: they might learn something too!

Most of the questions refer to drivers of all large vehicles. Questions specifically for PCV drivers are marked with a bus symbol.

Questions specifically for LGV drivers are marked with a lorry symbol.

Some of the questions in this book will not be used in Northern Ireland theory tests. These questions are marked as follows

NI EXEMPT

Section 1

Weights and dimensions

This section looks at rules on vehicle weights and dimensions.

The questions will ask you about

- vehicle size

  the dimensions of your vehicle

- stowage and loading

  the importance of a secure load

- excessive exhaust smoke

  the effect that poorly maintained engines can have on the air around you

- vehicle markings

  the requirement for clear markings showing vehicle size and dimensions.

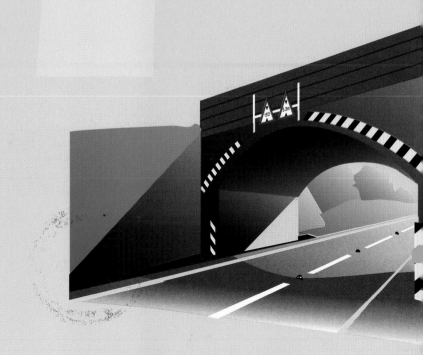

questions   answers

Q. 1.1

Mark one answer

Maximum authorised mass refers to the weight of

- [ ] your vehicle with passengers but no luggage
- [ ] your vehicle without passengers or luggage
- [ ] your vehicle with luggage but no passengers
- [ ] Your vehicle with both luggage and passengers

Answer

✓ Your vehicle with both luggage and passengers

Weight limits are imposed on roads and bridges for two reasons

- the structure may not be capable of carrying greater loads
- to divert larger vehicles to more suitable routes.

You're responsible for knowing the weight of your vehicle. Be aware of and understand the limits relating to any vehicle you drive.

The unladen weight can be found on the side of your vehicle.

Q. 1.2

Mark one answer

Fifteen passengers on your vehicle would increase the weight by about

- [ ] 0.5 tonnes
- [ ] 1 tonne
- [ ] 2.5 tonnes
- [ ] 3 tonnes

Answer

✓ 1 tonne

You must also be aware of the maximum authorised mass (MAM), which refers to the weight of your vehicle with both passengers and luggage.

Fifteen passengers would add approximately 1 tonne to the weight of your vehicle. You should also allow for any luggage that they may be carrying.

Q. 1.3

Mark one answer

As a guide, how many passengers equal about one tonne?

- [ ] 15
- [ ] 20
- [ ] 25
- [ ] 30

Answer

✓ 15

Your bus will move away more slowly and handle differently when fully laden with passengers and their luggage. You'll have to make allowances for this, especially when moving off uphill.

questions   answers

Q. 1.4

Mark one answer

Certain weight limit signs do not apply to buses. How would the driver know?

- ■ By a plate fitted beneath the weight limit sign
- ■ By the colour of the weight limit sign
- ■ By a plate attached to the vehicle
- ■ By a certificate carried by the driver

Answer

☑ **By a plate fitted beneath the weight limit sign**

Some weight restrictions apply to large goods vehicles (LGVs) alone and not to passenger carrying vehicles (PCVs). Look out for a plate beneath a restriction sign that indicates this.

Road signs show weight restrictions in various ways, and you should make yourself familiar with all of them, so that you're in no doubt about their meaning and relevance.

Q. 1.5

Mark one answer

What does this sign mean?

- ■ No entry for two-axled trailers
- ■ No entry for vehicles with two-speed axles
- ■ Maximum gross weight of 2 tonnes
- ■ Axle weight limit of 2 tonnes

Answer

☑ **Axle weight limit of 2 tonnes**

Always look out for road signs, but be especially aware of those that refer to large or heavy vehicles. Get into the habit of checking for signs at junctions. There might be an indication on the junction layout sign. Before you turn, ensure that the road you're using doesn't have any restrictions for the vehicle you're driving.

questions   answers

Q. 1.6

Mark one answer

This sign means no entry for goods vehicles

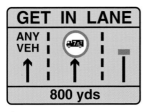

▮ under 7.5 tonnes maximum authorised mass

▮ over 7.5 tonnes maximum authorised mass

▮ over 7.5 metres overall height ·

▮ under 7.5 metres overall height

Answer

☑ **over 7.5 tonnes maximum authorised mass**

It's essential that all limits are complied with, in order to avoid overloading and possible prosecution.

Weight restrictions normally apply to the plated weight of a vehicle, often referred to as maximum authorised mass (MAM).

Q. 1.7

Mark one answer

Your lorry is over 7.5 tonnes maximum authorised mass. This sign means you may use

```
GET  IN  LANE
ANY I        I
VEH I  (7.5T) I   ▬
    ↑  I  ↑  I  ⊺
      800 yds
```

▮ either the left-hand or middle lane

▮ only the left-hand lane

▮ only the middle lane

▮ any of the lanes

Answer

☑ **only the left-hand lane**

Lanes at roadworks often carry weight restrictions to keep larger vehicles in the left-hand lane. The width of the lanes through the roadworks are very often narrowed and therefore not wide enough for large vehicles to overtake each other safely. Always look for restriction signs at roadworks. They are usually placed well in advance to give you time to move safely into the correct lane.

questions   answers

Q. 1.8

Mark one answer

You are driving a lorry with a maximum authorised mass of 7 tonnes. What is the maximum speed limit on a single carriageway?

- 30 mph
- 40 mph
- 50 mph
- 60 mph

Answer

✓ **50 mph**

Vehicles up to 7.5 tonnes MAM are allowed to travel at speeds of up to 50 mph on single carriageway roads.

Q. 1.9

Mark one answer

What is the national speed limit on a single carriageway road for a rigid lorry weighing more than 7.5 tonnes maximum authorised mass?

- 30 mph
- 40 mph
- 50 mph
- 60 mph

Answer

✓ **40 mph**

Vehicles exceeding 7.5 tonnes MAM are restricted to a maximum of 40 mph on single carriageway roads.

Q. 1.10

Mark one answer

Which of these lorries may normally use the right-hand lane of a three-lane motorway?

- Under 7.5 tonnes

- Over 7.5 tonnes

- Under 7.5 tonnes

- Over 7.5 tonnes

Answer

✓ Under 7.5 tonnes

Vehicles under 7.5 tonnes MAM may normally use the right-hand lane on a motorway, providing they are not pulling a trailer.

Be careful that you don't pull out into the path of faster traffic and make other drivers brake sharply to avoid a collision.

Q. 1.11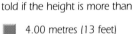

Mark one answer

You are driving a lorry over 7.5 tonnes maximum authorised mass. On a three-lane motorway you can only use the right-hand lane

- [ ] to overtake slower lorries
- [ ] when the left-hand lane is closed
- [ ] if you do not go faster than 60 mph
- [ ] if you are not towing a trailer

Answer

- [✓] **when the left-hand lane is closed**

Use of the right-hand lane on motorways with three or more lanes is not normally permissable for vehicles over 7.5 tonnes MAM, except in special circumstances.

Q. 1.12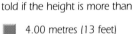

Mark one answer

You are driving a lorry with a high load. Telephone companies on the route must be told if the height is more than

- [ ] 4.00 metres (13 feet)
- [ ] 4.30 metres (14 feet 2 inches)
- [ ] 5.00 metres (16 feet 6 inches)
- [ ] 5.25 metres (17 feet 6 inches)

Answer

- [✓] **5.25 metres (17 feet 6 inches)**

When planning the movement of loads over 5.25 metres (17 feet 6 inches) high, telephone companies should be told of your intended route. You should tell them in plenty of time prior to making the journey.

questions

answers

Q. 1.13

Mark one answer

What does this sign mean?

- Slippery road
- Double bend
- Overhead electrified cable
- Cable laying ahead

Answer

✓ **Overhead electrified cable**

Look out for restrictions that you may not have seen on a map. These may be temporary or, in the case of this sign, permanent. You should also exercise care when entering

- loading bays
- bus and coach stations
- depots
- refuelling areas
- service station forecourts or any premises that have
- overhanging canopies.

Be careful when driving under

- bridges
- overhead cables
- overhead pipelines
- overhead walkways

or through road tunnels.

Q. 1.14

Mark one answer

This sign means

- no vehicles over 14 feet 6 inches wide
- no vehicles over 14 feet 6 inches high
- road humps 14 feet 6 inches apart
- weight limit of 14.6 tonnes

Answer

✓ **no vehicles over 14 feet 6 inches high**

Always be aware of the height of the vehicle you're driving, especially if you drive a variety of types of vehicle, or the loads you carry vary in shape or height.

Special maps are published that show weight and height limits on roads in the UK.

questions answers

Q. 1.15

Mark one answer

This sign warns of

■ low bridge ahead

■ accident ahead

■ tunnel ahead

■ accident blackspot ahead

Answer

☑ **tunnel ahead**

There may also be additional signs showing height and width restrictions.

If you're driving a high vehicle, make sure that there's enough headroom available for you to proceed through the tunnel.

Q. 1.16

Mark one answer

This sign means

400 yds

■ length of tunnel

■ length of low bridge

■ distance to tunnel

■ distance to low bridge

Answer

☑ **distance to tunnel**

The tunnel may have restrictions with regard to the available width of headroom for high vehicles.

The advance warning gives you the opportunity to find another route if your vehicle is too high or wide to proceed through the tunnel.

questions

answers

Q. 1.17

Mark one answer

The height of your vehicle is 4.3 metres (14 feet). What action should you take on the approach to this bridge?

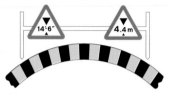

Keep to the centre of the arch and give way to oncoming traffic

Drive through slowly, keeping to the left of the marked limits

Keep to the centre of the arch and take priority over oncoming traffic

Drive through quickly, keeping to the left of the marked limits

Answer

☑ **Keep to the centre of the arch and give way to oncoming traffic**

The headroom under bridges in the UK is at least 5 metres (16 feet 6 inches) unless marked otherwise. But remember, this might mean the maximum height at only the highest point of an arch.

If your vehicle collides with a bridge, you must report the incident to the police. If a railway bridge is involved, you should also report it to Railtrack on 0345 114 141. In Northern Ireland you must report it to NIR as well as the police immediately.

Q. 1.18

Mark three answers

You are driving a vehicle higher than 3.0 metres (10 feet). Extra care must be taken when driving

through arched bridges

through road tunnels

near airports

near overhead cables

up steep hills

over narrow bridges

Answers

☑ **through arched bridges**

☑ **through road tunnels**

☑ **near overhead cables**

Care must be exercised when approaching any hazard where height is limited. Know the height of your vehicle, and don't take any risks. Stop if you're in any doubt, and if you're not sure that it's safe, take another route.

questions answers

Q. 1.19

Mark one answer

Unless otherwise shown, the headroom under bridges in the UK is at least

- 5.5 metres (18 feet)
- 4.0 metres (13 feet)
- 4.1 metres (13 feet 4 inches)
- 5.0 metres (16 feet 6 inches)

Answer

☑ **5.0 metres (16 feet 6 inches)**

Every year there are more than 750 accidents where vehicles hit railway or motorway bridges, most involving buses, coaches and lorries. Don't let one of them be yours. Not only can it cause major disruption, but if you're carrying passengers it could kill or injure them. There are also the costs involved in making the bridge safe, re-aligning railway tracks and ensuring the safety of rail passengers.

Q. 1.20

Mark one answer

What is the minimum height of an unmarked bridge?

- 4.5 metres (15 feet)
- 4.7 metres (15 feet 6 inches)
- 4.8 metres (16 feet)
- 5.0 metres (16 feet 6 inches)

Answer

☑ **5.0 metres (16 feet 6 inches)**

If there isn't a minimum height shown on the bridge the headroom (in the UK) will be at least 5 metres (16 feet 6 inches).

If you hit a railway bridge, or see another vehicle hit one, call Railtrack on 0345 114 141 and report the incident. In Northern Ireland you must report it to NIR and the police immediately.

Q. 1.21

Mark one answer

Your vehicle collides with a bridge. You must report it to

- the police
- the local authority
- your local garage
- the fire brigade

Answer

☑ **the police**

If it's a railway bridge, you must also inform Railtrack on 0345 114 141. In Northern Ireland you must report it to NIR as well as the police immediately.

questions

answers

Q. 1.22

Mark three answers

Your vehicle has collided with a railway bridge. You must telephone the railway authority to inform them of the

- [ ] damage caused
- [ ] type of bridge
- [ ] vehicle height
- [ ] bridge number
- [ ] vehicle number
- [ ] bridge location

Answers

- [x] **damage caused**
- [x] **bridge number**
- [x] **bridge location**

It's vital that the railway authority are given this information promptly, so that they can take action to prevent railway passengers being put at risk.

Q. 1.23

Mark one answer

Bells hanging across the road warn of

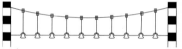

- [ ] a weight restriction
- [ ] trams crossing ahead
- [ ] overhead electric cables
- [ ] a railway level crossing

Answer

- [x] **overhead electric cables**

If your vehicle exceeds the safe travelling height beneath electrified overhead cables, bells suspended over the road will give you an audible warning. If your vehicle disturbs the bells you must stop immediately and seek advice.

questions   answers

Q. 1.24

Mark one answer

What does this sign mean?

- ▪ The width of the road is 6 feet 6 inches (2 metres)
- ▪ No vehicles over 6 feet 6 inches (2 metres) wide
- ▪ No vehicles over 6 feet 6 inches (2 metres) high
- ▪ Trailer length must not exceed 6 feet 6 inches (2 metres)

Answer

☑ **No vehicles over 6 feet 6 inches (2 metres) wide**

You must always be aware of the dimensions of your vehicle. Look out for road signs that show a width restriction. There will be an indication of this at the entrance to the road. Don't get into a situation where you have to reverse out of a narrow road or alley because you haven't seen a sign.

Q. 1.25

Mark one answer

What does this sign mean?

- ▪ Vehicle carrying dangerous goods in packages
- ▪ Vehicle broken-down ahead
- ▪ Holiday route
- ▪ Emergency diversion route for motorway traffic

Answer

☑ **Emergency diversion route for motorway traffic**

Major road works often cause complicated diversions for large vehicles. Drivers may be advised to follow a special symbol until the original road is rejoined.

Look for the yellow and black

- • square
- • triangle
- • diamond
- • circle

symbols, combined with additional information, to help you rejoin your route.

questions   answers

Q. 1.26

Mark one answer

This sign on a motorway means

- 11 tonnes weight limit
- stop, all lanes ahead closed
- leave the motorway at the next exit
- lane ahead closed

Answer

☑ **lane ahead closed**

Warning lights show when there are dangers ahead, such as

- lane closures
- accidents
- fog
- icy roads.

Q. 1.27

Mark one answer

You are driving on a motorway. You see this sign. It means end of

- restriction
- crawler lane
- weight limit
- hard shoulder

Answer

☑ **restriction**

Look out for variable-message warning signs advising you of

- lane closures
- speed limits
- hazards.

questions   answers

Q. 1.28

Mark one answer

You are driving a long vehicle. Your main concern at this hazard is your vehicle's

- ▓ height
- ▓ width
- ▓ weight
- ▓ length

Answer

☑ **length**

Always be alert for situations where the size of your vehicle can get you into difficulties. You should know the weight, width, length, height and ground clearance of your vehicle. If in doubt, don't attempt to go where you may have to reverse an unreasonable distance.

Q. 1.29

Mark three answers

When driving a low loader you should be aware of grounding on

- ▓ level crossings
- ▓ traffic calming humps
- ▓ yellow rumble strips
- ▓ hatched road markings
- ▓ hump back bridges

Answers

☑ **level crossings**

☑ **traffic calming humps**

☑ **hump back bridges**

Traffic calming measures are becoming more common. You should know the size of your vehicle and plan well ahead. Look out for signs informing you of hazards that will affect your vehicle. Change your route if necessary rather than take risks.

Q. 1.30 🚚

Mark one answer

You are driving a low loader. You see this sign. Your main concern is

- ▓ the ground clearance
- ▓ the weight limit
- ▓ the height limit
- ▓ the load

Answer

☑ **the ground clearance**

As the driver of a low loader you have a special responsibility to be aware of the dimensions, including ground clearance, of your vehicle. When planning your route you will have to consider some of the following hazards

- weight
- length
- height
- ground clearance.

questions   answers

Q. 1.31

Mark one answer

You are driving a vehicle that is over 17 metres (55 feet) long. What should you do at a level crossing?

- Cross over using your horn and hazard warning lights

- Stop before the crossing and phone the signal operator

- Increase your speed to clear the crossing quickly

- Stop before the crossing and look both ways before going on

Answer

☑ **Stop before the crossing and phone the signal operator**

If your vehicle is over 17 metres (55 feet) long and you wish to cross a level crossing, you must stop before the level crossing and telephone the signal operator. There may be a risk of grounding as you drive your vehicle across.

Q. 1.32

Mark one answer

When lorries and their loads exceed a certain length the police must be notified and an attendant carried. Which of the following lengths would this apply to?

- 15.5 metres (51 feet)

- 16.5 metres (54 feet)

- 19.4 metres (63 feet 6 inches)

- 27.4 metres (90 feet)

Answer

☑ **27.4 metres (90 feet)**

If your vehicle is over 27.4 metres (90 feet) in length you must notify the police before you undertake a journey. Such vehicles are designed to carry exceptionally long loads only. The vehicle will need an attendant, and should be clearly marked with the appropriate boards to indicate its exceptional size.

Q. 1.33

Mark three answers

In which of the following places might vehicles over a certain length be restricted?

- ☐ On ferries
- ☐ At freight terminals
- ☐ In road tunnels
- ☐ On dual carriageways
- ☐ On motorways
- ☐ On level crossings

Answers

- ☑ **On ferries**
- ☑ **In road tunnels**
- ☑ **On level crossings**

Look out for restrictions for long vehicles. There are few, compared to width or height restrictions, but they're found where turning facilities are restricted or there's a risk of grounding.

Q. 1.34 🚚

Mark one answer

What types of fastenings or restraints should you use when carrying a heavy load of steel?

- ☐ Chains
- ☐ Straps
- ☐ Ropes
- ☐ Sheeting

Answer

- ☑ **Chains**

YOU are responsible for the safety of the load you're carrying. At no time should the load endanger other road users. It's therefore vital that you ensure your load is secure and safely distributed on your vehicle. The method to ensure this will differ according to

- bulk
- weight
- the type of vehicle you're driving (flat bed, curtain side, etc.)
- the nature of the load.

questions   answers

Q. 1.35

Mark one answer

Ideally how should you secure an ISO steel cargo container onto your vehicle or trailer?

■ Using battens and chocks

■ Using straps

■ Using twist locks

■ Using ropes

Answer

✅ **Using twist locks**

If you're carrying a steel ISO (International Standards Organisation) cargo container, ropes or straps won't be strong enough to take the strain. This type of load requires a special type of restraint using twist locks.

Q. 1.36

Mark one answer

How wide can a load be before you must have side markers?

■ 2.0 metres (6 feet 6 inches)

■ 2.9 metres (9 feet 6 inches)

■ 3.5 metres (11 feet 6 inches)

■ 4.3 metres (14 feet 2 inches)

Answer

✅ **2.9 metres (9 feet 6 inches)**

If your load is over 2.9 metres (9 feet 6 inches) wide it then must display side markers. Make sure that they're clearly visible, at both the front and rear, and that they indicate the actual width projection.

Q. 1.37

Mark one answer

You must drive your lorry at lower speed limits when its load is wider than

■ 2.7 metres (9 feet)

■ 3.4 metres (11 feet)

■ 4.0 metres (13 feet)

■ 4.3 metres (14 feet 2 inches)

Answer

✓ **4.3 metres (14 feet 2 inches)**

Wide loads that are 4.3 metres (14 feet 2 inches) to 5 metres (16 feet 6 inches) wide are subject to the following speed limits

- 30 mph on motorways
- 25 mph on dual carriageways
- 20 mph on all other roads.

Q. 1.38

Mark three answers

You are driving a lorry with a wide load. The width of the load is between 3.5 metres (11 feet 6 inches) and 4.3 metres (14 feet 2 inches). Which three of the following apply?

■ Side markers must be shown

■ The police must be notified

■ An attendant must be carried

■ Reduced speed limits apply

■ Department of Transport approval must be obtained

Answers

✓ **Side markers must be shown**

✓ **The police must be notified**

✓ **An attendant must be carried**

Side markers must comply with regulations so that they show clearly on either side of the projection to the front and rear. All marker boards must be independently lit at night.

Q. 1.39

Mark one answer

Triangular projection markers are required when your load is wider than 2.9 metres (9 feet 6 inches). What colour are these?

■ Black/yellow

■ Red/yellow

■ Black/white

■ Red/white

Answer

✓ **Red/white**

The marker boards should be red and white. To ensure that they're seen clearly by other road users they must be kept clean and independently lit at night and in poor visibility.

questions answers

Q. 1.40

Mark one answer

You are driving a lorry carrying a load which is 4.5 metres (14 feet 9 inches) wide. What is your maximum allowed speed on a motorway?

- 10 mph
- 20 mph
- 30 mph
- 40 mph

Answer

☑ **30 mph**

Speed limits imposed on vehicles carrying abnormal loads can be frustrating for other drivers, but don't be tempted to exceed the speed limit.

Remember, the more weight you are carrying, the longer it will take you to stop safely.

Q. 1.41

Mark one answer

What is the maximum speed limit on a dual carriageway for a lorry carrying a load which is 4.5 metres (14 feet 9 inches) wide?

- 15 mph
- 25 mph
- 35 mph
- 45 mph

Answer

☑ **25 mph**

Dual carriageways have more places where crossing traffic can be a danger. Don't exceed the speed limits imposed on your loaded vehicle. The distance you need to stop will increase significantly with each extra mile per hour.

Q. 1.42

Mark one answer

Markings are required on the rear of lorries over 7.5 tonnes maximum authorised mass.What colour are these?

- Red/white
- Red/yellow
- Black/yellow
- Black/white

Answer

☑ **Red/yellow**

All vehicles over 7.5 tonnes must have markings on the rear of the vehicle. These are to inform other road users of the different characteristics of your vehicle.

These markings are rectangular and coloured red and yellow. They should be kept clean so that they can be seen clearly at all times, especially at night and in poor visibility.

Q. 1.43

Mark one answer

A passenger comments on exhaust smoke in the vehicle. You should

☐ report it as soon as you return to the depot

☐ stop and have the fault put right

☐ avoid heavy revving of the engine when stationary

☐ have the emissions checked at the next vehicle inspection test

Answer

☑ **stop and have the fault put right**

All road users should try to reduce the effects that vehicles have on the environment. Larger vehicles have larger engines and therefore produce more exhaust fumes. Try to cut down on the amount of fumes that your vehicle produces, and don't increase them by

* revving the engine
* long periods of static running
* ignoring comments about excessive smoke by passengers or other road users.

Q. 1.44

Mark one answer

Thick black smoke is coming from the exhaust of your vehicle. You should

☐ continue on to the nearest garage

☐ return to your depot and report the problem

☐ stop in a safe place and get help

☐ drive slowly with your hazard warning lights on

Answer

☑ **stop in a safe place and get help**

Causing excessive smoke is an offence and could contribute to causing an accident. Mechanical defects could become dangerous if ignored. You could also end up creating traffic chaos if your vehicle breaks down in a difficult location.

questions   answers

Q. 1.45

Mark one answer

At this roundabout you intend to take the fourth exit. On this road there is a limit on

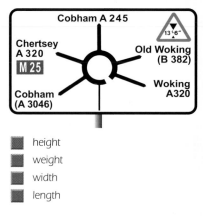

Cobham A 245

Chertsey A 320

M 25

Cobham (A 3046)

Old Woking (B 382)

Woking A320

- ◼ height
- ◼ weight
- ◼ width
- ◼ length

Answer

☑ **height**

Be alert for signs giving you forward information of bridge heights. As a professional driver you should always know the height of your vehicle or load. If you aren't sure of the safe height, STOP and check. Don't take chances.

Q. 1.46

Mark one answer

When using passing places on narrow roads you will MOST need to be aware of your vehicle's

- ◼ length
- ◼ roof height
- ◼ ground clearance
- ◼ weight

Answer

☑ **length**

On single-track roads, if your vehicle is too long to get completely into a passing place you may need to wait opposite it to allow a following or opposing road user to pass. On this type of road you need to plan and look well ahead so as to avoid meeting another road user at an inappropriate place.

Q. 1.47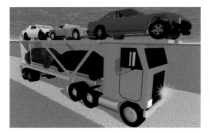

Mark one answer

When this vehicle turns, the overhang of the top deck will swing through

- a greater arc than the cab
- a lower arc than the cab
- a smaller arc than the cab
- the same arc as the cab

Answer

☑ **a greater arc than the cab**

As the top deck is longer than the cab and trailer, it will take up more room as the vehicle turns.

You must make sure before turning that you've allowed for the wider swing of the deck. Even though your cab is well clear, the overhanging deck could hit telegraph poles or traffic signs as you go through the corner.

Q. 1.48

Mark one answer

You are the driver of an articulated car transporter. When turning corners, you should be aware that the overhang of the top deck swings through a

- smaller arc than the cab
- shorter arc than the cab
- lower arc than the cab
- greater arc than the cab

Answer

☑ **greater arc than the cab**

The longer top deck needs a wider turning circle than the cab below it. To avoid hitting lamp posts or telegraph poles etc., you must be careful to allow for this overhang when turning.

questions

answers

Q. 1.49

Mark one answer

The driver of a car transporter must be most aware of the trailer front-overhang when

▢ overtaking

▢ turning

▢ loading

▢ braking

Answer

☑ **turning**

The long overhang at the front of a car transporter can cause problems where street furniture such as lamp posts and traffic signs are sited close to junctions. Particular problems may be encountered when there are Keep Left bollards in the middle of the road you are turning right into. Plan your route carefully to avoid situations where you may collide with hazards or have to reverse or turn round.

Q. 1.50

Mark one answer

When driving in traffic on a motorway you see a lorry too close behind. You should

▢ increase your distance from the vehicle in front

▢ touch the brake pedal sharply to show your brake lights

▢ briskly accelerate away from the vehicle behind

▢ switch your rear fog lamps on and off

Answer

☑ **increase your distance from the vehicle in front**

The faster the traffic is moving, the greater the distance which needs to be kept between vehicles to maintain safety margins. As a minimum always apply the two second rule in good, dry conditions. In extremely poor weather conditions you'll need up to ten times the stopping distance that you need in the dry.

questions answers

Q. 1.51

Mark one answer

You are driving a vehicle pulling a trailer in the left hand lane of a three lane motorway. You see this sign. You should

- [ ] move to the right-hand lane
- [ ] move to the hard shoulder and stop
- [ ] slow down and stay in the lane you are in
- [ ] slow down and leave the motorway at the next exit

Answer

☑ **move to the right-hand lane**

Temporary lane closures allow you to use the far right-hand lane when towing a trailer. Always check your mirrors carefully before changing lane, and don'tcut across the path of faster traffic. Look and signal early, and remember how quickly vehicles can approach from behind. The sooner you indicate, the more time other drivers will have to prepare.

Q. 1.52

Mark one answer

You are driving on a motorway. Your stopping distance can increase by up to ten times if the road surface is

- [ ] bumpy
- [ ] icy
- [ ] worn
- [ ] wet

Answer

☑ **icy**

Winter weather conditions affect all types of roads. Don't be misled by other drivers who are driving too fast.

All but the gentlest braking will lock your wheels on ice. If your front wheels lock, you can't steer. If you can't steer, you can't keep out of trouble.

Q. 1.53

Mark one answer

You are driving on the motorway in icy conditions. Your stopping distance can increase by up to

- [ ] 2 times
- [ ] 4 times
- [ ] 10 times
- [ ] 20 times

Answer

☑ **10 times**

Adequate separation distances are vital when driving on icy roads. You can never have too much safe space around your vehicle in these conditions. Motorways that appear wet may in fact be frozen.

Remember, all braking should be carried out gently to reduce the risk of losing control.

questions answers

Q. 1.54

Mark one answer

When towing a trailer the maximum speed allowed on a motorway is

- 40 mph
- 50 mph
- 60 mph
- 70 mph

Answer

☑ **60 mph**

On motorways with more than two lanes, caravans or trailers must not be towed in the outside lane unless other lanes are closed.

Q. 1.55

Mark one answer

On a motorway, how far from the exit is the first sign showing the junction number?

- Half a mile
- One mile
- Two miles
- Three miles

Answer

☑ **One mile**

Motorway traffic travels at higher speeds, and advance signs warning of junctions are vital to enable you to be in the correct lane in good time to take your exit. One mile before the exit you will see a junction sign with road numbers. Half a mile before the exit the sign will also include the names of places accessible from that junction.

Q. 1.56

Mark one answer

In which one of these places may you park large vehicles at night without lights on?

- In an 'off road' parking area
- On a road with a 20 mph speed limit
- At least 10 metres (32 feet 6 inches) away from any junction
- In most lay-bys

Answer

☑ **In an 'off road' parking area**

Off-road lorry/coach parks are often well lit and patrolled by police or security firms.

Never leave your vehicle unlit on a public road or lay-by after dark.

questions

answers

Q. 1.57

Mark three answers

Which of the following is most likely to cause danger to a group of horse riders?

- Powerful brake lights
- Size of your vehicle
- Noise of your vehicle
- The hiss of air brakes
- Leaving plenty of room
- Reacting in good time

Answers

- ☑ **Size of your vehicle**
- ☑ **Noise of your vehicle**
- ☑ **The hiss of air brakes**

The size of your vehicle can be intimidating, as well as reducing the amount of room left for others. Any noise can easily startle horses. You should take care to leave as much room as you can for riders, and keep the noise to a minimum by gentle use of the brakes and, if necessary stopping and turning your engine off.

Q. 1.58

Mark three answers

Which of these should you do when passing sheep on a road?

- Pass quickly and quietly
- Tap your horn once
- Drive very slowly
- Allow plenty of room
- Be ready to stop

Answers

- ☑ **Drive very slowly**
- ☑ **Allow plenty of room**
- ☑ **Be ready to stop**

Animals can be very unpredictable. You should give them as much room as you can, keep speed and noise down to a minimum to avoid panicking them, and always be ready to stop if necessary.

Q. 1.59

Mark three answers

You should show extra consideration for pedestrians when driving past

- mobile shops
- open moorland
- shopping areas
- ice cream vans
- motorway service areas
- suspension bridges

Answers

- ☑ **mobile shops**
- ☑ **shopping areas**
- ☑ **ice cream vans**

In all three of these situations, pedestrians may suddenly step out into the road. In particular, where mobile shops or ice cream vans are concerned, there may be children hidden from view who could suddenly run into your path. Always keep your speed down, and be extra observant when approaching these situations.

questions answers

Q. 1.60

Mark one answer

At a toucan crossing you should look out for pedestrians and

 horse riders

■ cyclists

■ motorcyclists

■ trams

Answer

✓ **cyclists**

A toucan crossing is traffic light controlled, but differs from a pelican crossing by not having a flashing amber light in the sequence.

Cyclists and pedestrians share the crossing and get the green signal together. Cyclists are permitted to ride across. The signals are push-button operated.

Q. 1.61

Mark one answer

On which of the following pedestrian crossings can a cyclist ride across, without dismounting, when pedestrians are crossing over?

 Toucan

■ Pelican

■ Puffin

■ Zebra

Answer

✓ **Toucan**

Toucans are shared crossings, where cyclists may ride across alongside pedestrians. Look out for them where you see signs and markings for cycle tracks.

Q. 1.62

Mark one answer

Certain types of crossings are shared by pedestrians and cyclists. Which one of these may a cyclist ride across at?

 Puffin

■ Zebra

■ Pelican

■ Toucan

Answer

✓ **Toucan**

Where a cycle track meets a busy road you may also find a toucan crossing. They're similar to other types of crossing, but have no flashing amber signal.

questions answers

Q. 1.63

Mark one answer

Ahead of you, in the middle of the road, there is a slow-moving motorcyclist. You are unsure what the rider is going to do. You should

- [ ] pass on the left
- [ ] pass on the right
- [ ] move closer
- [x] stay behind

Answer

 stay behind

Be patient, the rider may have a mechanical problem or be looking for a street name or house number. In these circumstances the only thing to be sure about is that your course of action doesn't put the rider at risk.

Q. 1.64

Mark one answer

You are about to overtake a motorcyclist. They look over their right shoulder. It is most likely that

- [x] the rider intends moving to the right
- [ ] something has fallen from the machine
- [ ] the drive chain is slack
- [ ] the rear tyre is flat

Answer

 the rider intends moving to the right

Anticipating the rider's next action in good time could prevent a serious accident, and the assessment you make is part of the forward planning of your overtaking manoeuvre.

Q. 1.65

Mark one answer

Having just overtaken a motorcyclist on a motorway you MUST always check the

- [ ] speedometer
- [x] left mirror
- [ ] right mirror
- [ ] road ahead

Answer

 left mirror

When overtaking with a long vehicle it is very important to be aware of the position of the road user you are overtaking. You must carefully check the nearside mirror to ensure that you have passed safely before returning to the left.

Motorcyclists require special attention as they are more vulnerable and may be affected by buffeting from your vehicle.

questions

answers

Q. 1.66

Mark one answer

'Red Routes' tell you that

- special waiting restrictions apply
- part-time traffic lights operate
- drivers have to pay a toll
- night-time and weekend weight limits apply

Answer

✓ **special waiting restrictions apply**

The main types of 'Red Route' controls are

- double red lines
- single red lines
- parking boxes
- loading boxes (red and white).

Red loading boxes allow up to 20 minutes for loading outside of rush hours.

White loading boxes allow up to 20 minutes for loading at any time during the day.

Q. 1.67

Mark one answer

When approaching a zebra crossing you should

- stop before the zig-zag lines
- wave pedestrians across the road
- sound the horn and flash headlights
- be prepared to stop in good time

Answer

✓ **be prepared to stop in good time**

Always keep your speed down on the approach to zebra crossings. This will allow you to stop safely if necessary.

On the approach look well ahead for anyone about to cross.

Q. 1.68

Mark one answer

You are driving behind a moped. You want to turn left at a junction just ahead. You should

- stay behind until the moped has passed the junction
- overtake the moped before the junction
- pull alongside the moped and stay level until just before the junction
- sound your horn as a warning and pull in front of the moped

Answer

✓ **stay behind until the moped has passed the junction**

Planning your driving will ensure that you anticipate where the moped rider will be in relation to the junction as you arrive to turn left.

Overtaking prior to making a left turn is selfish and could result in an avoidable accident, particularly when driving a long vehicle.

Q. 1.69

Mark one answer

Why should you allow EXTRA room to motorcyclists who are riding through road works?

- ■ There may be a reduced speed limit
- ■ There may be temporary traffic lights
- ■ They may swerve to avoid potholes
- ■ The traffic may be in single file

Answer

✓ **They may swerve to avoid potholes**

Motorcyclists ride through narrow gaps in traffic and generally don't take up as much room as a car.

However, other factors, including road surface, can affect their stability. It is wise to give them an extra safety margin when possible.

Q. 1.70

Mark one answer

At roadworks motorcyclists might swerve to avoid potholes. You should

- ■ give them extra room
- ■ keep alongside them
- ■ try to pass them
- ■ stay close behind them

Answer

✓ **give them extra room**

Always try to anticipate the other road user's next move. Good forward planning can help you to keep other road users out of trouble. Information to help you achieve this is available if you look for it; keep your eyes moving and watch for clues.

A motorcyclist taking a 'lifesaver' look over his/her shoulder could be showing their intention to change direction.

Q. 1.71

Mark one answer

You are scheduled to make a delivery. You arrive at your destination during the morning rush hour. The road is edged with double red lines. You should

- ■ unload only within a 'white box' area
- ■ unload only within a 'red box' area
- ■ delay your delivery until after the rush hour
- ■ limit your stop to a maximum of 30 minutes

Answer

✓ **unload only within a 'white box' area**

White boxes allow you to unload at any time, but during the day the length of stay is restricted to a maximum of 20 minutes.

At other times, such as between 7 pm and 7 am, and on Sundays, unrestricted stopping is allowed.

questions answers

Q. 1.72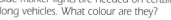

Mark one answer

You are driving a bus on a local service. You can use this lane

■ between 4 pm and 6.30 pm only

■ before 4 pm and after 6.30 pm only

■ at any time of the day

■ any time except Saturdays

Answer

✓ **at any time of the day**

As a local service bus driver you may use the bus lane at any time.

The restrictions apply to other road users to keep it clear for you at peak times.

Don't be tempted to speed when driving up the inside of slow-moving or stationary traffic. Be alert for pedestrians who may be trying to cross the road.

Q. 1.73

Mark one answer

Side marker lights are needed on certain long vehicles. What colour are they?

■ White

■ Amber

■ Red

■ Green

Answer

✓ **Amber**

Side marker lights are important at night. When you emerge or turn across traffic they help to alert other road users to your presence.

Make sure that they are kept clean at all times.

Q. 1.74

Mark one answer

Another vehicle has overtaken you and has pulled in too close in front. You should

 slow down

■ drive on close behind

■ overtake the vehicle

■ flash your headlights

Answer

✓ **slow down**

Tailgating is dangerous. Even if you feel aggrieved by the actions of another driver, following too close places you in unnecessary danger. Your view of the road ahead will be seriously reduced, and you won't be able to see or plan effectively. Some police forces have mounted campaigns to video and prosecute offenders.

questions

answers

Q. 1.75

Mark one answer

A large vehicle is most stable when driven in a straight line under

- harsh acceleration
- gentle braking
- gentle acceleration
- harsh braking

Answer

☑ **gentle acceleration**

The hallmark of a professional driver is being in the correct gear at the correct speed for all situations, and maintaining optimum progress smoothly and safely at all times.

Continuing commitment and practice are necessary to acquire the skills required to be called 'professional'.

Q. 1.76

Mark one answer

You are driving a lorry with a maximum authorised mass of more than 7.5 tonnes. What is the national speed limit on a dual carriageway?

- 40 mph
- 50 mph
- 60 mph
- 70 mph

Answer

☑ **50 mph**

Be considerate to other road users who may be travelling faster. Don't hog the middle or outside lane unnecessarily.

Make good use of your mirrors before signalling, in good time, your intention to change lanes.

Q. 1.77

Mark one answer

The national speed limit for buses and coaches on a dual carriageway is

- 55 mph
- 60 mph
- 65 mph
- 70 mph

Answer

☑ **60 mph**

Don't be tempted to drive on the limiter when using dual carriageway roads. The speed limit for passenger carrying vehicles is 60 mph.

Be considerate to faster moving traffic by not using the middle or outside lanes unnecessarily.

questions

answers

Q. 1.78

Mark one answer

You should be careful NOT to allow your vehicle to spill diesel fuel onto the road. It can be a serious risk ESPECIALLY to

- motorcycles
- empty tankers
- towed vehicles
- fire engines

Answer

✓ **motorcycles**

Those on two wheels don't have the same stability as other vehicles. Where the road surface has been made slippery, they're particularly vulnerable to skidding, and could fall from the vehicle altogether.

Q. 1.79

Mark one answer

You are driving a petrol tanker. 'Roll-over' is least likely to occur on vehicles fitted with

- tandem axles with double wheels
- tandem axles with air suspension
- tri-axles with single wheels
- tri-axles with double wheels

Answer

✓ **tri-axles with single wheels**

The type of suspension fitted to a vehicle will influence its resistance to roll-over. Modern tri-axle semi-trailers fitted with single wheels on each side extend the tracking width available, compared to twin-wheeled units, and are more stable.

Q. 1.80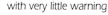

Mark one answer

You are driving a petrol tanker. The change from 'rear wheel lift' to 'roll-over' occurs

- only at roundabouts
- with very little warning
- with plenty of warning
- only when fully loaded

Answer

✓ **with very little warning**

The transition from rear wheel lift to roll-over is more rapid on vehicles equipped with air suspension systems.

Make sure you take advantage of any extra training that may be available to drivers of this type of vehicle.

questions   answers

Q. 1.81

Mark one answer

You are the driver of a refrigerated vehicle loaded with hanging meat carcasses. You should be especially careful when turning corners because of the

■ wave effect
■ camber effect
■ gravity effect
■ pendulum effect

Answer
☑ **pendulum effect**

As you turn a corner, the hanging meat carcasses will all swing to one side of your vehicle adding extra pulling forces towards the outside of the curve. The faster you turn a corner, the greater this force will be. Even after taking the corner the carcasses will continue to swing back and forth like pendulums, making the vehicle unstable.

Keeping your speed down while cornering will help prevent your vehicle from being in danger of turning over.

Q. 1.82

Mark one answer

At overnight stops many drivers park with their rear doors close to another lorry. This is to

■ keep the load safe
■ ensure a clear path
■ keep 'same company' lorries together
■ stop the theft of their fuel

Answer
☑ **keep the load safe**

Load security is extremely important. Make sure you park legally and preferably, in a well lit area.

Some lorry parks are patrolled regularly by the police or security services.

questions answers

Q. 1.83

Mark one answer

You are driving in a town. Ahead is a stationary bus showing this sign. You should

- accelerate quickly
- stop behind the bus and wait until it moves off
- drive past slowly
- drive normally, the driver will look after the children

Answer

✓ **drive past slowly**

You must be very careful when approaching any hazard where children are concerned, and even more so when the view is restricted.

Children getting off the bus will be hidden from your view, and they may not be able to see you. Even if they can see you, they may still suddenly run across the road.

It's vitally important that you drive slowly in this situation. Look under the bus, if you can, for signs of feet heading towards the road, and consider sounding the horn, if necessary, to help make the children aware that you're there.

Always be ready to stop.

Q. 1.84

Mark two answers

You are driving a vehicle with excessive exhaust smoke. Which of the following is correct?

- You risk being reported
- You risk reducing your vision ahead
- You could cause the brakes to fade
- You are breaking the law

Answers

✓ **You risk being reported**

✓ **You are breaking the law**

Apart from the fact that excessive smoke causes pollution, it can also make it more difficult for those following you to see properly. As soon as you become aware of excessive smoke you should take steps to have the problem attended to as soon as possible.

Q. 1.85

Mark one answer

You have been convicted of a drink-drive offence whilst driving your car, and banned from driving. This ban will affect

-  all your driving entitlements
- only your car entitlement
- only your lorry entitlement
-  only your bus entitlement

Answer

✓ **all your driving entitlements**

The dangers of drink-driving are well publicised. Anyone convicted of this serious offence will lose entitlement to drive any motor vehicle on the road.

Q. 1.86

Mark three answers

You are following this scooter on a poor road surface. You should

- overtake without any delay
- stay close behind until you can pass
- make sure you stay well back
- look out as they may wobble
- sound your horn as you get close
- be aware they may suddenly swerve

Answers

- ☑ **make sure you stay well back**
- ☑ **look out as they may wobble**
- ☑ **be aware they may suddenly swerve**

On a poor road surface, the rider may need to move out to avoid potholes. You may not always get much warning.

Look out for signs that the rider maybe about to move out - a look to the right or 'lifesaver' check may indicate this. You should also keep a watch on the road surface yourself, to try and predict what path the rider may take.

While the road conditions persist, you should stay well back, allowing the rider plenty of room.

Q. 1.87

Mark one answer

You should be extra careful when following riders of scooters as they may suddenly

- look down
- give signals
- swerve
- accelerate

Answer

- ☑ **swerve**

Scooter riders may suddenly change direction to avoid potholes or raised covers on the road. They can also be blown off course in windy conditions, especially when passing junctions or gaps in buildings, where they may be exposed to sudden gusts.

questions   answers

Q. 1.88

Mark one answer

You are following a scooter. The rider has left it too late to avoid potholes in the road. You should be aware that the rider may suddenly

 accelerate

■ slow down

■ overtake

■ turn left

Answer

☑ **slow down**

A rider on two wheels may need to slow down quickly to avoid a pothole.

Wherever the road surface is poor, you should always be prepared for those on two wheels to make sudden movements, and stay well back to allow for this.

Q. 1.89

Mark one answer

You are driving on a motorway. There has been an accident on the other side of the carriageway. You should take extra care as traffic in your lane may

■ leave at the next exit

 slow down to have a look

■ pull out to overtake

■ stop on the hard shoulder

Answer

☑ **slow down to have a look**

Despite the dangers, many people cannot resist the temptation to slow down for a good look at the scene of an accident. Further collisions can sometimes occur as a direct result of this.

Keeping a safe following distance and planning well ahead should enable you to keep out of trouble in situations like this.

Q. 1.90

Mark one answer

You are driving on a motorway. There has been an accident on the opposite carriageway. What should you do?

■ Concentrate on your driving

■ Slow down to look across

■ Switch on your hazard lights

■ Stop on the hard shoulder

Answer

☑ **Concentrate on your driving**

Drivers slowing down to watch what's happening on the other carriageway can often cause further accidents, when other 'rubber-necking' motorists run into the back of them through not looking where they're going.

It's far safer for you to simply concentrate on what's happening on your own side of the motorway.

Q. 1.91

Mark one answer

You are driving on a motorway. There has been an accident on the opposite carriageway. Busy traffic ahead is slowing to look. You should

 concentrate on the road ahead

slow down to take a look

pull up on the hard shoulder

overtake using the hard shoulder

Answer

✓ **concentrate on the road ahead**

'Rubber-necking' drivers at accident scenes can often end up having collisions themselves, when they allow their vehicle to wander or fail to notice that the driver ahead has slowed right down or stopped.

You need to keep your concentration in a situation like this and ignore what's happening on the other carriageway.

Q. 1.92

Mark one answer

On a motorway the colour of reflective studs on the right-hand edge of the carriageway is

amber

green

red

blue

Answer

✓ **amber**

Reflective studs on motorways and dual carriageways are provided to help drivers in bad visibility. The colour of reflective studs are

- red on the left-hand edge of the carriageway
- white to indicate lane markings
- green at slip roads and lay-bys
- amber on the right-hand edge of the carriageways marking the central reservation.

Q. 1.93

Mark one answer

You are driving on a three lane motorway. There are red reflective studs on your left and white reflective studs on your right. Which lane are you in?

Hard shoulder

Middle lane

Right-hand lane

Left-hand lane

Answer

✓ **Left-hand lane**

White reflective studs separate each of the lanes. Red studs mark the left-hand edge of the carriageway where the hard shoulder begins.

questions

answers

Q. 1.94

Mark one answer

On a motorway, green–yellow fluorescent studs

- [ ] mark the lanes in a contraflow system
- [ ] separate the slip road from the motorway
- [ ] mark access points for emergency services
- [ ] separate the edge of the hard shoulder from the grass verge

Answer

- [x] **mark the lanes in a contraflow system**

Roadworks can involve complex lane layouts. To make it easier for you as a driver, reflective green–yellow fluorescent studs are used to separate the lanes in a contra-flow traffic system.

Always look well ahead for traffic signs giving you advance information which may relate to the size or type of vehicle you are driving.

Q. 1.95

Mark one answer

Whilst driving at night you see a pedestrian wearing reflective clothing and carrying a red light. This means you are approaching

- [ ] men at work
- [ ] an organised walk
- [ ] an accident blackspot
- [ ] slow moving vehicles

Answer

- [x] **an organised walk**

Pedestrians who may need to walk in the road at night should wear bright or reflective clothing and carry lights. As a driver, though, you need to be aware that they may not always do this. Be particularly careful, slow down, and give the walkers plenty of room.

Q. 1.96

Mark one answer

Diamond shaped signs give instructions to drivers of

- [ ] lorries
- [ ] trams
- [ ] buses
- [ ] tractors

Answer

- [x] **trams**

You need to show caution when driving in areas where trams operate. You may not hear their approach, and they cannot change direction to avoid you.

There may also be crossing points where you will need to give way to them, or areas specifically reserved for trams which you are not allowed to enter.

Q. 1.97

Mark one answer

This sign means

☐ tramway speed limit

☐ distance to level crossing

☐ maximum passenger capacity

☐ goods vehicle weight limit

Answer

✓ **tramway speed limit**

Tramways are becoming increasingly common in large towns and cities, as the move to more environmentally-friendly transport continues.

They may either cross the road you're driving on, or share it with you. Always be aware of their virtually silent approach, and look out for places where you may be required to give way to them.

Q. 1.98

Mark one answer

Which of these should be fitted to a lorry with a maximum authorised mass of more than 7.500 kgs?

Answer

✓

Motor vehicles over 7,500 kgs maximum authorised mass (MAM) and trailers over 3,500 kgs (MAM) should have these markings fitted to the rear of the vehicle.

Q. 1.99

Mark one answer

Your vehicle is more than 3 metres (9 feet 10 inches) high. Where is this information usually displayed?

☐ On the tax disc

☐ On the weight plate

☐ In the drivers cab

☐ In the engine bay

Answer

✓ **In the drivers cab**

This information is usually displayed in the cab. It is a legal requirement that it can be read by the driver, when in the driving position. It is important to know this to avoid low bridges or obstacles such as overhead electrical cables.

questions   answers

Q. 1.100

Mark one answer

The D1 category licence allows you to drive buses with a maximum of

- [ ] 16 passenger seats
- [ ] 24 passenger seats
- [ ] 32 passenger seats
- [ ] 48 passenger seats

Answer

☑ **16 passenger seats**

The D1 category allows any bus with 9 – 16 passenger seats to be driven for hire or reward.

Q. 1.101

Mark one answer

How far can a load overhang at the rear before you must use triangular projection markers?

- [ ] 1 metre (3 feet 3 inches)
- [ ] 1.5 metres (5 feet)
- [ ] 2 metres (6 feet 6 inches)
- [ ] 2.9 metres (9 feet 6 inches)

Answer

☑ **2 metres (6 feet 6 inches)**

It's not only important that you're aware of the length of your vehicle, but other road users should also be informed. This is to enable them to understand the reason why you might take up certain positions before turning.

If the load on your vehicle overhangs by more than 2 metres (6 feet 6 inches) it must have marker boards.

Q. 1.102

Mark one answer

A driver should know the vehicle's unladen weight. Where can this information be found?

- [ ] On the dashboard of the vehicle
- [ ] On the driver's duty roster
- [ ] On the side of the vehicle
- [ ] On the depot noticeboard

Answer

☑ **On the side of the vehicle**

As a driver of a passenger carrying vehicle (PCV) you'll need to know about the

- weight (for restrictions)
- height (for clearances, etc.)
- width (for restrictions)
- length and ground clearance

of your vehicle (for humpback bridges, grass verges, kerbs, etc.).

Q. 1.103

Mark one answer

What does this sign mean?

- Warning of lorry crossing a one-way road
- No entry for vehicles over 32 feet 6 inches (10 metres) long
- No entry for vehicles over 32.6 tonnes
- Warning of lorry straight ahead

Answer

☑ **No entry for vehicles over 32 feet 6 inches (10 metres) long**

You need to know the length of your vehicle as well as the height and width. Places where the length of your vehicle will be relevant are

- road tunnels
- level crossings
- ferries
- bridges.

Q. 1.104

Mark one answer

What does this sign mean?

- Humpback bridge
- Risk of grounding
- Uneven road
- Road liable to subsidence

Answer

☑ **Risk of grounding**

If you see this sign, you must be alert to the danger of grounding. This can happen where there's a pronounced bump in the road, such as at a level crossing or a humpback bridge.

Drivers' hours and rest periods

This section looks at drivers' hours and rest periods.

The questions will ask you about

- **Driving limits**

  the EC driving limits and UK domestic hours rules

- **Keeping records**

  the records you must keep, and how long to keep them

- **Tachograph rules**

  the rules concerning the use of tachographs in the UK and abroad

- **Tiredness**

  the reasons for not driving when tired

- **Vehicle security**

  your responsibility for your vehicle and load.

questions answers

Q. 2.1

Mark three answers

Goods vehicle drivers' hours of work are controlled for three reasons. They are

- vehicle sympathy
- fair competition
- fair road use
- vehicle security
- road safety
- working conditions

Answers

☑ **fair competition**

☑ **road safety**

☑ **working conditions**

EC regulations set the maximum driving time and the minimum requirements for rest and break periods.

Q. 2.2

Mark two answers

Goods vehicle drivers' hours are controlled in the interests of

- fuel economy
- road safety
- traffic calming
- fair competition

Answers

☑ **road safety**

☑ **fair competition**

Drivers who break the rules are subject to heavy fines and could lose their licence to drive lorries.

Q. 2.3

Mark three answers

Why are drivers' hours under close control?

- To keep to a delivery schedule
- For fuel economy
- To save wear and tear
- For fair competition
- For road safety
- For safe working conditions

Answers

☑ **For fair competition**

☑ **For road safety**

☑ **For safe working conditions**

Altering drivers' hours' records with intent to deceive, or tampering with the tachograph, could lead to a prison sentence.

questions answers

Q. 2.4

Mark one answer

Under the rules for domestic drivers' hours you must

- keep a written record of hours worked
- only record any driving off public roads
- keep a written record of driving time only
- always use a vehicle fitted with a tachograph

Answer

☑ **keep a written record of hours worked**

Domestic rules apply to certain journeys within Great Britain which are not subject to EC rules.

Under domestic rules, if you drive both passenger and goods vehicles, you should keep written records of your hours of duty when driving goods vehicles.

Q. 2.5

Mark one answer

You are on a regular service and are not using a tachograph. What MUST you carry with you?

- Tachograph charts from the previous seven days
- Your bus driver's licence
- An extract from the duty roster and the service timetable
- Servicing and maintenance records

Answer

☑ **An extract from the duty roster and the service timetable**

Instead of using a tachograph you can carry an extract from the duty roster and a copy of the service timetable. The roster must show your name, the place where you're based and the schedule laid down in advance.

Q. 2.6

Mark two answers

A bus driver who is not using a tachograph on a regular service of over 50 km (31 miles) must carry which TWO of these?

- A drivers' hours record book
- An extract from the duty roster
- A copy of the service timetable
- Some small change
- A detailed route map

Answers

☑ **An extract from the duty roster**

☑ **A copy of the service timetable**

Under EC rules, drivers' activities are usually recorded by means of a tachograph. This is an instrument in the cab that records information about the vehicle and driver.

However, if you're a bus driver on a regular service over 50 km (31 miles) you may not be required to use one.

questions   answers

Q. 2.7

Mark two answers

What types of vehicle must be fitted with a tachograph when operating in the UK under EC rules?

- Light goods vehicles drawing a trailer exceeding 3.5 tonnes maximum authorised mass

- Only vehicles between 3.5 and 7.5 tonnes maximum authorised mass

- Vehicles over 3.5 tonnes maximum authorised mass

- Vehicles over 7.5 tonnes maximum authorised mass only used for driving instruction

- Vehicles manufactured before 1947

Answers

☑ **Light goods vehicles drawing a trailer exceeding 3.5 tonnes maximum authorised mass**

☑ **Vehicles over 3.5 tonnes maximum authorised mass**

EC rules on drivers' hours and tachographs apply to drivers of most heavy goods vehicles where the maximum authorised mass (MAM) limit (including any trailer) exceeds 3.5 tonnes. Domestic rules govern the remainder. You must be aware of which set of rules apply to the vehicle you're driving.

You'll be responsible if the information isn't recorded in the proper way.

Q. 2.8

Mark one answer

The driver of a bus with 18 seats on an excursion journey from London to Scotland should abide by which drivers' hours rules?

- AETR only
- Domestic
- EC only
- EC and AETR

Answer

☑ **EC only**

If you're driving a bus on an excursion journey (that is, not a regular journey) and your vehicle has 18 or more seats you must use EC rules and record the details on a tachograph chart.

Q. 2.9

Mark one answer

Who is responsible for the issue of tachograph charts to a bus/lorry driver?

- The driver's employer
- The Department of Transport
- The authorised calibration centre
- The local MOT testing station

Answer

☑ **The driver's employer**

Your employer is responsible for the issue of tachograph charts. You, the driver, must ensure that the correct information is recorded on the tachograph chart.

questions 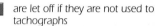 answers

Q. 2.10

Mark two answers

Drivers who break EC tachograph regulations

- are allowed three warnings
- may lose their licence
- will be heavily fined
- are let off if they are not used to tachographs

Answers

☑ **may lose their licence**

☑ **will be heavily fined**

You, the driver, must take responsibility to ensure that you comply with the drivers' hours and tachograph rules.

Q. 2.11

Mark one answer

Before starting driving, which of the following should you complete on the centre field of your tachograph chart?

- The place from which you start your day's journey
- Details of the goods carried
- The name and address of your employer
- The amount of daily rest taken prior to starting the shift

Answer

☑ **The place from which you start your day's journey**

Before departing on your journey you must record on the tachograph chart the date and the place where the use of the chart begins.

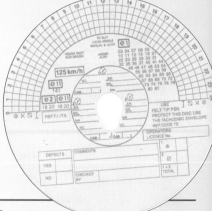

Q. 2.12

Mark one answer

You must have enough tachograph charts with you for your journey. You will need at least one for every

- 10 hours
- 24 hours
- 36 hours
- 48 hours

Answer

☑ **24 hours**

Your employer should supply you with enough tachograph charts for the entire journey. You'll need at least one for every 24 hours.

questions   answers

Q. 2.13

Mark two answers

When using a tachograph which of the following apply?

- You must carry enough approved charts
- Damaged charts can be used if they are clean
- Dirty charts can be used if they are undamaged
- All charts must be clean and undamaged

Answers

☑ **You must carry enough approved charts**

☑ **All charts must be clean and undamaged**

Make sure you carry enough approved tachograph charts for your journey. Keep your spare charts in a plastic wallet to ensure they remain clean and undamaged.

Q. 2.14

Mark one answer

One tachograph chart covers a period of

- 24 hours
- 48 hours
- 5 days
- 7 days

Answer

☑ **24 hours**

Your tachograph is a legal document; it is a record of your work covering a rolling 24-hour period. Drivers who break the rules are subject to heavy fines and could lose their vocational licence entitlement. Altering your tachograph chart with intent to deceive could lead to a prison sentence.

Q. 2.15

Mark one answer

You are driving a vehicle requiring the use of a tachograph. You must carry charts for the current week and the last

- day of the previous week on which you drove
- seven days on which you drove
- 14 days on which you drove
- 28 days on which you drove

Answer

☑ **day of the previous week on which you drove**

Vehicle Inspectorate (VI) executive agency enforcement staff and the police have powers to inspect drivers' hours and other documents. In Northern Ireland the inspections are carried out by the Department of the Environment for Northern Ireland (DOENI).

The obligation to make sure that all records are completed correctly falls on you, the driver, as well as the operator. There are heavy fines imposed for the misuse or falsification of charts.

questions answers

Q. 2.16

Mark one answer

Within how many days must drivers return completed tachograph charts to their employer?

 21 days

25 days

30 days

35 days

Answer

☑ **21 days**

An enforcement officer is entitled to inspect and copy any tachograph chart. The officer can detain a vehicle for inspection and, if a false record is suspected, the chart may be taken and kept for up to six months. The officer will either issue you with a receipt or write their name and telephone number on the back of the replacement chart.

To ensure that all records are kept up to date and available for inspection by enforcement staff, you must give completed charts to your employer within 21 days.

Q. 2.17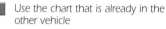

Mark one answer

During your working day you are changing to another vehicle with the same type of tachograph. What should you do with your tachograph chart?

Use the chart that is already in the other vehicle

Take the chart with you and use it in the other vehicle

Record your driving hours in a record book

Install a new chart in the other vehicle

Answer

☑ **Take the chart with you and use it in the other vehicle**

If you're changing vehicles during the working day, you should take your chart with you and use it in the next vehicle. This isn't always possible, however, as charts produced by different manufacturers may not be interchangeable. In this case you should use another chart, ensuring that all the information for the day is recorded.

Q. 2.18

Mark one answer

The tachograph on your vehicle becomes faulty. It can be repaired on return to base, if this is within

 one day

three days

one week

two weeks

Answer

☑ **one week**

If the tachograph on your vehicle becomes faulty you should take it to an approved tachograph repairer as soon as possible. If your vehicle can't return to your base within a week of discovery of the fault, the repair must be carried out while you're away on the journey. While the tachograph is faulty or broken you must keep a manual record of your activities on a temporary chart.

Q. 2.19

Mark one answer

Tachograph records must be available for inspection. An enforcement officer keeps one of your charts. Who should sign the back of the replacement chart?

 You, the driver

 Your transport manager

 The vehicle owner

 The officer

Answer

✓ **The officer**

If an enforcement officer retains a record chart, the driver should ask the officer to sign the back of the replacement chart with his name, telephone number and the number of charts retained.

This replacement chart must be used to continue the journey. You should always carry more blank charts than you need to use.

Q. 2.20

Mark two answers

When an enforcement officer keeps your tachograph records, the officer should sign the replacement chart with their

 name

 telephone number

 home address

 date of birth

Answers

✓ **name**

✓ **telephone number**

The enforcement officer should also record the number of charts retained. Alternatively, a receipt may be issued.

Q. 2.21

Mark one answer

You can find out when the tachograph was last recalibrated by

 a date on the tachograph chart

 contacting the vehicle's manufacturer

 checking the vehicle's service record

 a plaque on or near the tachograph

Answer

✓ **a plaque on or near the tachograph**

The installation plaque shows the date of the last six-yearly inspection.

questions

answers

Q. 2.22

Mark one answer

Your tachograph chart becomes dirty or damaged. What should you do?

- Continue with the same chart and enter the details in writing
- Use a spare chart and destroy the damaged chart
- Use a spare chart and attach it to the damaged one
- Continue to use the chart

Answer

☑ **Use a spare chart and attach it to the damaged one**

If your current tachograph chart becomes damaged you should start another and then attach it to the damaged one. Your records must be clear and up to date at all times.

It's sensible to carry more tachograph charts than you think you'll need for your journey. Then you'll be able to use a spare if one becomes dirty or damaged.

Q. 2.23

Mark one answer

Why should you carry spare tachograph charts?

- As a defence against a speeding prosecution
- To record when you have been in a traffic delay
- For recording extra loading duties and overtime
- To replace the original chart if it gets dirty

Answer

☑ **To replace the original chart if it gets dirty**

Your employer should supply sufficient approved charts for your journey, plus some spares in case any get damaged, or are taken by an authorised inspecting officer.

Q. 2.24

Mark one answer

Under EC rules a tachograph must be recalibrated every

- 4 years
- 6 years
- 8 years
- 10 years

Answer

☑ **6 years**

When a tachograph is installed and calibrated, an installation plaque is fixed near the tachograph. The installation plaque shows the date of the most recent tachograph calibration.

questions   answers

Q. 2.25

Mark one answer

Under EC rules a tachograph must be checked at an approved calibration centre every

- 2 years
- 5 years
- 7 years
- 10 years

Answer

☑ **2 years**

The two-yearly inspection is due two years after the date shown on the installation plaque, or two years after the date shown on the two-yearly inspection plaque.

Q. 2.26

Mark one answer

During your break your vehicle will be moved by another person. What should you do with the tachograph chart?

- Leave the chart in the vehicle and record the changes on the back
- Put in a new chart on your return to the vehicle
- Switch to rest mode to record the break
- Remove the chart and make a manual record of the break period

Answer

☑ **Remove the chart and make a manual record of the break period**

If your vehicle is likely to be used by another person while you're away from it, you should take your tachograph chart with you. Your break from driving should be entered on the reverse of the chart.

Q. 2.27

Mark one answer

Under EC rules a driver must take a break after a continuous driving period of

- 3 hours
- 4 hours
- 4.5 hours
- 5.5 hours

Answer

☑ **4.5 hours**

Whether you're driving a lorry or a bus it's essential that you don't become drowsy through driving for excessively long periods. EC rules are in place to prevent this happening. You must follow these rules, and ensure that the details of your journey are recorded. These details must be available for inspection by VI or DOENI enforcement staff. For this reason you should make sure that you know the rules relating to the vehicle you're driving and the journey you're making.

questions answers

Q. 2.28

Mark one answer

You have been driving non-stop since 5 am. The time is now 9.30 am. Under EC rules you must have a break of at least

- 15 minutes
- 30 minutes
- 45 minutes
- 60 minutes

Answer

☑ **45 minutes**

Your 45 minute break is a legal requirement under EC rules. It can be taken at the end of the driving period, or as two or three shorter breaks of at least 15 minutes during or immediately after the driving period. Remember that breaks of less than 15 minutes DO NOT count towards the 45 minute statutory break.

Q. 2.29

Mark one answer

You have been driving a lorry without a break for four and a half hours. Under EC rules a break must be taken. How long must it be?

- 30 minutes
- 35 minutes
- 40 minutes
- 45 minutes

Answer

☑ **45 minutes**

If you're driving under EC rules you must not drive continuously for more than four and a half hours without taking a break.

If you've driven continually for four and a half hours you must take a break of at least 45 minutes. Include your stops in the timetable when you're planning your journey.

Q. 2.30

Mark one answer

EC rules require that after driving continuously for the maximum period a bus driver must take a break. This must be at least

- 15 minutes
- 30 minutes
- 45 minutes
- 60 minutes

Answer

☑ **45 minutes**

Always park your vehicle in a safe place off the road. Try to find a place where you can get out of your vehicle for refreshment. This will help to ensure that you're fully refreshed.

If you're carrying passengers, they'll also be grateful for a break. Taking breaks at the correct time will ensure that your passengers are safe and comfortable.

Q. 2.31

Mark one answer

Under EC rules you can split your daily rest into two or three periods. Each period must be at least

 15 minutes

30 minutes

45 minutes

60 minutes

Answer

☑ **60 minutes**

If it is necessary to split your daily rest period, the following must be observed:

12 hours daily rest may be taken in two or three periods, the last of which must be at least eight consecutive hours.

The minimum rest period must be at least one hour.

Q. 2.32

Mark one answer

Under EC rules the break needed after a maximum period of driving may be replaced by several shorter breaks taken during the driving period. Each shorter break must be at least

 15 minutes

20 minutes

30 minutes

45 minutes

Answer

☑ **15 minutes**

A 45 minute continuous break can be replaced by several shorter breaks during the four and a half hours' driving period. These breaks must be at least 15 minutes.

Q. 2.33

Mark one answer

Under EC rules you can drive for a maximum of nine hours daily. How many days of the week can this be extended to ten hours?

One

Two

Three

Four

Answer

☑ **Two**

Under EC rules your normal daily driving must not exceed nine hours. This nine hours must be the time between

- any two daily rest periods
- a daily rest period and a weekly rest period.

It's permitted to extend these hours to ten hours twice a week.

questions   answers

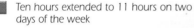

Q. 2.34

Mark one answer

Under EC rules what is the maximum daily driving time allowed?

 Nine hours extended to 11 hours on three days of the week

Ten hours extended to 11 hours on two days of the week

Nine hours extended to ten hours on two days of the week

Ten hours extended to 11 hours on three days of the week

Answer

☑ **Nine hours extended to ten hours on two days of the week**

You are allowed to extend your daily driving time twice a week to ten hours a day. If you drive your maximum hours each day for a six day week this brings your total driving time to the EC maximum of 56 hours.

A 'day' is generally any 24-hour period beginning with the resumption of other work or driving after the last daily or weekly rest period.

Q. 2.35

Mark one answer

Under EC rules your minimum daily rest is 11 hours. On three days of the week this may be reduced to

 seven hours

eight hours

 nine hours

 ten hours

Answer

☑ **nine hours**

Under EC rules you must have a minimum daily rest of 11 consecutive hours. This may be reduced to nine hours on not more than three days a week, as long as the reduction is compensated by an equivalent rest before the end of the following week.

Q. 2.36

Mark one answer

Under EC rules your daily rest can be reduced to 9 hours but NOT more often than

1 day per week

2 days per week

3 days per week

4 days per week

Answer

☑ **3 days per week**

Under EC rules any reduction in your daily rest must be compensated before the end of the following week.

Q. 2.37

Mark one answer

Under EC rules your normal daily rest period should be at least

- 8 hours
- 11 hours
- 13 hours
- 14 hours

Answer

☑ **11 hours**

Under EC rules you can reduce your daily rest period to nine hours up to three times in a week.

Q. 2.38

Mark one answer

Under EC rules what is the normal weekly rest that must be taken?

- 40 hours
- 41 hours
- 42 hours
- 45 hours

Answer

☑ **45 hours**

The working week is defined as the period between 00-00 hours on Monday and 24-00 hours on the following Sunday. When taking the weekly rest period, a daily rest period must normally be extended to at least 45 consecutive hours.

Q. 2.39

Mark one answer

You are taking a weekly rest period away from your normal base. Under EC rules the minimum number of consecutive hours this rest period must be is

- 18 hours
- 24 hours
- 36 hours
- 45 hours

Answer

☑ **24 hours**

Under EC rules reductions must be compensated by an equivalent period of rest taken before the end of the third week following the week concerned. It must be attached to a daily or weekly rest period of at least eight hours.

questions answers

Q. 2.40

Mark one answer

When a vehicle has two drivers each driver should

 share the same tachograph chart

use a separate tachograph chart for every driving period

use their own tachograph chart

not use the tachograph for such duties

Answer

✓ **use their own tachograph chart**

Your tachograph chart is your personal work record and, as such, should reflect the hours that you drive or carry out other work.

The law requires these charts to be held on file by your employer for a period of at least one year. Enforcement officers can require charts to be handed over for inspection.

Q. 2.41

Mark one answer

You are making a journey with a co-driver. When the other person is driving you may show some of this time as

 a daily rest period

a weekly rest period

a break in daily driving

driving time

Answer

✓ **a break in daily driving**

You may only record a break when you are not engaged in any other type of work. It is permissible to take a break on a double-manned vehicle while the vehicle is driven by the other crew-member. Any break must be a minimum of 15 minutes, otherwise it doesn't count.

Q. 2.42

Mark three answers

A tachograph will record

 load weight

driving time

fuel consumption

rest periods

engine temperature

vehicle speed

Answers

✓ **driving time**

✓ **rest periods**

✓ **vehicle speed**

The tachograph is designed to be used as a tool to help you be a safe and responsible driver.

Q. 2.43

Mark one answer

The tachograph will start recording as soon as the

 engine is started

 vehicle starts moving

ignition is switched on

chart is inserted

Answer

☑ **chart is inserted**

The tachograph will record a time trace on your chart. This accurately records the movement times of your vehicle.

Q. 2.44

Mark one answer

Which one of the following symbols on your tachograph indicates your break/rest period?

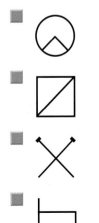

Answer

☑

A tachograph is fitted with a switch that allows you to select the task that you're undertaking. Time spent on that task is then recorded onto the chart automatically.

Each task has a different symbol. You should know the meaning so that your records are correct. The symbols are:

- driving
- other work
- on duty and available for work
- break or rest symbol.

questions answers

Q. 2.45

Mark one answer

What does this tachograph chart symbol mean?

- Driver at rest
- Chart not required
- Other work
- Driving

Answer

✓ **Driving**

Each activity has a different symbol on a tachograph chart. You should know what the different symbols mean so that you can select the correct one. You'll be responsible if you fail to record all your activities correctly.

Some new tachographs don't have a 'driving' mode switch. This is because these tachographs will automatically record driving time on the chart whenever the vehicle is moved, no matter what mode the switch is turned to.

Q. 2.46

Mark two answers

You are driving a vehicle with a tachograph. What do these symbols mean?

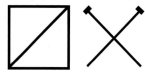

- Driving period
- Rest period
- Driver doing other work
- On duty and available for work

Answers

✓ **Driver doing other work**

✓ **On duty and available for work**

If you're working away from the vehicle and can't leave your tachograph chart in, you should take the chart with you and make a manual entry on the reverse side, for example OW (other work) 9.15 am to 10 am.

Q. 2.47

Mark three answers

The 'mode' switch on a tachograph is used to record

- driving
- illness
- taking a weekly rest period
- other work
- resting

Answers

✓ **driving**

✓ **other work**

✓ **resting**

It is important to change the mode switch to record your activities as they change during the working day. Failure to operate the mode switch could lead to a reprimand from your employer, or prosecution by the authorities.

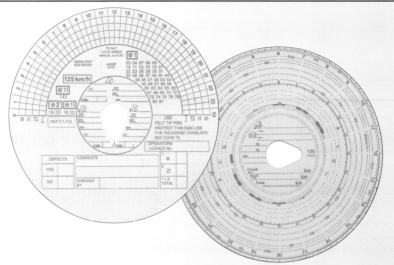

Q. 2.48

Mark one answer

Under EC rules what is the maximum number of days that you can drive in a week?

 Four

Five

Six

Seven

Answer

☑ **Six**

You're only allowed to drive for a maximum of six days in a working week. Your daily maximum driving hours, e.g.

- four days at nine hours and
- two days at ten hours

add up to 56 hours, which is your maximum driving time in a working week under EC rules.

Q. 2.49

Mark one answer

Under EC rules the maximum number of days that you can drive in any one week is normally

 four

five

six

seven

Answer

☑ **six**

Working a six-day week will allow you to reach the maximum driving time of 56 hours. This will limit your driving time to 34 hours in the following week.

questions   answers

Q. 2.50

Mark one answer

Under EC rules what is the maximum driving time allowed in a fortnight?

- 85 hours
- 90 hours
- 100 hours
- 105 hours

Answer

☑ **90 hours**

The maximum number of hours that you can drive in a fortnight is 90 hours. These hours don't have to be split evenly, but the total number of hours spent driving in any one week shouldn't exceed 56 hours.

Don't exceed your driving hours. You'll need to keep records of how many hours you drive in a day, a week and a fortnight. Learn the rules and adhere to them. Heavy fines can be imposed for failure to do so.

Q. 2.51

Mark one answer

At the end of your working week you have driven a total of 56 hours. What is the maximum number of hours that you can drive in the following week under EC rules?

- 34
- 36
- 38
- 40

Answer

☑ **34**

If you've driven a total of 56 hours in any one week you can only drive for 34 hours in the following week.

If your hours add up to a total of 56 in any one week you must make sure that you don't exceed the permitted hours the following week. Keep your own record to make sure that you don't exceed these hours.

Q. 2.52

Mark one answer

A driver's daily rest period may be taken in a parked vehicle if

- it is fitted with a bunk
- there is a smoke alarm fitted
- the vehicle is in an authorised coachpark
- there are no passengers on the vehicle

Answer

☑ **it is fitted with a bunk**

Some vehicles are fitted with sleeping accommodation for the driver. If your vehicle is fitted with this facility you're permitted to take your daily rest period there, provided your vehicle is stationary.

Q. 2.53

Mark one answer

An emergency situation has arisen. For safety reasons you will need to exceed the normal drivers' hours under EC rules. You should

 continue with the same tachograph chart and write an explanation on the back

◼ remove the tachograph chart and make a manual record of the rest of the journey

◼ continue; there is no need to give an explanation

◼ remove the tachograph chart and inform your employer of the reason

Answer

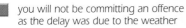 **continue with the same tachograph chart and write an explanation on the back**

As long as road safety is not put at risk, you may depart from the drivers' hours rules just enough to ensure the safety of people, the vehicle, or its load. In these circumstances you should note all the reasons on the back of your tachograph chart.

Q. 2.54

Mark one answer

You start your journey on a foggy night. You are delayed because of the fog and exceed your permitted hours. This means

◼ you will not be committing an offence as the delay was due to the weather

◼ you could be committing an offence as the delay could be foreseen

◼ your excess hours can be transferred to another day

◼ your excess hours will not apply because of the weather

Answer

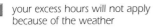 **you could be committing an offence as the delay could be foreseen**

When planning your journey you should allow for delays and unexpected hold-ups.

Don't let the time pressures related to your work cause you to rush to make up time. Act responsibly at all times. As a professional driver you should set the standards for others to follow.

questions   answers

Q. 2.55

Mark one answer

In an emergency situation you need to go over your normal drivers' hours. Under EC rules you should

- [ ] take no action, the tachograph chart will record this

- [ ] note the reasons on the back of the tachograph chart

- [ ] remove the chart from the tachograph before going over the hours

- [ ] note the reasons on the front of the tachograph chart

Answer

✓ **note the reasons on the back of the tachograph chart**

In an emergency, as long as road safety is not put at risk, a driver may depart from the drivers' hours rules just enough to get his load or passengers to a suitable stopping place.

Q. 2.56

Mark two answers

Which TWO of the following are most likely to cause tiredness?

- [ ] Making frequent and regular stops

- [ ] Driving breaks taken on board the vehicle

- [ ] Insufficient breaks from driving

- [ ] Modern vehicles with automatic gearboxes

- [ ] The cab becoming too warm

Answers

✓ **Insufficient breaks from driving**

✓ **The cab becoming too warm**

Tiredness will affect your concentration. It's most important that you don't allow yourself to become weary through not taking proper breaks or rest periods. As a professional driver you have a responsibility either for goods or for passengers, as well as for overall road safety.

Try to ensure that your vehicle is well ventilated. Open a window or turn down the heating to prevent yourself becoming drowsy.

Q. 2.57

Mark one answer

When driving, you start to feel tired or unable to concentrate. You should

- ■ stop as soon as it is safe to do so
- ■ wind down a window and carry on
- ■ switch on the radio and complete your journey
- ■ speed up to get to your destination sooner

Answer

☑ **stop as soon as it is safe to do so**

If you start to feel tired you should stop as soon as it's safe to do so, even if you aren't due a break.

Make sure that you get enough sleep the night before you're due to work, especially if you're on an early shift.

Q. 2.58

Mark one answer

You feel tired after driving for two and a half hours. What should you do?

- ■ Slow down to a safer speed
- ■ Reduce your planned driving time to three and a half hours
- ■ Stop as soon as it is safe to do so
- ■ Take a less busy route

Answer

☑ **Stop as soon as it is safe to do so**

Most accidents happen as a result of a lapse in concentration. Don't let this happen to you. If you start to feel tired you won't perform as well as you should. Your reactions will slow down and your anticipation and judgement of hazards will become flawed. It will be better for you, and for the safety of other road users, if you stop and rest as soon as it's safe to do so.

Q. 2.59

Mark one answer

You are driving on a motorway and suddenly become tired. What should you do?

- ■ Stop on the hard shoulder and rest
- ■ Leave by the next exit and find a place to stop
- ■ Stop on the next slip road and rest
- ■ Stop on the verge of the motorway and rest

Answer

☑ **Leave by the next exit and find a place to stop**

If you're driving for long distances on a motorway take plenty of rest stops. There have been many accidents blamed on drivers falling asleep at the wheel. If you feel yourself becoming 'mesmerised' stop at the next service area.

questions answers

Q. 2.60

Mark one answer

You are feeling tired when driving on a motorway. Where can you stop?

- On the hard shoulder
- At a service station
- On a slip road
- In a deceleration lane

Answer

✓ **At a service station**

Travelling long distances on a motorway can have a 'mesmerising' effect. Any lack of concentration, however brief, could lead to an accident. Stop as soon as you can, but don't stop on the hard shoulder. Leave the motorway by the next exit and pull over in a safe place to rest. Ideally you should use a service area, where you can have a rest and refreshment before you restart your journey.

Q. 2.61

Mark three answers

You are driving a lorry at night. What can you do to help you keep alert?

- Eat a heavy meal before setting off
- Keep plenty of cool fresh air moving through the cab
- Keep the cab warm and comfortable
- Take proper rest periods at correct intervals
- Drive faster to get to your destination sooner
- Walk around in fresh air at a rest stop

Answers

✓ **Keep plenty of cool fresh air moving through the cab**

✓ **Take proper rest periods at correct intervals**

✓ **Walk around in fresh air at a rest stop**

Driving at night can make you feel tired more quickly. If you're starting your shift at the end of the day, make sure that you have enough rest before you start work. You must be able to stay alert for the duration of your shift.

Make sure that you have good ventilation in the cab. This will help you to stay alert by making sure that there's enough fresh air. Stale, warm air will dull your senses and cause drowsiness.

Q. 2.62

Mark one answer

You are driving a lorry on a motorway and you are getting drowsy. There are no service areas or exits for some distance. What should you do?

☐ Stop on the hard shoulder and rest

☐ Open the window and turn the heating down

☐ Slow down and use the hazard warning lights

☐ Increase your speed to get to the next service area sooner

Answer

✓ **Open the window and turn the heating down**

During very cold weather it's tempting to have the heating in the cab turned on full. Try to be aware of the effect this can have on your reactions and anticipation. It may dull them by making you feel drowsy and tired.

Q. 2.63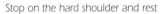

Mark one answer

You are driving a lorry. During the journey you are feeling ill and unable to concentrate. What should you do?

☐ Stop in a safe place and seek help

☐ Continue your journey and keep your windows open

☐ Increase your speed to finish your work earlier

☐ Keep stopping at regular intervals for rest

Answer

✓ **Stop in a safe place and seek help**

If you become unwell it will affect your concentration. You must be fully alert and ready for any hazards that might occur while you drive. Stop in a safe place and seek assistance. You may have to call out a relief driver to complete the journey for you.

Q. 2.64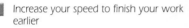

Mark one answer

What should you do if asked to leave your bus by an official who is not in uniform?

☐ Comply with the request

☐ Ask to see a warrant card

☐ Refuse to leave the vehicle

☐ Invite the official aboard

Answer

✓ **Ask to see a warrant card**

If you are asked to leave your vehicle by an official who's not in uniform, ask to see their warrant card. The official is likely to be a VI or DOENI enforcement officer or a police officer, but don't presume this.

questions 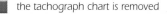 answers

Q. 2.65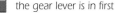

Mark one answer

When a bus is left unattended the driver MUST ensure that

- the tachograph chart is removed
- the gear lever is in reverse
- the gear lever is in first
- the parking brake is applied

Answer

☑ **the parking brake is applied**

Always ensure that your vehicle is safe when you leave it unattended. Always apply the parking brake and stop the engine.

Q. 2.66 🚚

Mark two answers

Which two of the following would NOT be helpful when trying to keep your load from being stolen?

- Giving a lift to a stranger
- Making sure all doors and windows are locked
- Discussing your load with members of the public
- Having a kingpin or drawbar lock fitted
- Parking in secure well-lit places when possible

Answers

☑ **Giving a lift to a stranger**

☑ **Discussing your load with members of the public**

Be careful of giving lifts to strangers. Some employers actively discourage this for very good reasons.

Careless chatter in the cab or to other drivers in the café can unwittingly give valuable information to the more unscrupulous members of society.

Q. 2.67 🚚

Mark one answer

When leaving your vehicle for an overnight stop, it is good practice to park with the

- rear doors close up to another vehicle
- rear doors well away from another vehicle
- front doors well away from another vehicle
- front doors close up to another vehicle

Answer

☑ **rear doors close up to another vehicle**

Being responsible for the safety of your vehicle, particularly when away from home, is very important.

questions   answers

Q. 2.68

Mark two answers

How can you reduce the risk of your lorry or trailer being stolen?

- ⬛ Fit an alarm and immobiliser
- ⬛ Fit a king pin lock to your trailer
- ⬛ Use the same route and rest periods
- ⬛ Park in quiet areas away from other vehicles

Answers

- ✅ **Fit an alarm and immobiliser**
- ✅ **Fit a king pin lock to your trailer**

Planning and taking sensible precautions can help to deter the most determined thief.

Q. 2.69

Mark one answer

A lorry driver must take care of his vehicle and load. Which of the following is NOT good practice?

- ⬛ Always parking it in a quiet area out of sight
- ⬛ Parking with the rear doors hard up against another vehicle
- ⬛ Avoiding using the same route and stops too often
- ⬛ Always asking to see the identity of any officer who may stop you

Answer

- ✅ **Always parking it in a quiet area out of sight**

Load security is one of the many responsibilities placed on the driver. When choosing a site to park your vehicle overnight, you should always look for a location which is legal and well-lit.

Many allocated lorry parks are patrolled by the police or security firms.

Q. 2.70

Mark three answers

You are parking overnight with a high-value load and intend sleeping in the cab. You should

- ⬛ lock doors but leave a window open for ventilation
- ⬛ ensure doors and windows will be secure
- ⬛ be in a reputable, lit lorry park
- ⬛ be in a quiet, unlit, non-residential area
- ⬛ stay at the same location regularly
- ⬛ block access to the rear door if possible

Answers

- ✅ **ensure doors and windows will be secure**
- ✅ **be in a reputable, lit lorry park**
- ✅ **block access to the rear door if possible**

Taking a few simple precautions will help to ensure your lorry and load are safe.

questions answers

Q. 2.71

Mark three answers

You are often involved in the carrying of high-value goods. What security measures can you adopt?

- Vary your routes and rest stops
- Always discuss details of your load
- Give lifts to anyone for added security
- Park overnight in well-lit areas
- Remove keys when not in attendance
- Keep your journeys to a strict routine

Answers

- ✓ **Vary your routes and rest stops**
- ✓ **Park overnight in well-lit areas**
- ✓ **Remove keys when not in attendance**

Use your common sense to plan your journeys.

Avoid developing a set routine or pattern by using different routes whenever possible.

Q. 2.72

Mark one answer

You have to leave your vehicle unattended for a very short time. You should

- avoid having to stop the engine
- leave keys available in case of obstruction
- keep the engine running but lock the doors
- be aware of the risks of theft or damage

Answer

- ✓ **be aware of the risks of theft or damage**

Take all the precautions you can to eliminate opportunities for theft. Lock your vehicle, especially when making deliveries which involve leaving the vehicle unattended.

Q. 2.73

Mark three answers

Before starting your engine your seat should be adjusted for

- height
- back support
- seat belt tension
- air ventilation
- distance from the controls
- leaving the cab

Answers

- ✓ **height**
- ✓ **back support**
- ✓ **distance from the controls**

Being seated properly is very important when driving long distances. A poor driving position can quickly cause fatigue.

Q. 2.74

Mark one answer

The audible warning device is operating as you reverse. You should be

- relying on a clear path behind
- expecting others to be aware of your course
- taking continuous, all-round observation
- concentrating solely on your blind areas

Answer

✓ **taking continuous, all-round observation**

Don't rely on an audible warning device to claim a right of way. It is your responsibility to be cautious and keep others safe.

Q. 2.75

Mark one answer

You have arrived at your destination. All your passengers want to leave the bus. Ideally their valuables should be

- placed on luggage racks
- taken with them
- placed on the seats
- left with you

Answer

✓ **taken with them**

Ideally passengers should take any personal property and valuables with them, unless they can be locked in secure luggage compartments.

Q. 2.76

Mark one answer

Which of the following can prevent you from obtaining a bus or lorry licence?

- heart disorders
- dyslexia
- skin problems
- stomach problems

Answer

✓ **heart disorders**

A number of reasons can prevent you from obtaining, or keeping, a bus or lorry licence. You must tell the Drivers' Medical unit at DVLA Swansea immediately, if you develop any serious illness or disability that is likely to last more than three months, and which could affect your driving. Partial blindness and mental disorders can also prevent you from obtaining a bus or lorry licence.

questions   answers

Q. 2.77

Mark one answer

You may be prevented from obtaining a lorry or bus licence if you have

 dyslexia

partial blindness

skin problems

stomach problems

Answer

☑ **partial blindness**

Other factors such as heart and mental disorders can also prevent you from obtaining a lorry licence. For enquiries about medical standards you should contact the Drivers' Medical unit, DVLA, Swansea.

Q. 2.78

Mark one answer

It is necessary to leave your trailer unattended. It should be parked

in a public car park

on the public highway

on secure premises

in a quiet residential area

Answer

☑ **on secure premises**

Instances of theft of vehicles and trailers are unfortunately common. You are responsible for the safety and security of your vehicle and trailer. Try to avoid leaving any trailer unattended unless on approved secure premises.

Q. 2.79

Mark one answer

You are planning to carry high value goods on a regular basis. You should seek advice from

other drivers in your area

your local crime prevention officer

other operators in your area

your local road safety officer

Answer

☑ **your local crime prevention officer**

Research has shown that more than 3000 lorries with an insured value of £30 million were stolen in the UK. in one year. To prevent their lorry becoming another statistic operators are advised to seek advice from the local crime prevention officer.

Q. 2.80

Mark one answer

Your trailer should be fitted with a kingpin or drawbar lock when

 driving on motorways

⬛ being driven abroad

⬛ partly loaded

 left unattended

Answer

✓ **left unattended**

Instances of theft are unfortunately common. You are responsible for your vehicle. You should ensure that a kingpin or drawbar lock is fitted to any trailer that has to be left unattended.

Q. 2.81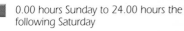

Mark one answer

A driver's week is defined as

⬛ 0.00 hours Monday to 24.00 hours the following Sunday

⬛ 0.00 hours Sunday to 24.00 hours the following Saturday

⬛ any seven consecutive days

⬛ any 56 hours driven

Answer

✓ **0.00 hours Monday to 24.00 hours the following Sunday**

A week is defined as a period between 0.00 hours on Monday to 24.00 hours the following Sunday.

Q. 2.82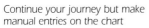

Mark one answer

When driving you notice your tachograph is not working. What should you do?

⬛ Stop immediately until it is repaired

⬛ Report it to the nearst police station

⬛ Telephone the vehicle inspectorate and report the fault

⬛ Continue your journey but make manual entries on the chart

Answer

✓ **Continue your journey but make manual entries on the chart**

If you cannot return to base within a week of the tachograph becoming defective, it must be repaired during the journey. While it is broken you must keep a manual record.

questions | answers

Q. 2.83

Mark one answer

Only lorries above a specific maximum authorised mass need a tachograph. That weight is

- [ ] 3.5 tonnes
- [ ] 5 tonnes
- [ ] 7.5 tonnes
- [ ] 10 tonnes

Answer
✓ **3.5 tonnes**

Normally, a tachograph should be fitted and in full working order if your vehicle is over 3.5 tonnes. You should be aware of how it works and the regulations that refer to it.

Q. 2.84

Mark one answer

The time is 10 am. You have been driving non-stop since 6 am. Under EC rules what is the longest you may now drive without a break?

- [ ] 15 minutes
- [ ] 30 minutes
- [ ] 40 minutes
- [ ] 45 minutes

Answer
✓ **30 minutes**

The maximum driving period under EC rules is four and a half hours after which you must have a minimum break of 45 minutes. Planning your route will allow you to take your statutory rest periods in a safe place, such as a service area, where you can get food, drink and a rest.

Q. 2.85

Mark one answer

Under EC rules you may drive for up to nine hours daily. On two days of the week this may be increased to a maximum of

- [ ] 9.5 hours
- [ ] 10 hours
- [ ] 11 hours
- [ ] 11.5 hours

Answer
✓ **10 hours**

Don't drive for more than the maximum hours allowed. You're permitted to extend the daily nine hours to ten hours twice a week.

Q. 2.86

Mark one answer

Only lorries above a specific maximum authorised mass need a tachograph. That weight is

◼ 3.5 tonnes

◼ 5 tonnes

◼ 7.5 tonnes

◼ 10 tonnes

Answer

☑ **3.5 tonnes**

Normally, a tachograph should be fitted and in full working order if your vehicle is over 3.5 tonnes. You should be aware of how it works and the regulations that refer to it.

Q. 2.87

Mark one answer

Your vehicle breaks down during a journey. You continue by driving in another vehicle with the same type of tachograph. What must you do with your tachograph chart?

◼ Leave it in the broken down vehicle

◼ Take it with you for security, but use a new chart in the new vehicle

◼ Telephone the Vehicle Inspectorate for permission to drive without a chart

◼ Take it with you, using it in the new vehicle

Answer

☑ **Take it with you, using it in the new vehicle**

When changing vehicles, you should also record the following information

• closing odometer reading

• registration number of new vehicle

• odometer start reading

• time of vehicle change.

Braking systems and speed limiters

This section looks at braking systems and speed limiters.

The questions will ask you about

- **Types of brake**
  the different types of braking systems used on vehicles

- **Maintenance and inspection**
  the importance of ensuring that your brakes are in good working order

- **Proper use of the brakes**
  when and how to use them

- **Tailgating**
  understanding that following too closely can lead to harsh braking and accidents

- **Freezing conditions**
  the effects of freezing weather on the braking system

- **Power steering**
  how the system works

- **Speed limiters**
  the law regarding speed limiters.

Q. 3.1

Mark one answer

On a three-line braking system to the trailer of a lorry what colour is the auxiliary line?

- Red
- Blue
- Green
- Yellow

Answer

☑ **Blue**

If you're driving an articulated vehicle or a trailer combination it's vital that you understand the rules that apply to coupling and uncoupling the brake lines. If you're taking a test with a trailer, you'll be expected to demonstrate this during your practical test. The lines must be connected strictly in accordance with the correct procedure. Study the information in *The Goods Vehicle Driving Manual* (published by The Stationery Office) to ensure that you know and understand the way this should be done.

Q. 3.2

Mark one answer

Air brake systems usually have two lines. What additional line is fitted on a three-line system?

- Emergency
- Service
- Electrical
- Auxiliary

Answer

☑ **Auxiliary**

The blue (auxiliary) line is not used when connecting to a two-line system. Follow the manufacturer's instructions about what to do with the third (blue) line.

Q. 3.3

Mark one answer

What could prevent air pressure building up in an air brake system in cold frosty weather?

- Moisture in the air may form bubbles in the brake fluid
- The air will contract, reducing the pressure
- The dampness may cause valves to rust
- Moisture drawn in with the air may freeze and cause a blockage

Answer

☑ **Moisture drawn in with the air may freeze and cause a blockage**

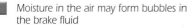

Large vehicles normally have braking systems that use compressed air to control the action of the brake shoes. The compressed air is built up by the vehicle's engine and stored in tanks on the chassis. This compressed air is, therefore, vital to the effectiveness of the brakes. You must understand the system and know how to keep it in good condition, so that the brakes won't fail when you need them.

questions answers

Q. 3.4

Mark one answer

You are about to set off in your bus in very frosty weather. You notice a lack of brake air pressure. What is the likely cause of this?

☐ Engine temperature too low

☐ Weak engine antifreeze mixture

☐ Brake pedal needs adjustment

☐ Frozen moisture in the storage tanks

Answer

✓ **Frozen moisture in the storage tanks**

Air braking systems use air from the atmosphere which contains moisture. All air braking systems are fitted with manual or automatic drain valves. Ensure the air tanks are drained daily to help prevent the system freezing in cold weather.

Q. 3.5

Mark one answer

What could prevent the build-up of brake air pressure on a bus in frosty weather?

☐ Lack of antifreeze in storage tanks

☐ Insufficient lagging of tanks and pipes

☐ Low engine revolutions

☐ Moisture freezing in the system

Answer

✓ **Moisture freezing in the system**

When the weather is frosty any moisture in the storage tanks may freeze and prevent pressure building up properly.

Q. 3.6

Mark one answer

In frosty weather, what precaution could a lorry driver take to prevent moisture freezing in brake air storage tanks?

☐ Drain the tanks daily

☐ Cover the tanks with a blanket

☐ Keep the engine at high revs when starting

☐ Pump the brakes

Answer

✓ **Drain the tanks daily**

You should make sure that you drain the tanks daily to avoid moisture freezing in the system. Most modern vehicles have an automatic draining system, which should be checked regularly.

Q. 3.7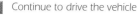

Mark one answer

What action would you take if a brake pressure warning device comes on?

- [ ] Continue to drive the vehicle
- [ ] Drain the air tanks
- [ ] Stop and get the fault put right
- [ ] Disconnect all the air lines

Answer

☑ **Stop and get the fault put right**

Air brake systems are fitted with a warning device that operates if the air pressure in the tanks drops below a safe level. This may be a warning buzzer and/or pressure gauges. You must always be aware of the function of all gauges on your vehicle, and check them as you drive.

Q. 3.8

Mark one answer

The brake air pressure warning light comes on whilst driving. You should

- [ ] stop and seek help without delay
- [ ] report the fault on return to your depot
- [ ] boost the pressure through added acceleration
- [ ] drain air tanks and continue normally

Answer

☑ **stop and seek help without delay**

If the warning light indicating a loss of brake pressure comes on, then you must stop and get the fault put right immediately. The safety of your load or, even more importantly, your passengers, will be at risk.

questions   answers

Q. 3.9

Mark one answer

When the brake air pressure warning light is operating, you should NEVER

- leave your vehicle
- release the parking brake
- switch your engine off
- engage the clutch

Answer

☑ **release the parking brake**

There may be sufficient pressure to release the parking brake even though the warning device is operating. In these circumstances the service brake may be ineffective.

Q. 3.10

Mark one answer

Your lorry does not have an anti-lock braking system fitted. You may prevent the wheels from locking under heavy braking by

- pushing the brake pedal harder until you stop
- depressing the clutch pedal as you brake
- rapid pumping of the brake pedal
- changing down through the gears as you brake

Answer

☑ **rapid pumping of the brake pedal**

Use maximum pressure to the point where the wheels are about to lock, momentarily release the brake pressure, quickly apply it again. This is a technique known as cadence braking.

Only use this method when the vehicle IS NOT fitted with an anti-lock braking system. It should only be used in an emergency situation to avoid skidding.

Q. 3.11

Mark one answer

Your vehicle has anti-lock brakes. You can

- stop in a shorter distance
- steer whilst braking
- drive faster on wet roads
- brake later than normal

Answer

☑ **steer whilst braking**

Although anti-lock braking gives you the ability to brake and steer, it should not be relied on to keep you out of trouble.

Good forward planning and anticipation will minimise the risk of skidding more effectively than relying on your braking system.

Q. 3.12

Mark one answer

Your vehicle is fitted with an anti-lock braking system. Its main purpose is to help you to

◻ drive at faster speeds

◻ brake much later than normal

◻ apply the brakes more quickly

◻ stop safely in an emergency

Answer

☑ **stop safely in an emergency**

Anti-lock braking systems work in a similar manner to cadence braking. Just as the wheels are about to lock, the sensor control releases the brake and immediately applies it again.

Q. 3.13

Mark one answer

An anti-lock braking system warning light fitted to a bus should go out

◻ when the brakes are used for the first time

◻ immediately after the anti-lock braking system comes into operation

◻ when road speed is 10 kph (6 mph) or more

◻ when the secondary braking system is used

Answer

☑ **when road speed is 10 kph (6 mph) or more**

Every vehicle fitted with anti-lock brakes must have a warning light fitted in the cab of the vehicle. Check this as part of your routine. Make yourself fully familiar with the warnings and gauges if you're driving the vehicle for the first time. Driving with defective anti-lock brakes may constitute an offence.

Warnings may differ between manufacturers, but should come on with the ignition. The light should go out when the vehicle reaches 10 kph (6 mph). Don't carry on any further if the light fails to go out. The safety of your passengers and all other road users will be at risk.

Q. 3.14

Mark one answer

As the driver of a vehicle fitted with an anti-lock braking system you should check it is working before each

◻ service

◻ day's work

◻ week's work

◻ journey

Answer

☑ **journey**

Modern anti-lock braking systems rely on electrical power for their operation. The satisfactory operation of the system can be checked from the warning signal on the dashboard. The warning signal should go out no later than when the vehicle has reached a speed of about 10 kph (6 mph).

questions   answers

Q. 3.15

Mark one answer

'Pumping' the brake pedal in a vehicle fitted with anti-lock brakes will cause

☐ increased effectiveness

☐ reduced effectiveness

☐ reduced brake wear

☐ increased brake wear

Answer

 reduced effectiveness

Always refer to the owner's handbook for details of the manufacturer's recommended method of use. Remember, anti-lock brakes will enhance your skills, NOT replace them.

Q. 3.16

Mark one answer

You are driving a vehicle fitted with anti-lock brakes. When braking in an emergency, you should

☐ 'pump' the brake pedal harshly

☐ apply minimum force to the brake pedal

☐ use the exhaust brake (retarder) then the footbrake

☐ apply firm continuous pressure to the brake pedal

Answer

 apply firm continuous pressure to the brake pedal

Always check with the vehicle manufacturer for details of their recommended method of use. Always plan well ahead to avoid 'emergency' situations developing.

Q. 3.17

Mark one answer

You are driving a vehicle not fitted with anti-lock brakes. How can 'wheel lock' be controlled during heavy braking?

☐ By using engine braking

☐ By cadence braking

☐ By braking suddenly

☐ By using clutch and brake together

Answer

 By cadence braking

Cadence braking is a special braking technique for slowing or stopping a vehicle without anti-lock brakes in slippery conditions. It is not a substitute for proper care and anticipation.

Q. 3.18

Mark one answer

Brake fade happens when the brakes get too

 hot

cold

dry

wet

Answer

 hot

Brake fade occurs when the brakes become too hot. Continuous use of the brakes can result in them becoming overheated and losing their effectiveness, especially on long downhill gradients.

Q. 3.19

Mark one answer

You have to stop quickly in an emergency. Which of the following are most likely to prevent 'wheel lock'?

Using the parking brake

Selecting neutral

Cadence braking

Changing up a gear

Answer

Cadence braking

The principle of cadence braking is to

* brake using maximum pressure to the point where the wheels are about to lock
* momentarily release the brake pressure
* quickly apply it again.

Q. 3.20

Mark one answer

What is 'brake fade'?

Reduction of air pressure

Smooth progressive braking

Reduction of braking effectiveness

Low hydraulic brake fluid level

Answer

Reduction of braking effectiveness

Make sure that you're in the correct gear before you negotiate downhill stretches of road. A low gear will assist with the braking and prevent the vehicle gaining momentum as you negotiate the hill. Look out for road signs. Look well ahead for a stretch of 'dead ground', which would indicate a dip or a hill.

Continually using the brakes could cause them to 'fade'. This will mean that they are less effective.

questions   answers

Q. 3.21

Mark two answers

To prevent brake fade you should

- use the endurance brake (retarder)
- apply the parking brake
- select a lower gear
- repeatedly pump the brake pedal
- select neutral for a short distance

Answers

☑ **use the endurance brake (retarder)**

☑ **select a lower gear**

Brake fade occurs due to the brakes overheating. Good forward planning and correct use of the gears to descend long hills, combined with proper use of the endurance brake (retarder), can help eliminate brake fade.

Q. 3.22

Mark one answer

What would cause the brakes to 'fade'?

- Contaminated brake linings
- Continuous use of the brakes
- Moisture in the storage tanks
- Brakes out of adjustment

Answer

☑ **Continuous use of the brakes**

It's important that you don't continually use the brakes. The brake shoes and drums can become hot from over-use and the friction material on the brake shoes can be affected by the heat generated, becoming shiny and slippery against the drums and, therefore, ineffective. This is referred to as 'brake fade'.

Q. 3.23

Mark one answer

To help to avoid 'brake fade' lorry drivers should ensure that

- the air tanks are drained before journeys
- air pressure is correct
- the handbrake is applied before stopping
- the appropriate gears are engaged before downhill gradients

Answer

☑ **the appropriate gears are engaged before downhill gradients**

It's important that you engage a low gear as you approach the hill to ensure the engine is building up air and can assist with braking. If the road has a long downhill gradient this is doubly important. You should be anticipating hazards like this as you drive. Good planning and preparation will ensure that you are always in the correct gear for the situation.

Q. 3.24

Mark one answer

'Brake fade' is a loss of effectiveness of the brakes, caused by their continuous use. When would this be most likely to happen?

 On a long journey

 On a long downhill gradient

 When approaching hazards

 On a long uphill gradient

Answer

✓ **On a long downhill gradient**

Continuous use of the brakes will cause them to overheat, and in extreme cases they'll become ineffective. When you're going downhill, the momentum of your vehicle will cause you to gather speed very quickly. Don't underestimate the importance of the correct use of your brakes.

Q. 3.25

Mark two answers

When driving down a steep hill the driver of a large vehicle should

 partly apply the parking brake

 have changed to a lower gear

 use an endurance brake (retarder)

 put the gear lever into neutral

 use as high a gear as possible

Answers

✓ **have changed to a lower gear**

✓ **use an endurance brake (retarder)**

Forward planning to deal with hazards is important at all times. To descend a long hill you should have taken note of any early warning signs. Plan your approach by reducing your speed and selecting the appropriate gear in good time.

Using an endurance brake (retarder), if fitted, will help control your speed.

Q. 3.26

Mark one answer

Your vehicle has anti-lock brakes. When stopping in an emergency this should allow you to

 brake more gently

 brake much later

 maintain steering control

 stop over a long distance

Answer

✓ **maintain steering control**

Anti-lock brakes are a driver aid; they shouldn't be used to get you out of trouble. Don't rely on being able to make sudden direction changes when braking.

questions   answers

Q. 3.27

Mark one answer

Your vehicle is fitted with an anti-lock braking system. When braking normally you should press the brake pedal

- [ ] in the usual way
- [ ] on and off rapidly
- [ ] quickly and firmly
- [ ] later than usual

Answer

 in the usual way

Anti-lock brakes don't remove the need for good driving practices, such as anticipating events and assessing road and weather conditions.

Q. 3.28

Mark one answer

Your vehicle has anti-lock brakes. This means that when you brake normally you will

- [ ] not need to alter the way you brake
- [ ] be able to brake much later
- [ ] need to brake more firmly
- [ ] not need to brake so early

Answer

☑ **not need to alter the way you brake**

Plan well ahead to enable you to brake normally. You shouldn't rely on anti-lock brakes to make up for deficiencies in your driving.

Q. 3.29

Mark one answer

You would see an escape lane

- [ ] outside a fire station
- [ ] alongside a bus lane
- [ ] before a motorway exit
- [ ] down a steep hill

Answer

☑ **down a steep hill**

The sign informs you of the direction of the road and shows a chequered area, usually straight ahead, which defines the escape route.

Q. 3.30

Mark one answer

You would use an escape lane

- ☐ where motorways merge
- ☐ when carrying a dangerous cargo
- ☐ when your brakes have failed
- ☐ for emergency vehicle repairs

Answer

- ☑ **when your brakes have failed**

On steep downhill sections of road you will sometimes see an escape lane. This is designed to give a 'run-off' area, usually straight ahead, to allow you to stop your vehicle in the event of an emergency.

Q. 3.31

Mark one answer

On steep hills an emergency area to be used only when your brakes have failed is called

- ☐ a buffer lane
- ☐ an escape lane
- ☐ a rumble strip
- ☐ the hard shoulder

Answer

- ☑ **an escape lane**

Do not park in the area designated as an escape lane. You are putting yourself and others in danger if a vehicle needs to use this 'run-off' area in an emergency.

Do NOT use it as a viewing area or for taking a rest period. Find an appropriate place to stop where you will not endanger other road users.

questions answers

Q. 3.32

Mark one answer

Your brakes fail down a very steep hill. Which of the following should you use?

- A buffer lane
- A crawler lane
- An escape lane
- A rumble strip

Answer

☑ **An escape lane**

The escape lane is intended to be used if your brakes fail. The escape lane route may take you to the left away from a steep descent. In the event of an emergency, look for the signs which will give you advance warning of where the escape lane is located.

Q. 3.33

Mark one answer

What causes brake fade?

- Continuous use of the brakes
- Repeated pumping of the brakes
- Loss of air pressure in the system
- Badly worn brake pads

Answer

☑ **Continuous use of the brakes**

The continuous use of the brakes on a long downhill gradient can cause them to overheat and could result in them becoming ineffective.

You should engage a low gear to enable the engine to assist with the braking. This will also ensure that there's enough air pressure building up in the tanks.

Q. 3.34

Mark one answer

The main cause of brake fade is

- the brakes overheating
- moisture in the air tanks
- oil on the brake linings
- the brakes out of adjustment

Answer

☑ **the brakes overheating**

Planning ahead will enable you to select an appropriate gear and use your endurance brake (retarder) to control the speed of your vehicle when travelling downhill.

This will help prevent your brakes overheating on long downhill gradients.

questions   answers

Q. 3.35

Mark one answer

Exhaust brakes give greatest efficiency when used

- ■ at high engine speed in low gears
- ■ at low engine speed in high gears
- ■ on stop-start town work
- ■ on high-speed motorway runs

Answer

☑ **at high engine speed in low gears**

Because excessive braking can have serious effects on the brakes, some vehicles are fitted with exhaust brakes. These brakes alter the engine's exhaust flow, using it to assist with the braking. They're most efficient when the engine is at high speed and in a low gear, such as when descending a long hill. Using the exhaust brakes can relieve the service brakes, preventing them from becoming hot and failing through over-use.

Q. 3.36

Mark one answer

An endurance brake (retarder) can be especially useful

- ■ when driving down long hills
- ■ when driving on steep cambers
- ■ to reduce gear changes
- ■ to improve fuel consumption

Answer

☑ **when driving down long hills**

Plan ahead and use your endurance brake (retarder) to help hold your speed in check on long downhill gradients. This can help prevent your brakes from overheating.

Q. 3.37

Mark one answer

You are driving down a long hill and want to avoid the brakes overheating. The vehicle's speed should be controlled by using the

- ■ anti-lock braking system
- ■ footbrake
- ■ secondary brake
- ■ endurance brake (retarder)

Answer

☑ **endurance brake (retarder)**

Systems that assist in controlling a vehicle's speed without using the wheel brakes are called endurance brakes or 'retarders'. Retarders operate by applying resistance via the transmission to the rotation of the vehicle's driven wheels. This may be achieved by

- increased engine braking
- exhaust braking
- transmission-mounted electromagnetic or hydraulic devices.

questions answers

Q. 3.38

Mark one answer

A system for controlling the vehicle's speed without using the footbrake is

- a secondary brake
- an endurance brake (retarder)
- a differential lock
- an emergency air system

Answer

✓ **an endurance brake (retarder)**

If your vehicle is fitted with any of these devices, you must become familiar with them before you make your journey. You won't lose respect by asking a colleague to show you, but you will if you have an accident through ignorance.

Q. 3.39

Mark two answers

An endurance brake (retarder) may work in which TWO of the following ways?

- Increasing engine braking
- Using an extra transmission device
- Sensing wheel speed
- Using the parking brake
- Using the secondary brake

Answers

✓ **Increasing engine braking**

✓ **Using an extra transmission device**

These systems provide a way of controlling a vehicle's speed without using the wheel-mounted brakes. When descending long hills the vehicle speed can be stabilised without using the service brakes.

Q. 3.40

Mark one answer

An endurance brake (retarder), when not combined with the footbrake, should be used

- on motorways only
- on long downhill slopes
- when braking quickly
- all the time when stopping

Answer

✓ **on long downhill slopes**

Mechanically operated endurance brakes (retarders) alter the engine exhaust gas flow. They are usually operated by a floor-mounted switch.

Electrically operated endurance brakes (retarders) can be combined with the use of the footbrake, or be operated via a multi-position dashboard-mounted lever which offers pre-defined stages of retardation.

Q. 3.41

Mark one answer

An endurance brake (retarder) should be used

- ▓ on motorways only
- ▓ when braking quickly
- ▓ when you stop or park
- ▓ on long downhill slopes

Answer

✓ **on long downhill slopes**

Your electrically operated endurance brake (retarder) may have a switch to enable or disable it.

For normal use it is advisable to leave it switched on, as it can considerably reduce brake wear.

Q. 3.42

Mark one answer

You are driving down a snow-covered hill. You should take extra care when using an independent endurance brake (retarder) because

- ▓ your brakes could overheat
- ▓ your speed could increase
- ▓ compressed air could escape
- ▓ the rear wheels could lock

Answer

✓ **the rear wheels could lock**

Select an appropriate gear in good time, and if your vehicle has a dashboard mounted lever, apply the endurance brake (retarder) in stages. Careful use is necessary when driving on extremely slippery surfaces to avoid applying too much too soon resulting in locking your drive wheels.

Q. 3.43

Mark two answers

An anti-lock braking system is most useful when you are driving in

- ▓ misty conditions
- ▓ falling snow
- ▓ drifting fog
- ▓ high winds
- ▓ heavy rain
- ▓ bright sunshine

Answers

✓ **falling snow**

✓ **heavy rain**

Do not rely on your anti-lock braking system to keep you out of trouble. It is your responsibility to plan ahead and drive according to the road and weather conditions at all times.

questions   answers

Q. 3.44

Mark one answer

When using an independent endurance brake (retarder) on slippery roads, you should take care to avoid the

 front wheels spinning

 rear wheels locking

■ four wheels sliding

■ four wheels spinning

Answer

✓ **rear wheels locking**

The endurance brake (retarder) usually operates by applying resistance via the transmission to the rotation of the vehicle's driven wheels.

Q. 3.45

Mark one answer

An endurance brake (retarder) operates by applying resistance to the driven wheels via

■ hydraulic lines

 the starter motor

■ air lines

■ the transmission

Answer

✓ **the transmission**

Transmission-mounted electromagnetic or hydraulically-operated endurance brakes (retarders) may be operated independently by a hand control or, alternatively, be built into the footbrake system.

Q. 3.46

Mark one answer

When using an exhaust brake (retarder), extra care must be taken on

■ uneven roads

■ slippery roads

■ downhill gradients

■ uphill gradients

Answer

✓ **slippery roads**

The exhaust brake (retarder) is usually a mechanical device. It works by either altering the engine exhaust gas flow or amending the valve timing to create a 'compressor' effect. The result is enhanced engine braking which helps to slow your vehicle.

questions   answers

Q. 3.47

Mark one answer

The principal braking system on a lorry is called the

- endurance brake (retarder)
- service brake
- parking brake
- hand brake

Answer

☑ **service brake**

The service brake

- is usually operated by the foot control
- is used to control the speed of the vehicle and to bring it to a halt safely
- may incorporate an anti-lock braking system.

Q. 3.48

Mark three answers

The three main braking systems fitted to lorries are known as

- over run
- cadence
- exhaust
- service
- secondary
- parking

Answers

☑ **service**

☑ **secondary**

☑ **parking**

The service brake performs the primary function of stopping the vehicle when you depress the footbrake. The secondary brake system is for use in the event of failure of the service brake.

The parking brake should normally only be used when the vehicle is stationary.

Q. 3.49

Mark one answer

The MOST powerful brake on a bus is normally the

- secondary brake
- anti-lock braking system
- endurance brake (retarder)
- service brake

Answer

☑ **service brake**

The most powerful and effective brakes on the vehicle are the service brakes, and these should be used in normal circumstances. Well-maintained brakes should apply an even pressure to all the wheels, providing an efficient, controlled stop.

questions   answers

Q. 3.50

Mark one answer

When making a short stop, facing uphill, you should

▪ hold the vehicle on the clutch

▪ hold the vehicle on the footbrake

▪ select neutral and apply the parking brake

▪ apply the parking brake after stopping

Answer

☑ **apply the parking brake after stopping**

If you have to make a stop on an uphill gradient, wait until the vehicle has come to a stop before applying the parking brake, just as you would normally.

Q. 3.51

Mark one answer

You are about to move off. Your vehicle has automatic transmission. Before you select drive (D) you must

▪ put your foot on the footbrake

▪ signal to move off

▪ alter your seat position

▪ adjust your mirrors

Answer

☑ **put your foot on the footbrake**

It is important to apply the footbrake before you engage 'D' or drive. This eliminates creep or roll-back out of control when you are expecting to move away. This can be dangerous if there's another road user close behind.

Q. 3.52

Mark three answers

Which THREE of the following are advantages of progressive braking when driving a bus?

▪ Passenger safety and comfort

▪ Increased air brake pressure

▪ Lower fuel consumption

▪ Reduced tyre wear

▪ Avoidance of 'brake fade'

Answers

☑ **Passenger safety and comfort**

☑ **Lower fuel consumption**

☑ **Reduced tyre wear**

As a driver of a bus, the safety and comfort of the passengers is your first priority. If you have the correct attitude when you're driving, your passengers will be assured of a comfortable and pleasant journey. By good forward planning and anticipation you'll be able to prevent harsh braking and late, sharp steering. These factors will also have a bearing on the maintenance and condition of your vehicle. Badly-driven vehicles cost more to run and maintain.

Q. 3.53

Mark two answers

Your vehicle is fully loaded. When dealing with bends all braking should be done

- as close to the bend as possible
- smoothly and in good time
- when driving in a straight line
- as you start to turn the wheel
- when halfway round the bend

Answers

✓ **smoothly and in good time**

✓ **when driving in a straight line**

Braking should always be

- progressive
- correctly timed
- smooth
- sensitive.

When a vehicle changes direction, forces are applied to it and its load. Sudden, excessive or badly timed braking can result in loss of control.

Q. 3.54

Mark one answer

You are driving a lorry fitted with a speed limiter. The limiter is set to comply with EC rules. This means you will not be able to exceed

- 50 mph (80 kph)
- 56 mph (90 kph)
- 60 mph (96 kph)
- 66 mph (106 kph)

Answer

✓ **56 mph (90 kph)**

EC regulations require the use of speed limiters on most lorries and buses, unless they are specifically exempt.

Lorries first used on or after 1st January 1988 capable of exceeding 56 mph (90 kph) and over 12 tonnes MAM must be limited under EC regulations to 56 mph (90 kph) (max).

Q. 3.55

Mark one answer

You are the driver of a 1996 bus, which must be fitted with a speed limiter. At what speed is the limiter set?

- 60 mph (96 kph)
- 62 mph (100 kph)
- 70 mph (112 kph)
- 75 mph (120 kph)

Answer

✓ **62 mph (100 kph)**

A speed limiter is designed to prevent the vehicle from exceeding a set limit.

questions   answers

Q. 3.56

Mark one answer

When a speed limiter is fitted to a bus, where must the setting be displayed clearly?

- In the driver's cab
- On the nearside of the vehicle
- On the rear of the vehicle
- On the driver's side at the front of the vehicle

Answer

☑ **In the driver's cab**

If there's a speed limiter fitted to the vehicle, there should be a notice clearly displayed in the driver's cab, showing the speed at which it's set.

Q. 3.57

Mark one answer

You are driving a vehicle fitted with a speed limiter. You should allow for its effects when

- cornering
- braking
- overtaking
- changing gear

Answer

☑ **overtaking**

Forward planning is important whenever you consider overtaking another road user. You should carefully assess the speed of the vehicle you intend to overtake. Remember that your vehicle speed is limited and this could considerably increase the distance and time needed to complete overtaking safely.

Q. 3.58

Mark one answer

A lorry is overtaking you on a two-lane motorway. It does not have the speed to get past. What should you do?

- Continue at the same speed
- Be prepared to reduce your speed
- Increase your speed and force the lorry to drop back
- Brake hard to allow the other driver to cut in

Answer

☑ **Be prepared to reduce your speed**

Always be prepared to give way to overtaking lorries or buses. Maintaining your speed will only block the motorway to other traffic unnecessarily.

Remember, you may find yourself in a similar situation when the limiter on your vehicle will not allow you enough speed to complete an overtaking manoeuvre.

Q. 3.59

Mark one answer

You must be aware of the effect a speed limiter has on your vehicle, especially when you intend to

- ▨ brake
- ▨ change gear
- ▨ overtake
- ▨ reverse

Answer

☑ **overtake**

Plan well ahead before overtaking. Your vehicle speed limiter may cause you difficulties if you attempt to pass another vehicle when climbing a hill.

Q. 3.60

Mark one answer

You are driving on a motorway in a vehicle fitted with a speed limiter. You should be aware of

- ▨ the lower running costs
- ▨ the smoother ride
- ▨ the limited power available when overtaking
- ▨ the increased fuel consumption

Answer

☑ **the limited power available when overtaking**

When driving on a motorway, the speed difference between two large vehicles can be extremely small. If you wish to overtake, plan well ahead to avoid causing a long tailback of frustrated drivers.

Q. 3.61

Mark one answer

What is the national speed limit for a lorry over 7.5 tonnes on a motorway?

- ▨ 50 mph (80 kph)
- ▨ 55 mph (88 kph)
- ▨ 60 mph (96 kph)
- ▨ 70 mph (112 kph)

Answer

☑ **60 mph (96 kph)**

Be aware of, and obey, all speed limits. Think about this when you're considering overtaking. On a motorway a lorry's speed shouldn't exceed 60 mph (96 kph).

questions   answers

Q. 3.62

Mark one answer

At 50 mph (80 kph) what gap should you leave behind the vehicle in front on a dry, level road?

- One vehicle length
- Two vehicle lengths
- A minimum one-second gap
- A minimum two-second gap

Answer

☑ **A minimum two-second gap**

'Tailgating' – travelling too close to the vehicle in front – is a common and very dangerous practice. It often happens on motorways. Don't do it.

Tailgating is often the cause of serious accidents. It's essential that you understand the distance it will take for you to stop if you have do so in an emergency. Always leave a safety margin.

Q. 3.63

Mark one answer

You are behind a large vehicle. How can you improve your view ahead?

- Stay further back
- Move over to the right
- Move over to the left
- Overtake as soon as you can

Answer

☑ **Stay further back**

Leaving a safety margin will improve your view of the road ahead. Staying back from the vehicle in front will allow you more room to react to hazards that might occur.

A good way to check whether you're too close to another vehicle is by using the two-second rule. Pick an object some distance ahead, such as a bridge, sign or lamp-post. As the vehicle in front passes it, begin to say 'Only a fool breaks the two-second rule'.

If you pass the object before you've finished saying it YOU'RE TOO CLOSE. Drop back and try the test again.

questions answers

Q. 3.64

Mark two answers

You should overtake at night only when

- ▉ you can see well ahead
- ▉ you can do so without cutting in
- ▉ there is an overtaking lane
- ▉ you are outside built up areas
- ▉ the road is well lit

Answers

- ☑ **you can see well ahead**
- ☑ **you can do so without cutting in**

It is more difficult to judge speed and distance accurately in the dark. Darkness can also hide bends and dips in the road. Plan ahead, and be sure that you have time and space to complete your overtaking safely.

Q. 3.65

Mark one answer

You are driving a lorry at a speed of 50 mph (80 kph) in good, dry conditions. What distance should you stay behind the vehicle in front?

- ▉ At least 20 metres (66 feet)
- ▉ At least 30 metres (98 feet)
- ▉ At least 40 metres (131 feet)
- ▉ At least 50 metres (164 feet)

Answer

- ☑ **At least 50 metres (164 feet)**

You should always leave a safety margin between you and the vehicle in front. This gap will give you a better view of the road ahead. It will also allow you more time to react if the traffic in front changes speed or direction.

Q. 3.66

Mark one answer

You are driving a lorry and trailer. You change to a lower gear when going too fast. This could cause the

- ▉ vehicle to jack-knife
- ▉ engine to stall
- ▉ brakes to fail
- ▉ trailer to uncouple

Answer

- ☑ **vehicle to jack-knife**

Jack-knifing is usually more likely to occur with an unladen vehicle, particularly when not travelling in a straight line. Severe braking or selection of a gear too low for your road speed can cause the tractor unit to be pushed by the semi-trailer pivoting around the coupling (fifth wheel).

questions answers

Q. 3.67

Mark three answers

Trailer swing is more likely to occur on a lorry and draw bar combination when

- braking on a bend
- oversteering at speed
- the brakes are out of adjustment
- braking lightly several times
- steering at slow speed and fully loaded
- an endurance brake (retarder) is fitted

Answers

- ✓ **braking on a bend**
- ✓ **oversteering at speed**
- ✓ **the brakes are out of adjustment**

All braking and changes of direction should be carried out smoothly and under full control. Make sure all the brakes are properly adjusted.

Q. 3.68

Mark three answers

An articulated vehicle is more likely to jack-knife when

- unladen
- manoeuvring slowly
- braking sharply
- fully loaded
- on a bend
- fitted with an endurance brake (retarder)

Answers

- ✓ **unladen**
- ✓ **braking sharply**
- ✓ **on a bend**

A combination of sharp braking and excessive steering can cause your vehicle to become unstable. Jack-knifing is more likely to occur when the vehicle is empty.

Q. 3.69

Mark one answer

When driving in snow, stopping distances may be increased by up to how many times, compared with a dry road?

- Two
- Four
- Five
- Ten

Answer

- ✓ **Ten**

In icy or snowy weather your stopping distance can increase by up to ten times. Because snowy weather increases the distance needed to stop, you must look well ahead and leave a good safety margin. It's easy to underestimate the different stopping distances needed in bad weather. You should be aware that ten times the normal stopping distance is a long way.

Q. 3.70

Mark one answer

When required to slow down or stop on an icy road you should make sure that

- braking is gentle and in good time
- retarders are always used
- downward gear changes are made
- the parking brake is used in a rapid on-and-off movement

Answer

☑ **braking is gentle and in good time**

When you have to slow down or stop you should avoid harsh, late braking. If you're planning ahead with good anticipation you can reduce the need to brake harshly. Brake gently and in good time to ensure control of your vehicle. This is particularly important on icy or slippery roads.

Q. 3.71

Mark two answers

You are driving a vehicle in icy weather. All braking must be done

- suddenly
- by 'pumping' the brakes
- gently
- by using the gears first
- over longer distances

Answers

☑ **gently**

☑ **over longer distances**

All braking should be

- controlled
- in good time
- when travelling in a straight line.

Avoid braking and turning at the same time. Look well ahead to assess and plan your actions.

Q. 3.72

Mark one answer

After driving through a flood what should you do?

- Carry out an emergency stop
- Drive in low gear with the footbrake lightly applied
- Avoid braking until the brakes are dried out
- Pump the footbrake when approaching hazards

Answer

☑ **Drive in low gear with the footbrake lightly applied**

If you have to drive through a flood, do so with caution. Ensure that the brakes on your vehicle haven't been impaired by the deep water. Once out of the flood drive in a low gear with the brakes gently applied. Don't forget to consider what's behind you before doing so.

questions

answers

Q. 3.73

Mark one answer

Coasting downhill could seriously affect the correct working of the

 air-brakes

 cooling system

tachograph

electrical systems

Answer

☑ **air-brakes**

Air-brake systems rely on engine-driven compressors to replenish the air in the brake reservoir tanks. Coasting and relying on the brakes to control your speed could result in loss of sufficient air pressure to operate the brakes effectively, particularly if the compressors are worn.

Q. 3.74

Mark one answer

Your vehicle has power-assisted steering. Its main purpose is to

reduce tyre wear

assist with braking

reduce driver effort

assist road holding

Answer

☑ **reduce driver effort**

The main purpose of power-assisted steering is to reduce driver effort.

When cornering it is possible to over-steer and scrub the front tyres, resulting in excessive wear.

Q. 3.75

Mark three answers

Many vehicles are fitted with power-assisted steering. You need to be aware that this

causes less tyre wear

prevents you from oversteering

 makes it easier for you to steer

senses when you start to turn the wheel

only works at high speeds

makes the steering seem light

Answers

☑ **makes it easier for you to steer**

☑ **senses when you start to turn the wheel**

☑ **makes the steering seem light**

Power-assisted steering only operates when the engine is running. If a fault develops, much greater effort is required to turn the steering wheel.

Do not attempt to drive a vehicle if you are aware of a fault in the power steering system.

Q. 3.76

Mark two answers

You hit the kerb at speed. You should, as soon as possible, check your vehicle for any damage to the

 exhaust

 brakes

 tyres

 steering

 lights

Answers

☑ **tyres**

☑ **steering**

'Kerbing' a large vehicle at speed can split the tyre or put the steering and suspension geometry out of alignment.

You should have it checked as soon as possible; sudden deflation of the front tyre on a large vehicle can result in a loss of steering control.

Q. 3.77

Mark one answer

Which of the following is most likely to cause a burst tyre when driving?

▪ Frequent gear changing in varying conditions

▪ Running at a constant high speed

▪ Always operating in cool weather

▪ Mixing tyres with different tread depth

Answer

☑ **Running at a constant high speed**

Tyres can become very hot and disintegrate under sustained high-speed running. Check for excessive heat when you stop for a break.

Q. 3.78

Mark one answer

What could seriously lessen the grip your vehicle has on the road?

▪ A multi-axle trailer

▪ An evenly distributed load

▪ Unchecked tyre pressures

▪ A poorly maintained engine

Answer

☑ **Unchecked tyre pressures**

Wrong tyre pressures will affect the handling and control of your vehicle. Check the tread depth and inspect for cuts and damage whenever you check the tyre pressures. Always use an accurate gauge. Try to check the tyres when they are cold.

questions   answers

Q. 3.79

Mark one answer

When can a 'selective' or 'block' gear change be used?

- ☐ To change gear down only
- ☐ To change gear up only
- ☐ To change gear to a low speed only
- ☐ To change gear either up or down

Answer

- ☑ **To change gear either up or down**

Recognising the opportunities to make selective gear changes can reduce driver effort. Planning ahead will enable you to make the most of any opportunities to put this into practice.

Q. 3.80

Mark one answer

You are driving a vehicle which has a two-speed axle. This

- ☐ halves the number of gears
- ☐ doubles the number of gears
- ☐ engages the diff-lock
- ☐ releases the diff-lock

Answer

- ☑ **doubles the number of gears**

An electrical switch actuates a mechanism in the rear axle which doubles the choice of gear ratios. This can significantly improve the performance of a heavily-laden vehicle.

Q. 3.81

Mark one answer

Your vehicle is fitted with a 'diff-lock'. You would normally use it when

- ☐ driving on straight roads
- ☐ towing an empty trailer
- ☐ driving on muddy construction sites
- ☐ uncoupling a trailer

Answer

- ☑ **driving on muddy construction sites**

The differential gears in the drive axle allow the drive wheels to rotate at different speeds, which is very important to enable you to negotiate corners and bends safely. The 'diff-lock' effectively locks the driven wheels together, so that power is transmitted equally to both. This is very useful in slippery or muddy conditions where otherwise the drive wheels can spin at different speeds and result in a loss of traction.

Q. 3.82

Mark one answer

Your lorry is stuck in snow. You use the diff-lock to move off. When should you switch the diff-lock off?

- Only after selecting top gear
- Once the engine has warmed up
- As soon as the vehicle is moving
- As soon as the snow has cleared

Answer

✓ **As soon as the vehicle is moving**

You must always disengage the diff-lock as soon as the vehicle is moving.

The differential allows the rear wheels to revolve at different speeds, which allows the vehicle to be steered.

Attempting to turn with the diff-lock engaged could have disastrous consequences, as your vehicle will try to go straight on.

Q. 3.83

Mark one answer

On a vehicle with automatic transmission you would use 'kickdown' to

- give quicker acceleration
- apply the emergency brakes
- stop more smoothly
- go down a steep hill

Answer

✓ **give quicker acceleration**

Dependant upon road speed, depressing the accelerator pedal firmly to the floor will activate a switch which allows the gearbox to select a lower gear for improved acceleration.

Q. 3.84

Mark one answer

The bus you are driving is fitted with an automatic gearbox. When would you use kickdown?

- When stopping in an emergency
- When changing to a higher gear
- When driving at slow speed
- When needing brisk acceleration

Answer

✓ **When needing brisk acceleration**

The kickdown facility on an automatic gearbox allows a lower gear to be engaged to allow rapid acceleration (e.g., for overtaking). This is achieved by pressing the accelerator to the floor.

questions

answers

Q. 3.85

Mark one answer

You are driving a modern vehicle. You notice the steering feels heavy. What is the most likely cause?

 Faulty power steering

 An icy road

 A burst rear tyre

A wet road

Answer

☑ **Faulty power steering**

Many large vehicles are fitted with power-assisted steering. Any fault should be investigated and repaired as soon as possible.

Q. 3.86

Mark one answer

Your coach is fully laden. You notice the steering feels heavy. What is the most likely reason?

An icy road

A burst rear tyre

Faulty power steering

Too many passengers

Answer

☑ **Faulty power steering**

An engine-driven oil pump operates hydraulic rams which assist the movement of steering components. This helps you by reducing the effort required to steer a large vehicle.

Q. 3.87

Mark one answer

Your vehicle suffers a tyre blow-out. What is likely to create a hazard for other road users?

Scattered debris

Skid marks

Suspension failure

Axle damage

Answer

☑ **Scattered debris**

When a tyre explodes, fragments are thrown over a wide area. This can cause serious problems for other drivers. Always check your tyre pressures and look for cuts or damage to the tyres. Frequent checks can prevent a blow-out from happening.

Q. 3.88

Mark one answer

When should you check the wheel nuts on your vehicle?

 Just before any journey

Only before long trips

Only every 1000 miles (1600 km)

Just before a major service

Answer

✓ **Just before any journey**

Always have a walk round and visually check wheel nuts whenever you take a break.

It's important after a wheel has been replaced to re-check wheel nuts shortly after their initial tightening. Wheel nuts must always be tightened to the torque specified by the manufacturer.

Q. 3.89

Mark one answer

You are driving a new articulated lorry which is fully laden. You notice the steering feels heavy. What is the most likely reason?

The road is icy

Faulty power steering

A tyre on the trailer has burst

The load on the trailer has shifted

Answer

✓ **Faulty power steering**

Any suspected failure of the power steering should be investigated as soon as possible. Many large vehicles can become undriveable if it fails completely.

Q. 3.90

Mark one answer

Your tractor unit has three air lines. You are connecting to a trailer with two air lines. What colour is the line you should NOT connect to the trailer?

Red

Yellow

Black

Blue

Answer

✓ **Blue**

When connecting three lines to a two line trailer, the third (blue) line is the one that should NOT be connected to the trailer. It is vitally important to follow the manufacturer's advice as it may be necessary to reconnect the extra line to the tractor unit.

questions answers

Q. 3.91

Mark one answer

The emergency line is common to both two and three line brake systems. What is its colour?

- Red
- Blue
- Black
- Yellow

Answer

✓ **Red**

The red emergency line is common to both two and three line braking systems. ALWAYS set the parking brake before disconnecting any brake lines.

Q. 3.92

Mark one answer

On an articulated lorry which has a three line connection, the red line is the

- emergency line
- service line
- auxiliary line
- electrical line

Answer

✓ **emergency line**

The red emergency line is common to both two and three line brake systems. The other colours are

- auxiliary – blue
- service – yellow.

Q. 3.93

Mark one answer

You are driving a tractor unit fitted with two air lines. You want to couple up to a trailer with three air lines. How should this be done?

- The trailer auxiliary line should be left unconnected
- The trailer service line should be left unconnected
- Only the service line should be connected
- Only the auxiliary line should be connected

Answer

✓ **The trailer auxiliary line should be left unconnected**

A two line system comprises of

- emergency – red line
- service – yellow line.

It is vitally important that you understand the rules that apply to safely connecting and mixing two and three line systems.

Q. 3.94

Mark one answer

The correct procedure for stopping a lorry equipped with an anti-lock braking system in an emergency is to

- apply the footbrake firmly in a pumping action until the vehicle has stopped
- apply the footbrake firmly and continuously until the vehicle has stopped
- apply the footbrake and handbrake until the vehicle has stopped
- apply the handbrake only

Answer

☑ **apply the footbrake firmly and continuously until the vehicle has stopped**

If you're driving a vehicle with anti lock brakes and you feel the vehicle beginning to skid, you should keep your foot firmly on the brake pedal until the vehicle stops. This will allow the system to work.

Although anti lock brakes on a vehicle makes a contribution to safe braking, it doesn't take away the need to drive with good planning and anticipation, which should greatly reduce the need to brake harshly. Reliable and efficient equipment is essential, but it's your action that can prevent an accident.

Attitude and alertness

This section looks at alertness and attention when you're driving.

The questions will ask you about

- **Consideration**

  considering other road users. Being positive but treating them as you would wish to be treated

- **Positioning**

  not following too closely. As well as being dangerous it can feel threatening to the driver in front

- **Courtesy**

  not using the size of your vehicle to intimidate other road users

- **Priority**

  being calm and tolerant if others break the rules or don't understand the position you need to take on the road.

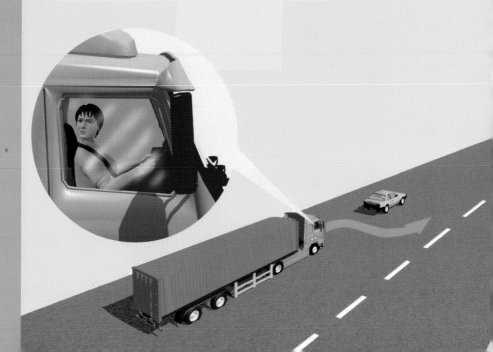

Q. 4.1

Mark one answer

You are driving along this road. The red van cuts in close in front of you. What should you do?

- Accelerate to get closer to the red van
- Give a long blast on the horn
- Drop back to leave the correct separation distance
- Flash your headlights several times

Answer

☑ **Drop back to leave the correct separation distance**

There are times when other drivers make incorrect or ill-judged decisions. Be tolerant and don't react aggressively or retaliate. Always consider the safety of other road users, your passengers and yourself.

Q. 4.2

Mark two answers

While driving you approach a large puddle that is close to the left-hand kerb. Pedestrians are close to the water. You should

- ignore the puddle
- brake suddenly and sound your horn
- slow down before the puddle
- try to avoid splashing the pedestrians
- wave at the pedestrians to keep back

Answers

☑ **slow down before the puddle**

☑ **try to avoid splashing the pedestrians**

The effect of your vehicle driving through a puddle will be to throw water onto the pavement. If there are pedestrians close by they could be splashed with the water. Be considerate. If necessary, and it's safe to do so, avoid driving through it.

questions answers

Q. 4.3

Mark one answer

A long, heavily-laden lorry is taking a long time to overtake you. What should you do?

 Speed up

Slow down

Hold your speed

Change direction

Answer

 Slow down

A long lorry with a heavy load will need more time to pass you than a car. It won't be able to accelerate to pass you quickly, especially on an uphill stretch of road. Ease off the accelerator and allow the lorry to pass.

Q. 4.4

Mark one answer

You are driving a slow-moving vehicle on a narrow road. When traffic wishes to overtake you should

take no action

put your hazard warning lights on

stop immediately and wave them on

pull in safely as soon as you can do so

Answer

 pull in safely as soon as you can do so

Try not to hold up a queue of traffic. This might lead to other road users becoming impatient. If you're driving a slow-moving vehicle and the road is narrow, look out for a safe place to pull in.

Q. 4.5

Mark one answer

You are driving a slow-moving vehicle on a narrow winding road. In order to let other vehicles overtake you should

wave to them to pass

pull in when you can

show a left turn signal

keep left and hold your speed

Answer

 pull in when you can

Don't frustrate other road users by driving for long distances with a queue of traffic behind you. This could cause them to lose concentration or make ill-judged decisions.

Q. 4.6

Mark one answer

What should you use your horn for?

- To alert others to your presence
- To allow you right of way
- To greet other road users
- To signal your annoyance

Answer

☑ **To alert others to your presence**

Don't use it to

- greet others
- show impatience
- give or claim priority.

Your horn shouldn't be used between 11.30 pm and 7 am in a built-up area or when your vehicle's stationary – unless a moving vehicle poses a danger.

Q. 4.7

Mark two answers

You are following a car driven by a learner driver. You cannot overtake it. You should

- flash your lights so that the driver sees you
- be patient and stay well behind
- switch your hazard lights on and stay well behind
- be ready for mistakes made by the driver
- drive along the centre line of the road

Answers

☑ **be patient and stay well behind**

☑ **be ready for mistakes made by the driver**

Learner drivers are often nervous. If you stay well back this will avoid accidents occuring if mistakes are made by the learner driver. Remember, you were in that situation once.

Q. 4.8

Mark one answer

You are signalled to stop by a police car. You should

- brake harshly to a stop
- drive on until you reach a side road
- pull up on the left when it is safe to
- stop immediately wherever you are

Answer

☑ **pull up on the left when it is safe to**

If a police car signals for you to stop you should always find a safe place on the left and pull over.

questions

answers

Q. 4.9

Mark one answer

A police car is following you. The police would like you to stop. They will do this by flashing their headlights and

☐ signalling with the right indicator

☐ signalling with the left indicator

☐ switching their hazard flashers on

☐ switching their rear fog lights on

Answer

 signalling with the left indicator

Indicating to the left shows that the police want you to pull in. You should find a safe place to stop before doing so.

Q. 4.10

Mark one answer

Large vehicles have many blind spots. What does 'blind spot' mean?

☐ An area of road covered by your right-hand mirror

☐ An area of road covered by your left-hand mirror

☐ An area of road that cannot be seen in your mirrors

☐ An area of road that is not lit by your headlights

Answer

 **An area of road that cannot be seen in your mirrors**

Blind spots can occur when bodywork interferes with your view through the mirrors. Vehicles with different shapes have different blind spots.

Q. 4.11

Mark one answer

You are driving a vehicle fitted with a hand held telephone. To answer it you should

☐ find a safe place to stop

☐ reduce your speed to less than 30mph

☐ steer your vehicle with one hand

☐ be very careful when dealing with junctions

Answer

 find a safe place to stop

Telephone calls can distract you, and mean that you are not in proper control of your vehicle. You must exercise proper control of your vehicle at all times. If you need to use any telephone in the vehicle, find a safe place to stop first.

Q. 4.12

Mark one answer

You have a mobile telephone fitted in your vehicle. It should only be used when you are

- ■ stopped in a safe place
- ■ travelling slowly
- ■ on a motorway
- ■ in light traffic

Answer

☑ **stopped in a safe place**

If you have stopped your vehicle, then you can concentrate on your telephone call. If you use your phone while driving, you have not got control of your vehicle and could be distracted, causing it to be involved in a crash.

Q. 4.13

Mark one answer

A pelican crossing that crosses the road in a STRAIGHT line and has a central island MUST be treated as

- ■ one crossing in daylight only
- ■ one complete crossing
- ■ two separate crossings
- ■ two crossings during darkness

Answer

☑ **one complete crossing**

The lights that control the crossing show to both directions of traffic. If a pedestrian from either side is still crossing when the amber light is flashing, you must wait.

Q. 4.14

Mark one answer

At a pelican crossing the flashing amber light means you should

- ■ stop, if you can do so safely
- ■ give way to pedestrians already on the crossing
- ■ stop and wait for the green light
- ■ give way to pedestrians waiting to cross

Answer

☑ **give way to pedestrians already on the crossing**

Pelican crossings are light-controlled crossings where pedestrians use push-button controls to change the signals. Pelican crossings have no red-and-amber stage before green. Instead, they have a flashing amber light, which means you must give way to pedestrians on the crossing.

If it's clear, you may go on.

questions   answers

Q. 4.15

Mark one answer

At zebra crossings you should

- rev your engine to encourage pedestrians to cross quickly
- park only on the zigzag lines on the left
- always leave it clear in traffic queues
- wave pedestrians to cross if you intend to wait for them

Answer

✓ **always leave it clear in traffic queues**

Look well down the line of traffic ahead so that you don't stop over the crossing, which should be left clear so that pedestrians are able to cross.

Q. 4.16

Mark one answer

In fast traffic a two-second gap may be enough only when conditions are

- dry
- wet
- damp
- foggy

Answer

✓ **dry**

You must be aware that when the weather is bad, you will have to keep a greater distance from the vehicle in front. It will take you further to stop. In wet weather it will take twice as far, in icy weather it could increase to ten times.

Q. 4.17

Mark one answer

At puffin crossings which light will not show to a driver?

- Flashing amber
- Red
- Steady amber
- Green

Answer

✓ **Flashing amber**

A flashing amber light is shown at pelican crossings, but puffin crossings are different. They are controlled electronically, and automatically detect when pedestrians are on the crossing.

The phase is shortened or lengthened according to the position of the pedestrians.

Q. 4.18

Mark one answer

You are approaching a red light at a puffin crossing. Pedestrians are on the crossing. The red light will stay on until

 you start to edge forward on to the crossing

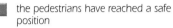 the pedestrians have reached a safe position

the pedestrians are clear of the front of your vehicle

a driver from the opposite direction reaches the crossing

Answer

☑ **the pedestrians have reached a safe position**

The electronic device will automatically detect that the pedestrians have reached a safe position. Don't proceed until the green light shows and it's safe to do so.

Q. 4.19

Mark one answer

You could use the 'two-second rule'

before restarting the engine after it has stalled

to keep a safe distance from the vehicle in front

before using the 'Mirror, Signal, Manoeuvre' routine

when emerging on wet roads

Answer

☑ **to keep a safe distance from the vehicle in front**

To measure this, choose a reference point, such as a bridge, sign or tree. When the vehicle ahead passes the object, say to yourself 'Only a fool breaks the two-second rule.' If you reach the object before you finish saying this you're TOO CLOSE.

Q. 4.20

Mark one answer

Following a large goods vehicle too closely is dangerous because

your field of vision is seriously reduced

slipstreaming will reduce wind effect

your engine will overheat

your brakes need a constant cooling effect

Answer

☑ **your field of vision is seriously reduced**

Staying back will increase your view of the road ahead. This will help you to see any hazards that might occur and allow you more time to react.

questions  answers

Q. 4.21

Mark one answer

You are following a vehicle on a wet road. You should leave a time gap of at least

 one second

two seconds

three seconds

four seconds

Answer

☑ **four seconds**

Wet roads will increase the time it will take you to stop. The 'two-second rule' will double to AT LEAST FOUR SECONDS.

Q. 4.22

Mark one answer

You are overtaking a lorry. You see the driver flash the headlights. What should you do?

Move back to the left when it is safe to do so

Indicate left and move back slowly

Act immediately on the other driver's signal

Flash your rear lights on and off twice

Answer

☑ **Move back to the left when it is safe to do so**

Never presume what someone means when they flash their headlights. Wait until it is safe to complete your manoeuvre.

Q. 4.23

Mark one answer

A coach is overtaking you. When it is safe for the coach to move back to the left you should

 do nothing and let the driver decide

switch your sidelights on and off

flash your headlights once

flash your headlights twice

Answer

☑ **do nothing and let the driver decide**

Allow the coach driver to make the decision to complete his manoeuvre.

Q. 4.24

Mark three answers

Which THREE of the following emergency vehicles will use blue flashing beacons?

 Motorway maintenance

Bomb disposal team

Blood transfusion

Police vehicle

Breakdown recovery vehicle

Answers

☑ **Bomb disposal team**

☑ **Blood transfusion**

☑ **Police vehicle**

Try to move out of the way of emergency vehicles with blue flashing beacons. Do so safely and without delay.

Q. 4.25

Mark one answer

When being followed by an ambulance showing a flashing blue beacon you should

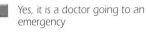 pull over as soon as safely possible to let it pass

accelerate hard to get away from it

ignore it if possible, and let it pass if forced to

brake harshly and immediately stop in the road

Answer

☑ **pull over as soon as safely possible to let it pass**

Pull over where the ambulance can pass safely. Check that there are no bollards or obstructions in the road that will prevent it doing so.

Q. 4.26

Mark one answer

You see a car showing a flashing green beacon. Should you give way to it?

Yes, it is a doctor going to an emergency

Yes, it is a fire crew support vehicle

No, it is a slow-moving vehicle

No, it is a breakdown vehicle

Answer

☑ **Yes, it is a doctor going to an emergency**

Give way by pulling over and letting the vehicle pass. Think about this; don't just stop suddenly. Choose a place as soon as you can where you enable the doctor's vehicle to pass safely.

questions   answers

Q. 4.27

Mark one answer

What type of emergency vehicle is fitted with a green flashing beacon?

 Fire engine

Road gritter

Ambulance

Doctor's car

Answer

☑ **Doctor's car**

A green flashing light on a vehicle means the driver or passenger is a doctor on an emergency call. Give way to them if it's safe to do so. Be aware that the vehicle may be travelling quickly or may stop suddenly.

Q. 4.28

Mark one answer

A bus is stopped at a bus stop ahead of you. Its right-hand indicator is flashing. You should

flash your headlights and slow down

slow down and give way if it is safe to do so

sound your horn and keep going

slow down and then sound your horn

Answer

☑ **slow down and give way if it is safe to do so**

Give way to buses whenever you can do so safely, especially when they signal to pull away from bus stops. Look out for people leaving the bus and crossing the road. Don't

• flash your headlights

• sound your horn

• give any other misleading signals.

Q. 4.29

Mark one answer

A bus lane on your left shows no times of operation. This means it is

not in operation at all

only in operation at peak times

in operation 24 hours a day

only in operation in daylight hours

Answer

☑ **in operation 24 hours a day**

You should always be aware of the times when bus lanes are operating. The absence of a plate indicating any times of operation means that the bus lane operates all the time.

Q. 4.30

Mark one answer

At a puffin crossing what colour follows the green signal?

 Steady red

Flashing amber

Steady amber

Flashing green

Answer

✓ **Steady amber**

Puffin crossings have infra-red sensors which detect when pedestrians are crossing and hold the red traffic signal until the crossing is clear. The use of a sensor means there is no flashing amber phase as there is with a pelican crossing.

Q. 4.31

Mark one answer

You stop for pedestrians waiting to cross at a zebra crossing. They do not start to cross. What should you do?

Be patient and wait

Sound your horn

Drive on

Wave them to cross

Answer

✓ **Be patient and wait**

If you stop for pedestrians and they don't start to cross don't

- wave them across
- sound your horn.

This could be dangerous if another vehicle's approaching and hasn't seen or heard your signal.

Q. 4.32

Mark one answer

You should beckon pedestrians to cross the road at

 pedestrian crossings

no time

junctions

school crossings

Answer

✓ **no time**

Beckoning pedestrians to cross can be dangerous. Other road users may not have seen your signal and you might lead the pedestrians into danger.

questions   answers

Q. 4.33

Mark one answer

You should never wave people across at pedestrian crossings because

 there may be another vehicle coming

☐ they may not be looking

☐ it is safer for you to carry on

☐ they may not be ready to cross

Answer

✅ **there may be another vehicle coming**

If it's safe you should always stop for pedestrians waiting at pedestrian crossings. Don't wave them to cross the road since another driver may not

• have seen them

• have seen your signal

• be able to stop safely.

Q. 4.34

Mark three answers

You should NOT park your vehicle or trailer

☐ at an overnight service area

☐ near the brow of a hill

☐ opposite a traffic island

☐ in front of an entrance to a property

☐ in a factory yard

Answers

✅ **near the brow of a hill**

✅ **opposite a traffic island**

✅ **in front of an entrance to a property**

Do not park where you would endanger or inconvenience others. If your choice of parking place obstructs drivers, riders or pedestrians, move to a more suitable area.

Q. 4.35

Mark three answers

You are driving close to the kerb in a busy shopping area. What dangers should you be most aware of?

☐ Traffic lights suddenly changing to green

☐ The amount of fuel being used when driving slowly

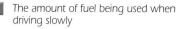 Pedestrians stepping off the edge of the pavement

☐ The nearside mirror striking the heads of pedestrians

☐ Cyclists moving up the left side of your vehicle

Answers

✅ **Pedestrians stepping off the edge of the pavement**

✅ **The nearside mirror striking the heads of pedestrians**

✅ **Cyclists moving up the left side of your vehicle**

When you need to drive close to the kerb, be aware of the dangers. Pedestrians may step off the kerb. The nearside mirror may be at head height and cyclists may be tempted to pass you on your left if you are driving slowly in congested conditions.

questions answers

Q. 4.36

Mark one answer

You have stopped for an elderly pedestrian who is slowly crossing the road. Traffic behind you is being held up. What should you do?

 Edge slowly forward and make them hurry

 Remain where you are and allow them to cross in their own time

 Steer slowly around them to ease the build up of traffic

 Get out of your vehicle and wave them across

Answer

✓ **Remain where you are and allow them to cross in their own time**

Elderly pedestrians can be very vulnerable when crossing the road. Be patient and show courtesy and understanding.

Q. 4.37

Mark two answers

Mirrors fitted to your vehicle MUST be

 clean

properly adjusted

convex

tinted

concave

Answers

✓ **clean**

✓ **properly adjusted**

It is important to know what is happening behind as well as ahead. Your mirrors must be clean and properly adjusted.

Q. 4.38

Mark one answer

You are driving a slow moving vehicle along a narrow road. You should let other vehicles overtake by

 maintaining a steady speed

waving them past

giving a left turn signal

pulling in when you can

Answer

✓ **pulling in when you can**

Drivers behind you who have been waiting to pass for some time may make hasty decisions in an effort to overtake. If you see a queue of traffic building up behind give way as soon as you can by pulling in to the left.

questions answers

Q. 4.39

Mark one answer

When is a nearside mirror likely to endanger pedestrians?

 When stopping before a pedestrian crossing

When braking hard on a bend

When driving close to the kerb

When turning right at a roundabout

Answer

☑ **When driving close to the kerb**

You must be aware that a nearside mirror could strike the head of a pedestrian when you drive close to the kerb. This is especially so in built up, congested shopping areas.

Q. 4.40

Mark one answer

As you drive past a group of school children standing close to the kerb you should

check your offside mirror

check your nearside mirror

switch on your headlights

switch on your hazard lights

Answer

☑ **check your nearside mirror**

On approach you should consider if you need to use the horn as a warning (this may not be appropriate where animals are around). Always check your nearside mirror as you pass potential hazards on the left.

Q. 4.41

Mark one answer

You are on a wet level road. At 50 mph what gap should you leave from the vehicle in front?

One second minimum

Two seconds minimum

Three seconds minimum

Four seconds minimum

Answer

☑ **Four seconds minimum**

Stopping distances can at least double on wet roads. Always drive in accordance with the road and weather conditions.

Q. 4.42

Mark one answer

You are driving at the legal speed limit. A vehicle comes up quickly behind, flashing its headlights. You should

- accelerate to maintain a gap behind you

- touch the brake pedal sharply to show your brake lights

- maintain your speed and prevent the vehicle from overtaking

- allow the vehicle to overtake

Answer

☑ **allow the vehicle to overtake**

Don't enforce the speed limit by blocking another vehicle's progress. This will only lead to the other driver becoming more frustrated. Slow down and allow the other vehicle to pass.

Q. 4.43

Mark one answer

You are approaching a pelican crossing. The amber light is flashing. You MUST

- give way to pedestrians who are crossing

- encourage pedestrians to cross

- not move until the green light appears

- stop even if the crossing is clear

Answer

☑ **give way to pedestrians who are crossing**

While the pedestrians are crossing DON'T

- encourage people to cross by waving or flashing your headlights – others may misunderstand your signal

- rev your engine impatiently.

Q. 4.44

Mark one answer

A vehicle pulls out in front of you at a junction. What should you do?

- Swerve past it and sound your horn
- Flash your headlights and drive up close behind
- Slow down and be ready to stop
- Accelerate past it immediately

Answer

☑ **Slow down and be ready to stop**

Try to be ready for the unexpected. Plan ahead and learn to anticipate hazards. You'll then give yourself more time to react to any problems that might occur.

Be tolerant of other road users who don't behave correctly.

questions answers

Q. 4.45

Mark one answer

Which road users are more vulnerable at night in built up areas?

 Runners

Drivers of black taxi cabs

Double-deck vehicle drivers

Ambulance drivers

Answer

✓ **Runners**

Take extra care. Runners may be difficult to see in the dark.

Q. 4.46

Mark one answer

Which road users are more vulnerable at night in built up areas?

Drivers of black taxi cabs

 Pedestrians in dark clothing

Double-deck vehicle drivers

Ambulance drivers

Answer

✓ **Pedestrians in dark clothing**

Look out for pedestrians wearing dark clothing.

Q. 4.47

Mark one answer

Which road users are more vulnerable at night in built up areas?

Drivers of black taxi cabs

Double deck vehicle drivers

 Cyclists

Ambulance drivers

Answer

✓ **Cyclists**

Look out for cyclists who may not have lights on.

Carrying passengers

This section looks at the rules concerning carrying passengers.

The questions will ask you about

- **Passenger comfort**
  the safety and comfort of your passengers

- **Vehicle stability**
  high and long vehicles must not be allowed to become unstable

- **Driver attitude**
  a good attitude to passengers and other road users is important

- **Special passengers**
  some passengers might have special needs

- **Safety equipment**
  certain safety equipment must be carried on your vehicle, and it is recommended that other equipment is carried as well

Q. 5.1 🚌

Mark one answer

What would you have to be especially aware of when driving a double-deck bus on a road with a steep camber?

- ◼ Keep Left islands
- ◼ A smooth road surface
- ◼ Pedestrian crossings
- ◼ Overhanging trees

Answer

☑ **Overhanging trees**

Where a road has a steep camber, that is, where the road dips towards the kerb, there are dangers that you must be aware of. As the nearside wheels will be lower this causes the vehicle to lean towards the pavement or verge. You must therefore look out for

- • overhanging trees
- • lamp posts
- • bus stop roofs.

Q. 5.2 🚌

Mark one answer

As a bus driver your first consideration is to your

- ◼ timetable
- ◼ passengers
- ◼ employer
- ◼ workmates

Answer

☑ **passengers**

Consideration for your passengers can be shown in numerous ways. Be courteous at all times. Give them time to get seated before moving away.

Some passengers have special needs. Allow them to be independent, but be prepared to help if necessary.

Look out for those who may not be able to see or hear your bus coming.

Q. 5.3 🚌

Mark two answers

You are driving a double-deck bus. Passenger care is important. You should

- ◼ assist passengers with special needs
- ◼ provide a commentary of the route
- ◼ listen to passengers while driving
- ◼ help passengers unfamiliar with the service
- ◼ carry passengers luggage upstairs

Answers

☑ **assist passengers with special needs**

☑ **help passengers unfamiliar with the service**

Showing consideration to passengers goes a long way – whether they have special needs or not. Try to imagine what assistance you would like if you were in their position.

questions   answers

Q. 5.4 🚌
Mark one answer

As a bus driver your main responsibility is

- ▪ the safety and comfort of your passengers
- ▪ keeping to a strict timetable
- ▪ the collecting of fares
- ▪ the issuing of tickets

Answer

☑ **the safety and comfort of your passengers**

You should deliver them to their destination

- safely
- on time
- efficiently
- courteously.

Q. 5.5 🚌
Mark two answers

As a bus driver you should show care to your passengers. You can do this by

- ▪ stopping close to the kerb
- ▪ reaching destinations early
- ▪ not speaking when taking fares
- ▪ giving them time to get seated

Answers

☑ **stopping close to the kerb**

☑ **giving them time to get seated**

Ensure that you stop the vehicle where it is safe and convenient for your passengers to get on and off.

Acceleration as you move off can easily unsteady a passenger; try to wait until all passengers are seated or settled before moving off.

Q. 5.6 🚌
Mark one answer

What is the MAIN reason for using smooth acceleration when driving your bus?

- ▪ To reduce wear on the tyres
- ▪ To reduce wear on the engine
- ▪ To improve fuel consumption
- ▪ To improve passenger comfort

Answer

☑ **To improve passenger comfort**

Operators often publicise journeys as being

- comfortable
- convenient
- fast
- trouble free.

You are an important factor in delivering this standard of service.

questions   answers

Q. 5.7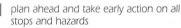

Mark two answers

When driving a bus, your main priorities should be

 the safety of your passengers

 the comfort of your passengers

keeping strictly to your timetable

greeting all passengers with a smile

making sure passengers take their luggage

Answers

☑ **the safety of your passengers**

☑ **the comfort of your passengers**

A bus driver should create the best possible image by setting a good example for others to follow.

Adopting the correct attitude will help you fulfil your main priority, which is the safety and comfort of your passengers.

Q. 5.8

Mark one answer

For the comfort of your passengers harsh braking should be avoided. You should

pump the brakes when approaching a bus stop or hazard

use the gears to slow down

use the parking brake just before stopping to avoid throwing passengers forward

plan ahead and take early action on all stops and hazards

Answer

☑ **plan ahead and take early action on all stops and hazards**

As the driver of a bus, your first duty is to your passengers. You're delivering a service to paying customers who wish to reach their destination comfortably and safely. Set yourself a high professional standard and take pride in your work.

You must ensure that you have a comprehensive knowledge of The Highway Code and other matters relating to vehicle and passenger safety.

Q. 5.9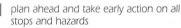

Mark one answer

A bus driver brakes harshly. Passengers may be thrown towards

the front of the bus

the rear of the bus

the nearside

the offside

Answer

☑ **the front of the bus**

When approaching hazards or bus stops you should always be aware of what your passengers are doing.

Late, harsh braking as they leave their seats can take passengers by surprise and cause them to fall over, possibly injuring themselves or others.

questions   answers

Q. 5.10

Mark one answer

How can you avoid harsh braking?

- Gently apply the parking brake
- Plan ahead and take early action
- Slow down by using your gears only
- Pump the brake pedal several times

Answer

☑ **Plan ahead and take early action**

Always look well ahead. Early planning and anticipation will help you to avoid braking harshly. As a bus driver you'll have paying customers on board, and they won't want to be thrown forward every time you deal with a hazard.

Q. 5.11

Mark two answers

On which TWO occasions would passengers be most likely to notice weight transfer?

- Braking
- Cornering
- Reversing
- Overtaking

Answers

☑ **Braking**

☑ **Cornering**

A smooth ride at all times is not always easy to achieve. However, driving in a professional manner will help you eliminate late braking and taking corners too fast.

Q. 5.12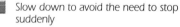

Mark one answer

Well ahead of you are traffic lights on green. What should you do in case the lights change to red?

- Accelerate to make sure you can cross before they change
- Slow down to avoid the need to stop suddenly
- Accelerate, but warn your passengers you may have to stop
- Carry on at a constant speed, but be ready to sound your horn

Answer

☑ **Slow down to avoid the need to stop suddenly**

If you're approaching a set of traffic lights and they've been on green for a while, anticipate their changing. Ease off the accelerator and be ready to come to a gradual stop if they change. Don't drive up to them trying to beat the red light. The lights will more than likely change as you come closer, causing you to brake late and harshly. Think of your passengers.

Q. 5.13

Mark one answer

A bus driver accelerates sharply. Passengers may be thrown towards

- the rear of the bus
- the front of the bus
- the nearside
- the offside

Answer

✓ **the rear of the bus**

After boarding passengers, accelerating to build up speed while they are still in the aisle can easily cause them to lose their balance and sustain unnecessary injury.

A few seconds' delay to allow them time to get seated will make little difference to your overall journey time.

BE PROFESSIONAL – BE PATIENT.

Q. 5.14

Mark one answer

A bus driver should avoid stopping harshly MOSTLY for the benefit of the

- tyres
- brakes
- passengers
- suspension

Answer

✓ **passengers**

Passengers are very vulnerable when they are standing in a moving vehicle. Inconsiderate use of the footbrake can easily cause injury to your passengers, especially the young or infirm, who may not wait until you have stopped before they leave their seat.

Consider that it may even be your driving style that has encouraged them to leave their seat early, because they don't want to feel responsible for holding you up.

Q. 5.15

Mark one answer

If a bus takes a bend too fast passengers may be thrown towards

- the outside of the bend
- the inside of the bend
- the front of the bus
- the rear of the bus

Answer

✓ **the outside of the bend**

Turning or travelling around bends too quickly will push passengers sideways. In addition, the weight of the passengers being transferred to one side of the vehicle will make it even more unstable. This in turn will make steering out of the bend more difficult.

questions

answers

Q. 5.16

Mark three answers

For the safety and comfort of your passengers you should

- brake smoothly
- think well ahead
- stop close to the kerb
- brake hard on a bend
- give change on the move
- drive with the door open

Answers

- ✓ **brake smoothly**
- ✓ **think well ahead**
- ✓ **stop close to the kerb**

How well you look after your passengers and drive your bus is a measure of your professionalism. Dealing competently and safely with hazards and other road users is expected. Making that extra effort, especially when under pressure, is appreciated by your passengers.

Q. 5.17

Mark two answers

Before moving off from a standstill, a bus driver should be especially aware of passengers who attempt to

- change seats
- smoke
- ask you questions
- get off
- get on
- refuse to pay

Answers

- ✓ **get off**
- ✓ **get on**

Check your nearside external and internal mirrors before you move away, to check for anyone attempting to board or leave your vehicle.

Always give passengers time to get seated safely before you move away.

Q. 5.18

Mark two answers

The driver of a bus should wear a seat belt if one is fitted UNLESS

- the seat belt is particularly uncomfortable
- the vehicle is being reversed
- a valid medical exemption certificate is held by the driver
- the belt is of the lap-only type
- the passengers carried are children

Answers

☑ **the vehicle is being reversed**

☑ **a valid medical exemption certificate is held by the driver**

If your vehicle is fitted with a seat belt you must wear it, unless you're exempt for medical reasons. Seat belts save lives. If the fitting of the belt is uncomfortable and it prevents you obtaining a safe driving position, report this to your employer. If it isn't right for you, it's likely that it won't be right for other drivers either.

Q. 5.19

Mark one answer

When seat belts are fitted in a bus your passengers SHOULD wear them

- on journeys over distances of 25 km(15.5 miles)
- only when travelling in EC countries
- only when travelling on motorways
- at all times

Answer

☑ **at all times**

As the driver of a bus you may be responsible for several passengers at any given time. If a situation occurs where you have to brake or steer harshly in an emergency, your passengers could be thrown about the vehicle in different directions. Due to the necessary fittings on board, such as luggage racks, handrails and poles, there's a great danger of injury. If seat belts are provided for passengers, they should wear them. Seat belts save lives.

Q. 5.20

Mark one answer

Which of the following is a legal requirement for every bus?

- A fire extinguisher
- A current timetable
- A mobile phone or radio
- A working tachograph

Answer

☑ **A fire extinguisher**

Every bus must carry a fire extinguisher. Make sure that you know where it's located and how to use it so that you're fully prepared in the event of a fire.

questions   answers

Q. 5.21

Mark three answers

The location of which of the following MUST be clearly labelled on a bus?

- Air vents
- First aid equipment
- Vehicle length
- Route timetables
- Fuel cut-off switch
- Fire extinguisher

Answers

☑ **First aid equipment**

☑ **Fuel cut-off switch**

☑ **Fire extinguisher**

Knowing the location of first aid equipment, the fuel cut-off device and the fire extinguisher is essential on every PCV that you drive.

Take time to familiarise yourself with their location whenever you drive a different vehicle.

When you take your PCV test you will be asked questions on safety.

Q. 5.22

Mark one answer

If a passenger carries a white stick with a red ring painted on it this shows the person is

- blind and deaf
- deaf only
- unable to climb steps
- blind only

Answer

☑ **blind and deaf**

Give extra care to those passengers who require more time or help to get on or off the vehicle. Recognise their disability and help them as much as you can.

There's a great deal of competition these days, and passengers often have a choice of how they travel. Take pride in your work and this will show through in the way that you deal with your passengers. They'll appreciate this, and travel with your company again.

Q. 5.23

Mark one answer

A passenger is boarding your bus. They are carrying a white stick with a red ring painted on it. What does this mean?

- They have a learning difficulty
- They have poor vision and hearing
- They have a physical disability
- They have a speech problem

Answer

☑ **They have poor vision and hearing**

Be prepared to help if they appear to need it, or ask for it. Always do your best to offer a smooth and comfortable ride to your passengers.

Q. 5.24

Mark one answer

A disabled passenger is boarding your bus. They tell you that getting on board is not a problem to them. You should

- let them board without help
- ask a passenger to help them
- leave your cab and help them
- do nothing, you cannot leave your seat

Answer

☑ **let them board without help**

Always be prepared to offer assistance if they ask for it, but allow them to show their independence, even if it delays you for a few seconds longer.

Q. 5.25

Mark one answer

A bus driver should never allow passengers to

- smoke in the saloon
- stand in the aisle
- stow their own luggage
- ride on an open platform

Answer

☑ **ride on an open platform**

A bus driver is responsible for the safety of passengers on board. Anyone standing on an open platform is at risk should the driver have to brake suddenly, or take a corner too quickly.

questions   answers

Q. 5.26

Mark three answers

As a bus driver, which of the following should you not do?

- Signal if necessary when pulling in
- Drive on before people are seated
- Issue tickets without looking at customers' faces
- Use smooth acceleration and anticipate braking needs
- Give time to passengers and show consideration
- Always rush to keep to a timetable

Answers

- ☑ **Drive on before people are seated**
- ☑ **Issue tickets without looking at customers' faces**
- ☑ **Always rush to keep to a timetable**

Nobody likes to be late, but a friendly face and showing your passengers some common courtesies will encourage them to use your service again.

questions   answers

Q. 5.27

Mark three answers

While you are collecting fares you should look at passengers when speaking to them. This will

- help you to recognise someone having difficulty

- show people you are in a rush to keep to a timetable

- show common courtesy and help the image of your company

- help deaf and hearing-impaired people to understand you

- help you decide whether people with a disability should get on the bus

Answers

✓ **help you to recognise someone having difficulty**

✓ **show common courtesy and help the image of your company**

✓ **help deaf and hearing-impaired people to understand you**

You are a representative of your company, so showing passengers that their custom is appreciated will encourage them to travel with you again.

Q. 5.28

Mark two answers

When dealing with passengers who are hard of hearing it is important that you

- shout as loudly as you can

- look at them when speaking to them

- hurry them to get seated

- are as helpful as possible

Answers

✓ **look at them when speaking to them**

✓ **are as helpful as possible**

Hard of hearing passengers may want to lip read. Make sure that they are able to see your face clearly as you speak.

questions   answers

Q. 5.29 🚌

Mark one answer

Your bus is fitted with lifts or ramps for the less able bodied. The equipment should only be operated by

- wheel chair attendants
- fully-trained people
- bus company employees
- accompanying nurses

Answer

✓ **fully-trained people**

Make sure that you are fully trained in the safe use of lifts, ramps and securing devices. If you drive a vehicle fitted with this equipment, never let untrained people operate it. Look out for the safety of others at all times.

Q. 5.30 🚌

Mark one answer

The purpose of a 'kneeling bus' is to

- improve passenger comfort on bumpy roads
- help with access under low bridges
- allow the step height to be raised and lowered
- give more clearance over speed ramps

Answer

✓ **allow the step height to be raised and lowered**

This type of bus can be especially useful for disabled passengers. Using air suspension, the front entrance can be lowered for easier access. Make sure you are properly trained to operate this equipment. Only use it for the intended purpose, and make sure it is in the correct position before continuing your journey.

Q. 5.31 🚌

Mark one answer

This sign fitted to the front and rear of a bus means that

- the bus may be carrying children
- children must be accompanied by an adult
- the bus is carrying blind people
- the driver will help disabled people

Answer

✓ **the bus may be carrying children**

If you're carrying children on your vehicle and it isn't on a scheduled route used by the general public, it must have a sign displayed to the front and rear.

When carrying children to and from school it's likely that you'll have to make several stops in places other than recognised bus stops. Think carefully before you stop.

Don't cause unnecessary inconvenience to other road users.

questions answers

Q. 5.32 🚌

Mark two answers

You are the driver of a bus displaying reflective yellow signs. You are permitted to use hazard warning lights when

- ☐ stationary and parked on the offside of the road
- ☐ stationary and children are boarding
- ☐ stationary and children are getting off
- ☐ slowing down to find a parking space
- ☐ slowing down in town centre traffic queues
- ☐ slowing down approaching a bus stop

Answers

- ☑ **stationary and children are boarding**
- ☑ **stationary and children are getting off**

Buses carrying children must display a distinctive yellow reflective sign on the front and rear, unless running a scheduled service for the general public.

Buses displaying the sign are permitted to use hazard warning lights when stationary for children to get on or off.

Q. 5.33 🚌

Mark one answer

Hazard warning lights may only be used at certain times. In addition, a bus displaying this sign may use them when

- ☐ stopped at a pedestrian crossing
- ☐ stopped and children are getting on or off the vehicle
- ☐ approaching a school crossing patrol
- ☐ there is a sign warning of a school ahead

Answer

- ☑ **stopped and children are getting on or off the vehicle**

You may be driving in the rush hour, when traffic is dense, so when you stop you're permitted to show your hazard warning lights. This will show other road users that children are getting on and off the vehicle. Look out for passing traffic and try to ensure that all your passengers get on and off safely.

questions

answers

Q. 5.34

Mark one answer

You are driving a bus. The bell rings four times. This means

☐ continue past the next bus stop

☐ the bus is full

☐ move off when safe

☐ there is an emergency

Answer

☑ **there is an emergency**

Four bell rings indicate that someone on the bus considers an emergency situation has occurred. As the driver, you must stop the vehicle safely, with consideration for your passengers, before investigating further.

Q. 5.35

Mark one answer

Your conductor rings the bell twice. This means

☐ carry on past the next bus stop

☐ stop immediately for an emergency stop

☐ pull in at the next bus stop

☐ move off when safe to do so

Answer

☑ **move off when safe to do so**

Make sure that you are both familiar with the correct signals. The conductor will ensure that all passengers are settled before signalling.

Q. 5.36 ⬛

Mark one answer

You are driving a bus. The bell rings three times. This means

☐ pull in at the next stop

☐ move away when safe

☐ an emergency on board

☐ your vehicle is full

Answer

☑ **your vehicle is full**

The bell system is used to inform you using a pre-determined set of codes. Never allow anyone to use the bells other than in the accepted way.

Q. 5.37

Mark one answer

Your bus has broken down at night in heavy rain. Why should you move your passengers to the front of the bus?

◼ To keep the bus stable

◼ To help you see clearly out of the back window

◼ To limit injuries in case of a rear-end collision

◼ To keep them informed about the breakdown

Answer

✓ **To limit injuries in case of a rear-end collision**

The safety of your passengers should be your first priority. You should take every precaution possible to ensure they are out of danger.

Q. 5.38

Mark one answer

You are driving a half-cab bus and have no contact with the passengers. This is only allowed if

◼ it is fitted with an interior mirror

◼ there is a chain or strap across the doorway

◼ a responsible person is in charge of them

◼ you make sure no one stands on the platform

Answer

✓ **a responsible person is in charge of them**

It's essential that the passengers on the vehicle are able to report any problems to a responsible person. This person should be aware of the correct bell signals so that they are able to communicate with the driver.

Q. 5.39

Mark one answer

You are driving a coach at night with passengers on board. You should never

◼ stop at service stations

◼ switch the radio on

◼ leave the interior in darkness

◼ close any curtains

Answer

✓ **leave the interior in darkness**

Passengers should be able to move about the vehicle in safety.

You should ensure that all interior lights are in working order before you start your journey.

questions

answers

Q. 5.40

Mark three answers

There is a fire on the upper deck of your double-deck bus. You should

- stop safely and quickly
- get everyone off the bus
- contact emergency services
- open all the windows
- move the passengers into the lower deck
- make sure passengers have their belongings

Answers

☑ **stop safely and quickly**

☑ **get everyone off the bus**

☑ **contact emergency services**

Fire can spread extremely quickly. Your first priority is the safety of your passengers.

If at all possible

- disconnect electrical lines
- cut off the fuel supply.

Fire can destroy a vehicle in an alarmingly short time.

Q. 5.41

Mark one answer

Frequent tyre checks are advised on three axle double deck vehicles because

- their tyres are more likely to deflate
- punctures can be difficult to detect
- blow-outs are more common on these vehicles
- their tyre air pressures are difficult to maintain

Answer

☑ **punctures can be difficult to detect**

Frequent tyre checks are advisable on multi-axled vehicles. The inside wheels on the twin rear axle are the most difficult to check. A deflated tyre will transfer the weight to the second tyre on a twin axle pair and could cause it to burst as they are not designed to run on their own.

Q. 5.42

Mark one answer

The driver of a coach should always wear gloves when

 loading and stowing passengers' luggage

operating a disabled passenger lift

checking the fuel cut off switch

topping up the oil or water levels

Answer

☑ **topping up the oil or water levels**

Even the best maintained vehicles accumulate a certain amount of grime around the engine oil fillers. By wearing gloves you can keep your hands and cuffs clean to present a smart appearance to your customers – the paying passengers.

Q. 5.43

Mark two answers

The driver of a coach should always wear gloves when

emptying the ticket machines

emptying waste systems

driving in cold weather

driving a vehicle without power steering

checking the fuel gauge

checking battery levels

Answers

☑ **emptying waste systems**

☑ **checking battery levels**

A few simple precautions are necessary when carrying out regular maintenance chores. Wearing gloves will help eliminate the risk of infections or conditions such as eczema or dermatitis.

Q. 5.44

Mark one answer

Kneeling buses are specifically designed to improve access for

the driver

extra luggage

elderly passengers

low bridges

Answer

☑ **elderly passengers**

Some buses are equipped with air or hydraulic systems that allow the step level to be lowered. They are known as kneeling buses. You MUST raise the step again before moving off.

questions   answers

Q. 5.45

Mark one answer

What are kneeling buses designed to improve?

■ Access for the disabled

■ Stability when cornering

■ Passenger comfort at higher speeds

■ Access for the driver

Answer

☑ **Access for the disabled**

Kneeling buses are equipped with air or hydraulic systems that allow the step level to be lowered. It improves access for disabled and elderly passengers but you MUST raise the step before moving off.

Q. 5.46

Mark one answer

Your double deck bus breaks down on a busy road. You should ask your passengers to move to the

■ rear of the bus

■ top deck

■ lower deck

■ front of the bus

Answer

☑ **front of the bus**

The greatest risk to a stationary bus is being hit from behind. Moving your pasengers forward could reduce the risk of injury.

Q. 5.47

Mark one answer

As you move off watch out, in particular, for any passengers who attempt to

■ smoke in the lower saloon

■ stand in the upper saloon

■ avoid paying the correct fare

■ board the bus

Answer

☑ **board the bus**

Always check your nearside mirror before moving away, a passenger may be attempting to open the door to board the bus or running to jump aboard an open platform. Also check for passengers trying to get off the bus as you move away.

Q. 5.48

Mark one answer

When you pull away from a bus stop watch out in particular for passengers who attempt to

◾ avoid paying the correct fare

◾ smoke in the lower saloon

◾ alight from the bus

◾ use an expired travel pass

Answer

☑ **alight from the bus**

Even though you have started to move off passengers may still attempt to alight from the bus. You should also check your nearside mirror for any passengers trying to get on.

Q. 5.49

Mark one answer

A passenger finds walking difficult. What could you do to help?

◾ Drive quickly so that passengers will not be on for long

◾ Wait until the passenger is sitting down before moving away

◾ Make sure they have a window seat

◾ Suggest they stand near the door

Answer

☑ **Wait until the passenger is sitting down before moving away**

Try to wait until your passengers have sat down before you move away. This is even more important if they are elderly or have difficulty walking. Don't forget the personal touch. Offer help when you think it might be needed, and remember, a smile goes a long way.

Safety and hazard awareness

This section looks at safety margins and judgement when you're driving.

The questions will ask you about

- **Anticipation**

  planning ahead to prevent last-second reactions

- **Hazard awareness**

  recognising a hazard ahead and preparing for it

- **Attention**

  looking out for problems ahead when you are driving

- **Speed and distance**

  travelling at the correct speed for the situation, leaving a safe distance to react if a problem arises

- **Reaction time**

  being aware that you need time to react

- **Alcohol and drugs**

  recognising that these will affect your reaction and perception time

- **Tiredness**

  not driving when you are tired, even if you are within your drivers' hours.

Q. 6.1

Mark three answers

Which THREE result from drinking alcohol and driving?

- [ ] Less control
- [ ] A false sense of confidence
- [ ] Faster reactions
- [ ] Poor judgement of speed
- [ ] Greater awareness of danger

Answers

- ☑ **Less control**
- ☑ **A false sense of confidence**
- ☑ **Poor judgement of speed**

You must understand the dangers of mixing alcohol with driving. One drink is too many if you're going to drive. Alcohol will reduce your ability to drive safely.

Q. 6.2

Mark three answers

Which THREE of these are likely effects of drinking alcohol on driving?

- [ ] Reduced co-ordination
- [ ] Increased confidence
- [ ] Poor judgement
- [ ] Increased concentration
- [ ] Faster reactions
- [ ] Colour blindness

Answers

- ☑ **Reduced co-ordination**
- ☑ **Increased confidence**
- ☑ **Poor judgement**

Alcohol can increase confidence to a point where a driver's behaviour might become 'out of character'. Someone who normally behaves sensibly suddenly takes risks and enjoys it. Never let yourself or your friends get into this situation.

Q. 6.3

Mark three answers

Drinking any amount of alcohol is likely to

- [ ] reduce your ability to react to hazards
- [ ] increase the speed of your reactions
- [ ] worsen your judgement of speed
- [ ] increase your awareness of danger
- [ ] give a false sense of confidence

Answers

- ☑ **reduce your ability to react to hazards**
- ☑ **worsen your judgement of speed**
- ☑ **give a false sense of confidence**

Never drink if you are going to drive. It's always the safest option not to drink at all. If you are convicted of drink-driving you will certainly lose your job, so don't be tempted – it isn't worth it.

questions

answers

Q. 6.4

Mark three answers

What else can seriously affect your concentration when driving, other than alcoholic drinks?

 Drugs

Tiredness

Tinted windows

Contact lenses

Loud music

Answers

☑ **Drugs**

☑ **Tiredness**

☑ **Loud music**

The least distraction can allow your concentration to drift. Think only about your driving, and nothing else, to stay in full control of your vehicle.

Q. 6.5

Mark one answer

How does alcohol affect your driving?

It speeds up your reactions

It increases your awareness

It improves your co-ordination

It reduces your concentration

Answer

☑ **It reduces your concentration**

Concentration and good judgement at all times are needed to be a good, safe driver.

Q. 6.6

Mark one answer

You have been convicted of driving whilst unfit through drink or drugs. You will find this is likely to cause the cost of one of the following to rise considerably. Which one?

Road fund licence

Insurance premiums

Vehicle test certificate

Driving licence

Answer

☑ **Insurance premiums**

You have proved yourself to be a risk to yourself and others on the road. For this reason insurance companies may charge you a high premium for the use of your own vehicle. You will certainly lose your job.

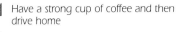
Q. 6.7

Mark one answer

What advice should you give to a driver who has had a few alcoholic drinks at a party?

 Have a strong cup of coffee and then drive home

 Drive home carefully and slowly

 Go home by public transport

 Wait a short while and then drive home

Answer

✓ **Go home by public transport**

Drinking black coffee or waiting a few hours won't make any difference. Alcohol takes time to leave the body. You might even be unfit to drive the following morning.

Q. 6.8

Mark one answer

A driver attends a social event. What precaution should the driver take?

 Drink plenty of coffee after drinking alcohol

 Avoid busy roads after drinking alcohol

 Avoid drinking alcohol completely

 Avoid drinking alcohol on an empty stomach

Answer

✓ **Avoid drinking alcohol completely**

This is always going to be the safest option. One drink could be too many.

Q. 6.9

Mark two answers

It is eight hours since you last had an alcoholic drink. Which of the following applies?

 You will certainly be under the legal limit

 You will have no alcohol in your system

 You may still be unfit to drive

 You may still be over the legal limit

Answers

✓ **You may still be unfit to drive**

✓ **You may still be over the legal limit**

Alcohol can take a long time to leave the body. You may feel alright to drive, but its effect will last for many hours.

questions   answers

Q. 6.10

Mark one answer

Your doctor has given you a course of medicine. Why should you ask if it is OK to drive?

- ▪ Drugs make you a better driver by quickening your reactions

- ▪ You will have to let your insurance company know about the medicine

- ▪ Some types of medicine can cause your reactions to slow down

- ▪ The medicine you take may affect your hearing

Answer

☑ **Some types of medicine can cause your reactions to slow down**

Always check the label of any medication container. The contents might affect your driving. If you aren't sure, ask your doctor or pharmacist.

Q. 6.11

Mark one answer

You have been taking medicine for a few days which made you feel drowsy. Today you feel better, but still need to take the medicine. You should only drive

- ▪ if your journey is necessary
- ▪ at night on quiet roads
- ▪ if someone goes with you
- ▪ after checking with your doctor

Answer

☑ **after checking with your doctor**

Take care, it's not worth taking risks. Always check to be really sure. The medicine may have an effect on you later in the day.

Q. 6.12

Mark two answers

You are not sure if your cough medicine will affect your driving. What TWO things could you do?

- Ask your doctor
- ▪ Check the medicine label
- ▪ Drive if you feel alright
- ▪ Ask a friend or relative for advice

Answers

☑ **Ask your doctor**

☑ **Check the medicine label**

If you're taking medicine or drugs prescribed by your doctor, check to ensure that they won't make you drowsy. If you forget to ask at the time of your visit to the surgery, check with your pharmacist.

Q. 6.13

Mark one answer

You take some cough medicine given to you by a friend. What must you do before driving?

 Drink some strong coffee

Ask your friend if taking the medicine affected their driving

Check the label to see if the medicine will affect your driving

Make a short journey to see if the medicine is affecting your driving

Answer

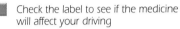 **Check the label to see if the medicine will affect your driving**

Never drive having taken drugs you don't know about. They might affect your judgement and perception and, therefore, endanger lives. ,

---

Q. 6.14

Mark two answers

You are driving along a motorway and become tired. You should

stop at the next service area and rest

leave the motorway at the next exit and rest

increase your speed and turn up the radio volume

close all your windows and set heating to warm

pull up on the hard shoulder and change drivers

Answers

stop at the next service area and rest

leave the motorway at the next exit and rest

If you have planned your journey properly to include rest stops, you will arrive at your destination in good time.

Q. 6.15

Mark one answer

You are about to drive home. You feel very tired and have a severe headache. You should

 wait until you are fit and well before driving

drive home, but take a tablet for headaches

drive home if you can stay awake for the journey

wait for a short time, then drive home slowly

Answer

wait until you are fit and well before driving

All your concentration should be on your driving. Any pain you feel will distract you. Change your plans and be safe.

questions   answers

Q. 6.16

Mark one answer

If you are feeling tired it is best to stop as soon as you can. Until then you should

 increase your speed to find a stopping place quickly

ensure a supply of fresh air

gently tap the steering wheel

keep changing speed to improve concentration

Answer

 ensure a supply of fresh air

If you're travelling on a long journey, plan your route before you leave. This will help you to

• be decisive at intersections and junctions

• plan your rest stops

• know approximately how long the journey will take.

Make sure that the vehicle you're travelling in is well ventilated. A warm, stuffy atmosphere can make you drowsy, which will impair your judgement and perception.

Q. 6.17

Mark one answer

Your reactions will be much slower when driving

if tired

in fog

too quickly

in rain

Answer

 if tired

Try to prevent becoming tired by

• taking plenty of rest stops

• allowing fresh air into the vehicle.

Q. 6.18

Mark one answer

You are driving on a motorway. You feel tired. You should

carry on but drive slowly

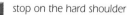 leave the motorway at the next exit

complete your journey as quickly as possible

stop on the hard shoulder

Answer

leave the motorway at the next exit

If you do feel tired and there's no service station for many miles, leave the motorway at the next exit. Find a road off the motorway where you can pull up and stop safely.

questions answers

Q. 6.19

Mark one answer

A driver pulls out of a side road in front of you. You have to brake hard. You should

 ignore the error and stay calm

 flash your lights to show your annoyance

 sound your horn to show your annoyance

 overtake as soon as possible

Answer

 ignore the error and stay calm

If you're driving where there are a number of side roads, be alert. Drivers approaching or emerging from the side road might not be able to see you. Be especially careful if there are a lot of parked vehicles. If a vehicle does emerge and you have to stop quickly

- try to be tolerant
- learn from the experience.

Q. 6.20

Mark one answer

A car driver pulls out causing you to brake. You should

 keep calm and not retaliate

 overtake and sound your horn

 drive close behind and sound your horn

 flag the driver down and explain the mistake

Answer

 keep calm and not retaliate

You have to understand that others on the road might disobey the rules or make an error of judgement at times. Try to accept this calmly, and learn from other people's mistakes.

Q. 6.21

Mark one answer

Another driver's behaviour has upset you. It may help if you

 stop and take a break

 shout abusive language

 gesture to them with your hand

 follow their car, flashing your headlights

Answer

 stop and take a break

Tiredness may make you more irritable than you would be normally. You might react differently to situations because of it. If you feel yourself becoming tense, take a break.

questions answers

Q. 6.22

Mark one answer

You are waiting at a T-junction. A vehicle is coming from the right with the left signal flashing. What should you do?

 Move out and accelerate hard

 Wait until the vehicle starts to turn in

Pull out before the vehicle reaches the junction

Move out slowly

Answer

✓ **Wait until the vehicle starts to turn in**

Try to anticipate the actions of other road users. Their signals might be misleading. When you're waiting at a junction, don't emerge until you're sure of their intentions.

Q. 6.23

Mark one answer

You should use rear fog lights when visibility is poor. At other times they can dazzle other drivers. This is most likely to happen

when it is foggy

in high winds

when it is raining

in bright sunshine

Answer

✓ **when it is raining**

Rear fog lights are very bright and can reflect off the wet surface and dazzle drivers behind.

Q. 6.24

Mark one answer

Before raising the body of a tipper lorry you should make sure the ground is

soft and level

soft and downhill

solid and uphill

solid and level

Answer

✓ **solid and level**

When discharging a load from a tipper vehicle the centre of gravity is raised to a critical position. It's vitally important the vehicle is on a level, solid surface before engaging the hoist mechanism.

Q. 6.25

Mark two answers

Your lorry has a sleeper cab. A quick sideways glance would be helpful especially

- after driving over a pedestrian crossing
- when traffic is merging from the right or left
- before climbing a steep hill
- when driving round sharp bends
- before changing lanes on a motorway

Answers

☑ **when traffic is merging from the right or left**

☑ **before changing lanes on a motorway**

The size and design of some cabs, especially a sleeper cab, can cause blind spots.

A quick sideways glance might show up something you cannot see in your mirrors.

Q. 6.26

Mark one answer

You are driving a lorry in a busy town. A driver pulls out in front of you. You have to brake hard. What should you do?

- Overtake as quickly as possible
- Stay calm and accept the error
- Flash your lights to show your annoyance
- Sound your horn and speed up

Answer

☑ **Stay calm and accept the error**

Some drivers might be hesitant or become confused at major junctions. Don't intimidate them by driving up too close or revving the engine.

Understand that other drivers might make mistakes.

Q. 6.27

Mark one answer

Baffle plates help reduce the load movement in lorries that are carrying

- containers
- cars
- animals
- liquids

Answer

☑ **liquids**

If the drivers of certain tanker vehicles relax the footbrake when braking to a stop there's a danger that the motion in the fluid load could force their vehicles forward. This is due to the wave effect created in the tank contents, especially where baffle plates are omitted from the design.

questions

answers

Q. 6.28

Mark one answer

You are driving in snow. Care should be taken when using the endurance brake (retarder) because it may cause

 the front wheels to lock

 an increase in speed

 the rear wheels to lock

 compressed air to escape

Answer

☑ **the rear wheels to lock**

When operating independent retarders care must be taken when descending snow covered gradients. The retarder could cause the rear wheels to lock.

Q. 6.29

Mark one answer

You are taking medication that could affect your driving. What should you do?

 Seek medical advice

 Make short journeys only

 Drive only at night

 Drink plenty of water

Answer

☑ **Seek medical advice**

Check all medicines. Consult your doctor or pharmacist if you are not sure.

Q. 6.30

Mark three answers

A vehicle travelling downhill will

 need more engine power

 need more braking effort

 take longer to stop

 need a shorter stopping distance

 require less braking effort

 increase speed quickly

Answers

☑ **need more braking effort**

☑ **take longer to stop**

☑ **increase speed quickly**

When a vehicle is stationary on level ground the only force acting on it is the downward pull of gravity. When travelling on a downhill gradient the effect of gravity will tend to

• make the vehicle's speed increase

• require more braking effort

• increase stopping distances.

Q. 6.31

Mark one answer

The road is wet. Why should you slow down as you approach this pedestrian?

▢ Because there are no road markings

▢ To avoid splashing them

▢ Because they have priority

▢ To encourage them to cross

Answer

☑ **To avoid splashing them**

Drive with consideration along wet roads especially if pedestrians are walking or standing near the kerb.

Q. 6.32

Mark one answer

You are driving on a motorway and feel tired. You should

▢ stop on the hard shoulder for a rest

▢ carry on, but drive slowly

▢ leave at the next exit

▢ try to complete your journey more quickly

Answer

☑ **leave at the next exit**

Don't continue to drive without taking your proper rest periods. Walking around in the fresh air during your break will help before setting off again.

questions answers

Q. 6.33

Mark one answer

You have driven a long distance and feel tired. Your tachograph shows that you have not exceeded your driving hours. What should you do?

■ Park in a suitable place and rest

■ Reduce your speed and drive more slowly

■ Carry on driving to use up your hours

■ Increase your speed and reduce your journey time

Answer

☑ **Park in a suitable place and rest**

The smallest lapse in concentration can result in loss of control. Pull up at the next safe place if you feel that you are losing concentration.

Q. 6.34

Mark two answers

Tailgating another vehicle is dangerous because

■ your job could be at risk

■ your braking time is increased

■ your view to the rear is reduced

■ your view ahead is reduced

■ your room for braking is reduced

Answers

☑ **your view ahead is reduced**

☑ **your room for braking is reduced**

Tailgating is very dangerous because there is no safety distance in which to stop between yourself and the driver in front. It also intimidates the driver you are following.

Q. 6.35

Mark four answers

Which of the following MUST be clearly displayed on your bus?

■ Seating and standing capacity

■ Location of all bus stops

■ Emergency exit location

■ The route timetable

■ Fuel cut-off switch

■ Electrical isolator switch

Answers

☑ **Seating and standing capacity**

☑ **Emergency exit location**

☑ **Fuel cut-off switch**

☑ **Electrical isolator switch**

Ensure that all information required on the vehicle, by law referred to as the 'legal lettering', is displayed

- seating / standing capacity
- emergency exit location
- fuel cut-off switch
- electrical isolator

Q. 6.36

Mark one answer

Hazard warning lights may be used while moving when

- you have just overtaken another vehicle
- you need to reverse for some distance
- traffic ahead is slowing quickly on a motorway
- one of your lights has failed

Answer

✓ **traffic ahead is slowing quickly on a motorway**

While moving, hazard warning lights may only be used on a motorway or unrestricted dual carriageway, to warn following drivers of a need to slow down, due to a temporary obstruction ahead.

Q. 6.37

Mark one answer

Wheel nuts should be checked shortly after

- driving down a steep hill
- initial tightening
- driving on a motorway
- unloading

Answer

✓ **initial tightening**

Always recheck wheel nuts shortly after their initial tightening. Make sure they are tightened to the torque specified by the manufacturer.

Q. 6.38

Mark one answer

On a six wheel double deck bus rear wheel punctures are

- much easier to detect
- more likely to happen
- more difficult to detect
- less likely to happen

Answer

✓ **more difficult to detect**

The handling of a six wheel bus or coach is not much different from a two axle vehicle, except that punctures can be more difficult to detect.

questions

answers

Q. 6.39

Mark one answer

Persistent misuse of drugs or alcohol may lead to

■ better concentration

■ better eyesight

■ withdrawal of a driving licence

■ faster reactions

Answer

 withdrawal of a driving licence

Persistent misuse of drugs and or alcohol may lead to the withdrawal of a driving licence. Your insurance premiums will probably increase as well.

Q. 6.40

Mark one answer

You are driving in town and see these lights flashing. What would you expect to see ahead?

■ Contra flow system

■ Uneven road surface

■ Children crossing the road

■ Roadworks ahead

Answer

 Children crossing the road

These lights warn of children likely to be crossing the road on their way to and from school. Slow down and watch out for children.

questions answers

Q. 6.41

You are two and a half times over the legal alcohol limit. You are disqualified from driving. Before regaining your licence who will you have to satisfy that you do NOT have an alcohol problem?

 The local hospital

■ Driver and Vehicle Licensing Agency's Medical Branch

■ Alcoholics Anonymous

■ The Vehicle Inspectorate

Answer

☑ **Driver and Vehicle Licensing Agency's Medical Branch**

If you are disqualified because you are two and a half times over the legal limit, you will have to satisfy the Driver and Vehicle Licensing Agency's Medical Branch that you do NOT have an alcohol problem, before your licence is returned.

Q. 6.42

Mark one answer

Where are these lights found?

■ On approach to a level crossing

■ Near a fire station

■ On approach to a motorway

■ Near a school

Answer

☑ **Near a school**

Flashing amber lights are found near schools. They warn you that children are likely to be crossing the road to and from school. Drive slowly until you are clear of the area.

Q. 6.43

Mark one answer

Another driver does something that upsets you. You should

 try not to react

■ let them know how you feel

■ flash your headlights several times

■ sound your horn

Answer

☑ **try not to react**

There are occasions when other drivers or riders make a misjudgement or a mistake. If this happens, try not to let it worry you. Don't react by showing anger. Sounding the horn, flashing your headlights or shouting at the other driver won't help the situation. Good anticipation will help to prevent these incidents becoming accidents.

Accident handling

This section looks at how to behave in the event of an accident.

The questions will ask you about

- **Reducing risk**

  good planning and anticipation, to lessen the risk of an accident

- **Injuries**

  what to do if someone is injured

- **Hazardous materials**

  actions to take concerning other road users, and reporting procedures

- **Casualties**

  treatment and reporting procedures

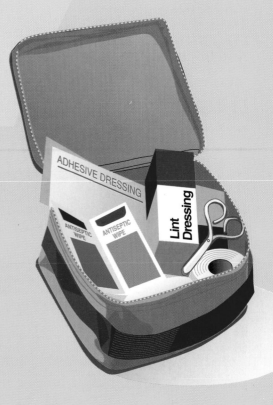

questions answers

Q. 7.1

Mark one answer

You have broken down on a two-way road. How far behind your vehicle should you place a warning triangle?

 25 metres (82 feet)

45 metres (147 feet)

2.5 car lengths

5 car lengths

Answer

☑ **45 metres (147 feet)**

Placing the triangle 45 metres back gives plenty of time to warn other drivers of the hazard ahead.

Q. 7.2

Mark one answer

In the UK the headroom under bridges, unless otherwise shown, is AT LEAST

4.8 metres (16 feet)

5 metres (16 feet 6 inches)

6 metres (19 feet 8 inches)

8 metres (26 feet 3 inches)

Answer

☑ **5 metres (16 feet 6 inches)**

Always be aware of the height of the vehicle you're driving. Don't forget if you're driving a high vehicle – there are over 750 incidents a year involving collisions with bridges. Every effort should be made to prevent these incidents occuring. If you hit a railway bridge it must be reported to

- Railtrack or Northern Ireland Railways (NIR)
- the police.

Failure to report an incident involving a railway bridge is an offence.

Q. 7.3

Mark one answer

NI EXEMPT

You are approaching a bridge that has NO height restriction on it. The height of the bridge will be at least

 3.6 metres (11 feet 10 inches)

 4.4 metres (14 feet 5 inches)

4.8 metres (16 feet)

5 metres (16 feet 6 inches)

Answer

☑ **5 metres (16 feet 6 inches)**

The headroom under bridges in the UK is at least 5 metres (16 feet 6 inches), unless otherwise indicated. Where the overhead clearance is arched, this headroom is normally only between the limits marked.

questions

answers

Q. 7.4

Mark one answer

NI EXEMPT

Your bus hits a low railway bridge. Nobody is injured. You should report the accident

- immediately, to your employer
- within 24 hours to Railtrack
- within seven days to the police
- immediately, to Railtrack

Answer

☑ **immediately, to Railtrack**

Due to the possibility of structural damage to the bridge you should inform the authorities immediately. You should telephone Railtrack's 24-hour bridge hotline number and report the incident. It's very important to do this as soon as possible so that all rail traffic is stopped.

In Northern Ireland you must report it to NIR and the police immediately.

Q. 7.5

Mark two answers

A laminated windscreen is one which

- will not shatter
- does not mist up
- has a plastic layer
- cuts down on glare

Answers

☑ **will not shatter**

☑ **has a plastic layer**

Windscreens are either laminated or toughened. The main difference is that toughened screens shatter, whereas a laminated screen will crack. A small crack will quickly become larger because the screen will flex as the vehicle is being driven.

Q. 7.6

Mark one answer

You have been involved in an accident and damaged some property. Your vehicle is still roadworthy. Nobody else is present. What should you do?

- Stop, then report the accident to the police within 24 hours
- Leave the scene. Do not report the accident if there are no witnesses
- Stop, then report the accident to the police after 48 hours
- Leave the scene. Do not report the accident if there were no injuries

Answer

☑ **Stop, then report the accident to the police within 24 hours**

If you are involved in an accident that causes damage or injury to a person or property, you **must** stop. You are also obliged to give your details to any one who has reasonable grounds to ask for them. If you don't do this, you must inform the police as soon as possible and within 24 hours.

questions answers

Q. 7.7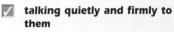

Mark one answer

Your bus is stopped at the scene of an accident. Why should you consider moving your passengers to the front of the bus?

- To improve weight distribution
- To reduce the risk of injury from behind
- To be nearer emergency exits
- To be witnesses of the accident

Answer

To reduce the risk of injury from behind

You'll need to decide whether it's appropriate for passengers to move to a safer position if another vehicle could run into the back of the bus.

Q. 7.8

Mark one answer

At the scene of an accident a person has become hysterical. You should calm them by

- leaving them to quietly recover
- shouting at them loudly
- giving them a hot drink
- talking quietly and firmly to them

Answer

talking quietly and firmly to them

Try to calm somebody who is hysterical by talking quietly and firmly to them.

Q. 7.9

Mark one answer

You are at an accident. Why may it be unwise to move a casualty?

- You could damage your back
- You could get blood on your hands
- You could be accused of an assault
- You could cause more injury

Answer

You could cause more injury

Be especially careful about moving casualties at the scene of an accident. Inexperienced handling of a casualty could cause more injury, or even prove to be fatal.

questions   answers

Q. 7.10

Mark one answer

There has been an accident. The driver is in contact with live electrical cables. Do not touch the driver unless you can use

 a metal pole

your bare hands

a damp piece of cloth

a length of wood

Answer

☑ **a length of wood**

If you arrive at the scene of an accident, don't touch any casualties who are in contact with live electricity. You should use a non-conducting item, such as a wooden sweeping brush. You must not give first aid until you are sure the electrical contact has been broken.

Q. 7.11

Mark two answers

You are at the scene of an accident and someone's arm is bleeding heavily. How could you help stop the bleeding?

 Raise the arm

Lower the arm

Place firm pressure on the wound

 Keep the wound free from pressure

Answers

☑ **Raise the arm**

☑ **Place firm pressure on the wound**

If you notice the limb bleeding heavily raise it to reduce the flow of blood.

Q. 7.12

Mark one answer

You arrive at the scene of a serious accident. Your FIRST priority should be to

your passengers

yourself

the emergency services

accident victims

Answer

☑ **your passengers**

In the event of an accident, keeping calm and in command of the situation could save lives.

Your passengers are your first priority. Make sure they are safe and call the emergency services.

Q. 7.13

Mark three answers

You are the first to arrive at the scene of an accident. Someone is unconscious. Which of the following should be given urgent priority to help them?

- [ ] Try to get them to drink water
- [ ] Look for any witnesses
- [ ] Clear the airway and keep it open
- [ ] Check that they are breathing
- [ ] Stop any bleeding
- [ ] Take the numbers of any vehicles involved

Answers

- [x] **Clear the airway and keep it open**
- [x] **Check that they are breathing**
- [x] **Stop any bleeding**

Gently tilt the head back as far as possible to clear the airway. Check for at least ten seconds that the casualty is breathing by looking for movement in the chest, listening for sounds and feeling for breath on your cheek. Apply pressure to any wound that is bleeding.

Q. 7.14

Mark one answer

You are driving a coach carrying elderly people. You arrive at the scene of an accident. The emergency services have already arrived. You should

- [ ] ask your passengers to find out what is happening
- [ ] not tell passengers anything in case you upset them
- [ ] leave the passengers on the bus and see what is happening yourself
- [ ] tell the passengers what is happening without upsetting them

Answer

- [x] **tell the passengers what is happening without upsetting them**

You should reassure passengers when letting them know what has happened. Confirm to them that the emergency services are in attendance.

questions   answers

Q. 7.15

Mark one answer

What must you do if you are involved in an accident?

■ Drive on for help

■ Inform the police within seven days

■ Stop at the scene of the accident

■ Drive to the nearest police station

Answer

✓ **Stop at the scene of the accident**

If your vehicle is involved in an accident you must stop. If the accident causes any damage or injury to another person, other vehicle, any animal not in your vehicle, or roadside property, you must

• stop at the scene

• give your own address and the vehicle owner's address, plus the registration number of the vehicle, to anyone having reasonable grounds to require it.

Q. 7.16

Mark one answer

NI EXEMPT

Your vehicle has been involved in an accident where someone is injured. You do not produce the required insurance certificate at the time of the accident. You must report the accident to the police as soon as possible, or in any case within

 24 hours

 48 hours

■ 72 hours

■ seven days

Answer

✓ **24 hours**

If you don't give your name and address at the time of the accident, report the accident to the police as soon as reasonably practicable. That is, as soon as possible, or in any case within 24 hours.

If any other person is injured and you don't produce your insurance at the time of the accident to the police or to any other person who has reasonable grounds to request it, you must also

• report the accident to the police as soon as possible, or in any case within 24 hours

• produce your insurance certificate to the police either when reporting the accident or within seven days (five days in Northern Ireland) at any police station you select.

Q. 7.17

Mark one answer

Your bus and other vehicles have been involved in an accident. You should

■ switch off their headlights

■ switch off the fuel supply

■ turn vehicles the right way up

■ always pull casualties out of their vehicles

Answer

☑ **switch off the fuel supply**

The risk of fire will be reduced if all fuel supplies are switched off.

Q. 7.18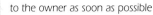

Mark one answer

NI EXEMPT

Your bus has hit a parked vehicle. The owner cannot be found. You must report the accident

■ to the police within seven days

■ to the owner as soon as possible

■ to the owner within seven days

■ to the police within 24 hours

Answer

☑ **to the police within 24 hours**

If you damage a parked vehicle and the owner isn't around, you must report it to the police. This applies to any property you might have damaged.

In Northern Ireland all accidents must be reported to the police immediately.

Q. 7.19

Mark one answer

At the scene of an accident you see a plain orange rectangle displayed on one of the vehicles. This tells you that the vehicle

■ is carrying dangerous goods

■ is carrying a First Aid kit

■ is carrying medical supplies

■ is unladen

Answer

☑ **is carrying dangerous goods**

Vehicles that carry dangerous goods have badges displayed on the side and rear. These are coloured orange and show the type of material that's being carried. Make a note of this and report it to the emergency services when you contact them.

questions   answers

Q. 7.20 🚌

Mark one answer

You are treating a passenger who is in shock. You should

- give them liquids
- keep them moving
- encourage them to sleep
- keep them warm

Answer

✓ **keep them warm**

Knowing what to do in the event of an accident could save lives. Stay calm and be in command of the situation. Call the emergency services. They're the experts and know how to deal with injured or shocked victims. First Aid is very important, but the correct procedure is vital.

Although not obviously injured, passengers may be suffering from shock. Reassure them and keep them warm. Don't give them anything to eat or drink.

Q. 7.21 🚌

Mark one answer

A passenger on your bus has stopped breathing. You help them by giving mouth to mouth resuscitation. When should you stop doing this?

- When they can breathe on their own
- When you think the passenger has died
- When their skin colour has turned blue
- When you think the ambulance is coming

Answer

✓ **When they can breathe on their own**

You should only stop resuscitation when the passenger can breathe on their own or a professional medical person can take over.

Q. 7.22

Mark one answer

Your bus is involved in an accident. You have a passenger who is unconscious but still breathing. What should you do?

- Get medical help
- Check their pulse
- Give them liquid
- Lay them on their back

Answer

☑ **Get medical help**

If one of your passengers is unconscious but breathing, get medical help immediately. Only move the casualty if there's danger of further injury. Call the experts: dial 999.

Study the section on First Aid in your copy of The Goods Vehicle Driving Manual or The Bus and Coach Driving Manual (both published by The Stationery Office). Please note that the advice given in these manuals is only a brief example of how you may deal with situations on the road. If you require further and more comprehensive details about First Aid, you can contact the

- St John Ambulance Association and Brigade
- St Andrew's Ambulance Association
- British Red Cross Association.

There's no substitute for proper training.

Q. 7.23

Mark two answers

There is a fire in your engine compartment. Which TWO of the following should you do?

- Open all windows
- Disconnect electrical leads
- Flag down a passing motorist
- Cut off the fuel supply
- Try to remove the load

Answers

☑ **Disconnect electrical leads**

☑ **Cut off the fuel supply**

If you suspect a fire try to isolate the source. If at all possible disconnect leads and cut off the fuel supply.

questions   answers

Q. 7.24

Mark one answer

You arrive at an accident where someone is suffering from severe burns. Which of the following would help?

 Douse the burns with cold water

Remove anything stuck to the burns

Burst blisters that form on the burns

Apply ointment to the burns

Answer

☑ **Douse the burns with cold water**

Cold water will cool the burning tissue, prevent further damage, reduce swelling, minimise shock and alleviate pain.

Q. 7.25

Mark one answer

A vehicle has rolled over and caught fire. The driver's hands and arms have been burned. You should NOT

douse the burns with cold water

lay the casualty down

remove smouldering clothing

remove anything sticking to the burns

Answer

☑ **remove anything sticking to the burns**

Do not remove anything sticking to the burn. You may cause further damage and introduce infection into the wound.

Q. 7.26

Mark one answer

You arrive at the scene of an accident. A pedestrian is bleeding heavily from a leg wound. What should you do?

Apply firm pressure to the wound

Dab the wound to stop the bleeding

Keep both legs flat on the ground

Wrap an ice pack near the wound

Answer

☑ **Apply firm pressure to the wound**

Control blood loss by applying pressure over the wound and raising the leg if possible.

Q. 7.27

Mark one answer

An accident has just happened. An injured person is lying in the busy road. What is the first thing you should do to help?

 Treat the person for shock

■ Warn other traffic

■ Place them in the recovery position

■ Make sure the injured person is kept warm

Answer

✓ **Warn other traffic**

You could do this by

- displaying an advanced warning signal, if you have one

- switching on hazard warning lights or other lights

- any other means that does not put you at risk.

Q. 7.28

Mark three answers

You are the first person to arrive at an accident where people are badly injured. Which THREE should you do?

■ Switch on your own hazard warning lights

■ Make sure that someone telephones for an ambulance

■ Try and get people who are injured to drink something

■ Move the people who are injured clear of their vehicles

■ Get people who are not injured clear of the scene

Answers

✓ **Switch on your own hazard warning lights**

✓ **Make sure that someone telephones for an ambulance**

✓ **Get people who are not injured clear of the scene**

If you're the first to arrive at the scene of an accident, further collisions and fire are the first concerns. Switching off vehicle engines will reduce the risk of fire.

Your hazard warning lights will let approaching traffic know that there's a need for caution.

Don't assume someone else has called the emergency services. Do it yourself.

questions answers

Q. 7.29

Mark two answers

You are at the scene of an accident and there are several bystanders. Which TWO of the following should you do first?

 Always pull people who are hurt out of their vehicles

 Ask the bystanders to check the casualties for signs of bleeding

 Make sure that the emergency services have been called for

 Keep the bystanders clear as they do not know first aid

Clear a parking area for ambulance and fire service crews

Answers

☑ **Ask the bystanders to check the casualties for signs of bleeding**

☑ **Make sure that the emergency services have been called for**

Encourage the bystanders to help. Do this calmly and decisively; they may be very willing to help, but don't know what to do.

Q. 7.30

Mark three answers

You arrive at a serious motorcycle accident. The motorcyclist is unconscious and bleeding. Your main priorities should be to

 try to stop the bleeding

make a list of witnesses

check the casualty's breathing

take the numbers of the vehicles involved

sweep up any loose debris

check the casualty's airways

Answers

☑ **try to stop the bleeding**

☑ **check the casualty's breathing**

☑ **check the casualty's airways**

At a road accident the danger of further collisions and fire need to be dealt with first. Injuries should be dealt with in the order

- Airway
- Breathing
- Circulation and bleeding.

Q. 7.31

Mark one answer

You arrive at an accident. A motorcyclist is unconscious. Your first priority is the casualty's

 breathing

 bleeding

broken bones

bruising

Answer

☑ **breathing**

The first priority when dealing with an unconscious person is to make sure they can breathe. This may involve clearing their airway if they're having difficulty or some obstruction is obvious.

At the scene of an accident you must make sure there is no danger from further collisions or fire before dealing with any casualties.

Q. 7.32

Mark three answers

At an accident a casualty is unconscious. Which three of the following should you check urgently?

- Circulation
- Airway
- Shock
- Breathing
- Broken bones

Answers

- ✓ **Circulation**
- ✓ **Airway**
- ✓ **Breathing**

An unconscious casualty may have difficulty breathing. Check that their tongue has not fallen back, blocking their airway. Do this by tilting the head back slightly.

Q. 7.33

Mark three answers

In first aid what does ABC stand for?

- Airway
- Bleeding
- Conscious
- Breathing
- Circulation
- Alert

Answers

- ✓ **Airway**
- ✓ **Breathing**
- ✓ **Circulation**

To check if a casualty is breathing put your face close to their mouth. Look, listen and feel for any sign of breathing.

Q. 7.34

Mark three answers

You arrive at the scene of an accident. It has just happened, and someone is unconscious. Which of the following should be given urgent priority to help them?

- Clear the airway and keep it open
- Try to get them to drink water
- Check that they are breathing
- Look for any witnesses
- Stop any heavy bleeding
- Take the numbers of vehicles involved

Answers

- ✓ **Clear the airway and keep it open**
- ✓ **Check that they are breathing**
- ✓ **Stop any heavy bleeding**

Stay with the casualty and send someone to ring for an ambulance.

Q. 7.35

Mark one answer

Which of the following safety checks is in the correct order?

▨ Breathing, Circulation, Airway

▨ Airway, Breathing, Circulation

▨ Circulation, Breathing, Airway

▨ Breathing, Airway, Circulation

Answer

✓ **Airway, Breathing, Circulation**

Remembering this important order of safety checks is easy as ABC.

Q. 7.36

Mark three answers

At an accident someone is unconscious. Your main priorities should be to

▨ sweep up the broken glass

▨ take the names of witnesses

▨ count the number of vehicles involved

▨ check the airway is clear

▨ make sure they are breathing

▨ stop any heavy bleeding

Answers

✓ **check the airway is clear**

✓ **make sure they are breathing**

✓ **stop any heavy bleeding**

Remember this procedure by saying ABC

• Airway

• Breathing

• Circulation.

Q. 7.37

Mark three answers

You have stopped at the scene of an accident to give help. Which THREE things should you do?

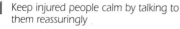 Keep injured people warm and comfortable

Keep injured people calm by talking to them reassuringly

Keep injured people on the move by walking them around

Give injured people a warm drink

Make sure that injured people are not left alone

Answers

✓ **Keep injured people warm and comfortable**

✓ **Keep injured people calm by talking to them reassuringly**

✓ **Make sure that injured people are not left alone**

If you stop at the scene of an accident to give help and there are casualties don't

• move injured people, unless further danger is threatened

• give the injured anything to drink.

Q. 7.38

Mark three answers

You arrive at the scene of an accident. It has just happened and someone is injured. Which of the following should be given urgent priority?

- Stop any severe bleeding
- Get them a warm drink
- Check that their breathing is OK
- Take numbers of vehicles involved
- Look for witnesses
- Clear their airway and keep it open

Answers

☑ **Stop any severe bleeding**

☑ **Check that their breathing is OK**

☑ **Clear their airway and keep it open**

When you have done this, call the emergency services, they are the experts.

If you feel you are not capable of carrying out first aid, then consider doing some training. It could save a life.

Q. 7.39

Mark two answers

At an accident a casualty has stopped breathing. You should

- remove anything that is blocking the mouth
- keep the head tilted forwards as far as possible
- raise the legs to help with circulation
- try to give the casualty something to drink
- keep the head tilted back as far as possible

Answers

☑ **remove anything that is blocking the mouth**

☑ **keep the head tilted back as far as possible**

These actions will ensure that the casualty has clear airways and is in the correct position if mouth to mouth ventilation is required.

questions answers

Q. 7.40

Mark four answers

You are at the scene of an accident. Someone is suffering from shock. You should

- reassure them constantly
- offer them a cigarette
- keep them warm
- avoid moving them if possible
- loosen any tight clothing
- give them a warm drink

Answers

- ✓ **reassure them constantly**
- ✓ **keep them warm**
- ✓ **avoid moving them if possible**
- ✓ **loosen any tight clothing**

The effects of trauma may not be immediately obvious. Prompt treatment can help to minimise the effects of shock.

- Lay the casualty down.
- Loosen tight clothing.
- Call an ambulance.
- Check their breathing and pulse.

Q. 7.41

Mark one answer

Which of the following should you not do at the scene of an accident?

- Warn other traffic by switching on your hazard warning lights
- Call the emergency services immediately
- Offer someone a cigarette to calm them down
- Ask drivers to switch off their engines

Answer

- ✓ **Offer someone a cigarette to calm them down**

Keeping casualties or witnesses calm is important, but never offer a cigarette because of the risk of fire. Check for any signs of shock, such as

- sweating
- clammy skin
- giddiness
- rapid or shallow breathing
- a weak pulse.

Q. 7.42

Mark two answers

When treating someone for shock you should

- reassure them
- loosen tight clothes
- walk them around
- give them a hot drink
- offer them an alcoholic drink

Answers

- ✓ **reassure them**
- ✓ **loosen tight clothes**

Keep talking to the casualty to keep them calm, don't leave them alone.

questions   answers

Q. 7.43

Mark two answers

There has been an accident. The driver is suffering from shock. You should

 give them a drink

reassure them

not leave them alone

offer them a cigarette

ask who caused the accident

Answers

✓ **reassure them**

✓ **not leave them alone**

They could have an injury that is not immediately obvious. Loosen any tight clothing and check that their breathing is not rapid or slow.

Q. 7.44

Mark one answer

You have to treat someone for shock at the scene of an accident. You should

 reassure them constantly

walk them around to calm them down

give them something cold to drink

cool them down as soon as possible

Answer

✓ **reassure them constantly**

You should lay the casualty down and loosen any tight clothing, whilst reassuring them. If possible, get someone else to call an ambulance to avoid leaving the casualty alone.

Q. 7.45

Mark one answer

You arrive at the scene of a motorcycle accident. No other vehicle is involved. The rider is unconscious, lying in the middle of the road. The first thing you should do is

 move the rider out of the road

warn other traffic

clear the road of debris

give the rider reassurance

Answer

✓ **warn other traffic**

The motorcyclist is in an extremely vulnerable position, exposed to further danger from traffic. The traffic needs to slow right down and be aware of the hazard in good time.

questions answers

Q. 7.46

Mark one answer

At an accident a small child is not breathing. When giving mouth to mouth you should blow

◼ sharply

◼ gently

◼ heavily

◼ rapidly

Answer

☑ **gently**

With a small child, breathe gently into the nose and mouth until you see the chest rise. Give five breaths, allowing two seconds for the lungs to inflate.

Q. 7.47

Mark three answers

To start mouth to mouth on a casualty you should

◼ tilt the head forward

◼ clear the airway

◼ turn them on their side

◼ tilt their head back

◼ pinch the nostrils together

◼ put their arms across their chest

Answers

☑ **clear the airway**

☑ **tilt their head back**

☑ **pinch the nostrils together**

Use your finger to check for and move any obvious obstruction in the mouth. It's important to ensure that the air ways are clear.

Q. 7.48

Mark one answer

You are giving mouth to mouth to a casualty. They are still not breathing on their own. You should

◼ give up if you think they are dead

◼ only keep trying for up to two minutes

◼ carry on until an ambulance arrives

◼ only keep trying for up to four minutes

Answer

☑ **carry on until an ambulance arrives**

Make sure that someone has called the emergency services. They have the expertise and equipment to deal with the situation.

questions   answers

Q. 7.49

Mark one answer

When you are giving mouth to mouth you should only stop when

 you think the casualty is dead

the casualty can breathe without help

the casualty has turned blue

you think the ambulance is coming

Answer

 the casualty can breathe without help

Don't give up. Look for signs of recovery and check the casualty's pulse. When the casualty starts to breathe, place them in the recovery position.

Q. 7.50

Mark one answer

You arrive at the scene of an accident. There has been an engine fire and someone's hands and arms have been burnt. You should NOT

douse the burn thoroughly with cool liquid

lay the casualty down

remove anything sticking to the burn

remove smouldering clothing

Answer

remove anything sticking to the burn

This could cause further damage and introduce infection to the wound. Your first priorities are to cool the burn and check the patient for shock.

Q. 7.51

Mark one answer

You arrive at an accident where someone is suffering from severe burns. You should

 apply lotions to the injury

burst any blisters

remove anything stuck to the burns

douse the burns with cool liquid

Answer

douse the burns with cool liquid

Try to find fluid that is clean, cold and non-toxic. Its coolness will stop the burn and relieve the pain. Keep the wound doused for at least ten minutes. If blisters appear, don't attempt to burst them, as this could lead to infection.

questions   answers

Q. 7.52

Mark two answers

You arrive at the scene of an accident. A pedestrian has a severe bleeding wound on their leg, although it is not broken. What should you do?

- Dab the wound to stop bleeding
- Keep both legs flat on the ground
- Apply firm pressure to the wound
- Raise the leg to lessen bleeding
- Fetch them a warm drink

Answers

- ☑ **Apply firm pressure to the wound**
- ☑ **Raise the leg to lessen bleeding**

As soon as you can, apply a pad to the wound with a bandage or a clean length of cloth. Raising the leg will lessen the flow of blood. Be aware that any restriction of blood circulation for more than a short period of time may result in long-term injury.

Q. 7.53

Mark one answer

You arrive at the scene of an accident. A passenger is bleeding badly from an arm wound. What should you do?

- Apply pressure over the wound and keep the arm down
- Dab the wound
- Get them a drink
- Apply pressure over the wound and raise the arm

Answer

- ☑ **Apply pressure over the wound and raise the arm**

If possible, lay the casualty down. Raising the arm above the level of the heart will reduce the flow of blood.

Q. 7.54

Mark one answer

You arrive at the scene of an accident. A pedestrian is bleeding heavily from a leg wound, but the leg is not broken. What should you do?

- Dab the wound to stop the bleeding
- Keep both legs flat on the ground
- Apply firm pressure to the wound
- Fetch them a warm drink

Answer

- ☑ **Apply firm pressure to the wound**

Lift the casualty's leg so that the wound is higher than their heart. This should reduce the flow of blood.

questions

answers

Q. 7.55

Mark one answer

At an accident a casualty is unconscious but still breathing. You should only move them if

 an ambulance is on its way

■ bystanders advise you to

■ there is further danger

■ bystanders will help you to

Answer

✓ **there is further danger**

Moving them could cause further injury. So it's important that this is only done if there is obvious danger to the casualty.

Q. 7.56

Mark one answer

At an accident you suspect a casualty has back injuries. The area is safe. You should

 offer them a drink

■ not move them

■ raise their legs

■ offer them a cigarette

Answer

✓ **not move them**

Talk to the casualty and keep them calm. If you attempt to move them it could cause further injury. Call an ambulance straightaway.

Q. 7.57

Mark one answer

At an accident it is important to look after the casualty. When the area is safe, you should

 get them out of the vehicle

■ give them a drink

■ give them something to eat

■ keep them in the vehicle

Answer

✓ **keep them in the vehicle**

Don't move casualties who are trapped in vehicles unless they are in danger.

questions answers

Q. 7.58

Mark one answer

You are driving on a motorway. A large box falls onto the carriageway from a lorry ahead of you. The lorry does not stop. You should

- drive to the next emergency telephone and inform the police

- catch up with the lorry and try to get the driver's attention

- stop close to the box and switch on your hazard warning lights until the police arrive

- pull over to the hard shoulder, then try and remove the box

Answer

☑ **drive to the next emergency telephone and inform the police**

Lorry drivers are sometimes unaware of objects falling from their vehicles. If you see something fall off a lorry onto the motorway, watch to see if the driver pulls over. If the lorry doesn't stop you should

- pull over onto the hard shoulder near an emergency telephone

- report the hazard to the police.

Q. 7.59

Mark one answer

You are driving along a motorway. The lorry in front switches on its hazard warning lights while it is still moving. What does this mean?

- there is a police car ahead

- the lorry is about to change lanes

- the lorry driver is leaving the motorway

- there is a hazard ahead

Answer

☑ **there is a hazard ahead**

The driver in front has spotted a hazard ahead. Slow down and be prepared to stop and react as appropriate.

Q. 7.60

Mark three answers

You are stopped by a police officer. Which of the following documents are the police most likely to ask you to produce?

- Insurance certificate

- Vehicle registration document

- Road fund licence

- Theory test certificate

- Driving licence

- Test certificate (MOT)

Answers

☑ **Insurance certificate**

☑ **Driving licence**

☑ **Test certificate (MOT)**

These documents must be produced at the time when asked for, or within seven days at any police station.

Q. 7.61

Mark one answer

When using an emergency telephone on a motorway where should you stand?

- In front of the barrier
- Facing the oncoming traffic
- With your back to the traffic
- Looking towards the grass verge

Answer

 Facing the oncoming traffic

Motorway phones are free and easily located. You should face the oncoming traffic while using them, so that you can see what is coming.

Q. 7.62

Mark one answer

You are allowed to use hazard warning lights while moving when

- towing another vehicle
- an overtaking lorry has cleared the front of your vehicle
- being towed by another vehicle
- traffic ahead on a motorway is slowing down quickly

Answer

traffic ahead on a motorway is slowing down quickly

Hazard warning lights may only be used while moving when driving on motorways, or unrestricted dual carriageways. You can only use them to warn drivers behind you of a hazard or obstruction ahead.

Vehicle condition

This section looks at the condition of your vehicle.

The questions will ask you about

- **Safety checks**

  checking brakes, steering and tyres, which are essential to ensure safe and legal driving

- **Legal requirements**

  knowing what the law demands to ensure that your vehicle is in a safe and roadworthy condition.

questions   answers

Q. 8.1

Mark four answers

You must inspect all tyres on your bus for

- signs of wear
- overheating
- maker's details
- correct pressure
- 'dust cap' in place
- objects between twin tyres

Answers

- ☑ **signs of wear**
- ☑ **overheating**
- ☑ **correct pressure**
- ☑ **objects between twin tyres**

An unroadworthy vehicle will endanger the lives of your passengers. You should always make these essential checks as a matter of routine.

Q. 8.2

Mark three answers

You are checking your vehicle's tyres before starting a long motorway drive. Each tyre should be checked for

- air pressure
- tracking
- tread wear
- tread pattern
- bulges
- valve clearance

Answers

- ☑ **air pressure**
- ☑ **tread wear**
- ☑ **bulges**

All tyres must be properly inflated and in good condition. Some motorways are littered with the remains of tyres that have disintegrated during long high-speed journeys.

Q. 8.3

Mark one answer

What is the main reason for cleaning your wheels and tyres when leaving a building site?

- It helps to keep the tyres in good condition
- So that the tyres will not cause damage to the road surface
- So that air pressure will not leak from the tyre valves
- It is illegal for you to spread mud on the road

Answer

- ☑ **It is illegal for you to spread mud on the road**

You must arrange for the mud to be cleared if your wheels leave mud behind. This slippery surface could cause danger to other road users.

questions

answers

Q. 8.4

Mark one answer

You should look at the rear wheels before leaving a building site to check that

- the diff-lock is engaged
- the diff-lock is disengaged
- the load-sensing valve is working
- bricks are not wedged between them

Answer

☑ **bricks are not wedged between them**

This will damage the tyres and could be thrown out as you increase your road speed. This could be dangerous to the drivers of following vehicles.

Q. 8.5

Mark one answer

You are driving on a muddy building site. Before driving on normal road surfaces you should

- disengage the diff-lock
- engage the diff-lock
- apply the steering lock
- disengage the twist lock

Answer

☑ **disengage the diff-lock**

Attempting to drive at normal speeds with this engaged is dangerous, it will severely affect your steering control. The diff-lock is designed to be used in slippery conditions, at low speed.

Q. 8.6

Mark one answer

You notice that two wheel nuts are missing from one of the wheels. What should you do?

- Continue your journey
- Drive to the nearest tyre depot
- Use a nut from another wheel
- Park and phone for assistance

Answer

☑ **Park and phone for assistance**

If you notice any missing wheel nuts, park and phone for assistance. It's essential that wheel fixings are tightened to the torque specified by the manufacturer, with an approved calibrated torque wrench.

As a professional driver you must ensure that your vehicle is in serviceable condition at all times. Checks should be made before you leave on any journey, but make a visual check every time you start up again after a rest stop. Don't take risks by driving a defective vehicle, however important your journey may seem at the time.

Q. 8.7

Mark three answers

Which THREE of the following items would make a tyre illegal for a large vehicle?

 Different makes of tyres on the same axle

- A lump or bulge
- A deep cut more than 25 mm (1 inch) long
- An exposed ply or cord
- Recut tyres
- A tread depth of 1.3 mm

Answers

☑ **A lump or bulge**

☑ **A deep cut more than 25 mm (1 inch) long**

☑ **An exposed ply or cord**

You should carry out checks on your tyres as part of your routine check of the vehicle.

A damaged or worn tyre can have major effects on the handling of your vehicle. Your vehicle will be a danger on the road if you drive it with defective tyres; it's also an offence.

Q. 8.8

Mark one answer

In very cold weather moisture may freeze in your vehicle's air storage tanks. Which of the following would help to prevent this?

- Covering the air tanks with a blanket
- Draining the tanks daily
- Using the brakes frequently
- Pumping the brakes

Answer

☑ **Draining the tanks daily**

In very cold weather moisture can build up in the storage tanks and freeze. Ice can form in the pipes, and this will result in loss of pressure or, worse, brake failure. Make sure that you drain the tanks daily as part of a routine. Most modern vehicles are fitted with automatic bleed valves. Check that they're working properly and that air-drying systems are effective.

Q. 8.9

Mark one answer

What does this warning light on the instrument panel mean?

- Low oil pressure
- Battery discharge
- Braking system fault
- Door open

Answer

☑ **Braking system fault**

You should be familiar with all warning lights and buzzers fitted to your vehicle. If you're driving the vehicle for the first time ensure that you know the function of each. If the brake warning light indicates a fault in the system, stop as soon as it's safe to do so. Report the fault, and don't continue until it has been corrected.

questions

answers

Q. 8.10

Mark one answer

You are driving along a motorway. The brake low-pressure warning device starts to operate. What should you do?

- [ ] Stop immediately in the lane you are in
- [ ] Continue slowly to the next service area
- [ ] Pull up on the hard shoulder as soon as possible
- [ ] Leave the motorway at the next exit

Answer

☑ **Pull up on the hard shoulder as soon as possible**

You should never take chances with the braking system. Pull up well to the left on the hard shoulder. Don't even attempt minor repairs on the motorway. Put on the hazard warning lights.

Contact the police using the nearest emergency telephone. They will contact a recovery contractor for you.

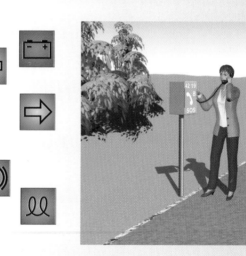

Q. 8.11

Mark one answer

You are driving a lorry along a motorway. You notice that tread is coming away from one of your tyres. What should you do?

- [ ] Stop on the hard shoulder and phone for assistance
- [ ] Stop on the hard shoulder and change the wheel
- [ ] Continue driving to the next service station
- [ ] Continue driving and leave by the next exit

Answer

☑ **Stop on the hard shoulder and phone for assistance**

It's dangerous to drive a defective vehicle. Continuous high speeds on the motorway can cause the tyres to become hot and shred. If you notice this in your mirrors you must stop on the hard shoulder as soon as it's safe to do so.

If you're on a motorway and you notice any defect on your vehicle, you must stop on the hard shoulder as soon as it's safe. Use the emergency telephone for assistance.

questions answers

Q. 8.12

Mark one answer

Your vehicle has broken down at night on a two-way road. You should try to park your vehicle

- on the left of the road
- partly on the pavement
- on a grass verge
- on the right of the road

Answer
☑ **on the left of the road**

You must ensure that your vehicle can be seen by other road users. Your reflectors should show red to the rear.

Q. 8.13

Mark one answer

When parked on the road at night buses and coaches must

- be under street lights
- be within 25 metres (82 feet) of a street light
- have all of the interior lights switched on
- have their sidelights on

Answer
☑ **have their sidelights on**

Make sure that all your lights are working, and that they are clean. Your vehicle may cause other road users to slow down or stop, so they must be able to see you in good time.

Q. 8.14

Mark two answers

Extra skills are needed when driving at night. The MAIN problems you will have to deal with are

- headlight dazzle
- other drivers speeding
- cold weather conditions
- dazzle from shop windows
- becoming tired

Answers
☑ **headlight dazzle**
☑ **becoming tired**

You must concentrate even harder than normal. The slightest distraction or break in your concentration can result in an accident.

questions

answers

Q. 8.15

Mark three answers

Normally white lights on a vehicle at night show you that the vehicle is

- moving away from you
- moving towards you
- ahead of you and braking
- stationary facing you
- stationary and facing away from you
- reversing towards you

Answers

- ✓ **moving towards you**
- ✓ **stationary facing you**
- ✓ **reversing towards you**

As well as being able to see well ahead, other road users must be able to recognise the size of your vehicle and which way you are going.

Q. 8.16

Mark three answers

When driving at night you should make sure all your lights are clean and working correctly. Why is this?

- To enable you to see ahead properly
- To prevent the battery from overcharging
- So that other road users can see the size of your vehicle
- So that the intensity of street lighting can be reduced
- To allow following drivers to use dipped headlights
- So that other road users are aware of your direction of travel

Answers

- ✓ **To enable you to see ahead properly**
- ✓ **So that other road users can see the size of your vehicle**
- ✓ **So that other road users are aware of your direction of travel**

See and be seen. Making your vehicle a hazard will endanger your passengers.

Q. 8.17

Mark one answer

Unless there is street lighting, why could it be dangerous to overtake at night when driving a bus?

- There may be unseen dips or bends in the road
- You may dazzle other drivers
- It is harder to concentrate
- It is harder to keep control in the dark

Answer

- ✓ **There may be unseen dips or bends in the road**

On unlit roads it is more difficult to see where the road bends or if there are junctions or dips. This could also prevent you from seeing oncoming traffic. Don't endanger your passengers. Unless the road is well lit or dual carriageway, ask yourself if overtaking is absolutely necessary.

Q. 8.18

Mark one answer

Whilst driving, your power-assisted steering suddenly fails. What should you do?

- ■ Continue driving to the nearest repair centre
- ■ Return to the depot
- ■ Continue your journey at a slower speed
- ■ Park and seek assistance

Answer

☑ Park and seek assistance

Power steering is designed to help the driver by reducing the effort required to turn the steering wheel. It uses hydraulic pressure to assist with the steering mechanism.

Hydraulic fluid is pressured by a pump that's driven by the vehicle's engine. The power-assisted steering only operates when the engine is running. If this system fails, the steering will become very stiff and difficult to turn. It may also be felt as a series of jerks.

You should park and seek assistance. The vehicle is designed to be used with this steering assistance, and driving it without might cause danger to other road users.

Q. 8.19

Mark one answer

You are driving a three-axle double-deck bus and using full steering lock. Why should you take extra care?

- ■ Passengers might alter the angle of tilt
- ■ The power steering might fail
- ■ You may damage the air suspension
- ■ You may scrub the rear tyres

Answer

☑ You may scrub the rear tyres

The course the wheels take on tight corners should be observed and allowed for when driving. Very low speed is advisable when the steering is on full lock.

Q. 8.20

Mark one answer

You are driving a three-axle double-deck bus and using full steering lock. To avoid rear tyre scrub you should use

- ■ the highest gear possible
- ■ a very low speed
- ■ the exhaust brake (retarder)
- ■ a steering ball

Answer

☑ a very low speed

This is advisable when negotiating tight corners.

questions answers

Q. 8.21

Mark two answers

Whilst driving your steering suddenly becomes heavy to turn. What could this indicate?

 A puncture in a front tyre

☐ Loss of air brake pressure

☐ A faulty parking brake

☐ A failure of power-assisted steering

Answers

☑ **A puncture in a front tyre**

☑ **A failure of power-assisted steering**

If the steering becomes heavy there are other possible causes you should be aware of. Your vehicle might have a puncture or the load might have shifted. In any case you should stop safely, investigate the cause, then seek assistance.

Q. 8.22

Mark one answer

What should you do if the brake pedal becomes 'hard'?

☐ Continue to drive and report it at the end of the day

☐ Pump the brake pedal continuously

☐ Drain the air tanks and then continue

☐ Park and telephone for assistance

Answer

☑ **Park and telephone for assistance**

Don't take risks. As soon as you detect a fault on your vehicle you must take action. Where the brakes are concerned, always park and get assistance. Always report minor faults as soon as you detect them. Minor faults can become major ones if they aren't seen to quickly.

Q. 8.23

Mark one answer

Air tanks on brake systems require draining because

 excess coolant may collect in them

☐ rain water can often seep in

☐ any engine leakages are directed here

☐ of moisture drawn in from the atmosphere

Answer

☑ **of moisture drawn in from the atmosphere**

This moisture condenses in the air and can be transmitted around a vehicle's braking system. This is especially dangerous in cold weather, as it can lead to ice building up in the valves and pipes.

Q. 8.24

Mark one answer

Whilst checking your vehicle you discover an air leak in the braking system. What should you do?

- Drive slowly to the nearest garage
- Check the leak from time to time on your journey
- Leave it parked and report it immediately
- Start your journey and report it on your return

Answer

☑ **Leave it parked and report it immediately**

Under no circumstances should you attempt to move or drive a vehicle with an air leak in the braking system.

Report the fault immediately, or arrange to have it repaired.

Place a warning sign in a prominent position in the cab informing other drivers to prevent them unwittingly moving the vehicle.

Q. 8.25

Mark one answer

The low air pressure buzzer sounds whilst you are driving. You should

- drive faster to increase the air pressure
- stop as soon as possible
- drive slowly to the nearest garage
- pump the footbrake pedal rapidly

Answer

☑ **stop as soon as possible**

Stop as quickly and safely as possible. Check your air gauges – the fault may be electrical. If in doubt get professional assistance to rectify the problem.

DO NOT drive the vehicle until it has been repaired properly.

Q. 8.26

Mark one answer

You are driving a large vehicle. A loud buzzer sounds in the cab. This is most likely to indicate low

- oil pressure
- air pressure
- tyre pressure
- fuel level

Answer

☑ **air pressure**

Warning buzzers are linked to many systems on modern vehicles.

A warning light on the dashboard may help you identify the system that has caused the problem.

Under no circumstances should you continue driving until the fault has been identified and rectified. Seek professional assistance if necessary.

questions

answers

Q. 8.27

Mark one answer

Your vehicle is fitted with a warning device, which sounds when reversing. When should you NOT use it in a built-up area?

- Between 10.30 pm and 6.30 am
- Between 11 pm and 6.30 am
- Between 11.30 pm and 7 am
- Between 12.30 am and 8 am

Answer

☑ **Between 11.30 pm and 7 am**

Some modern vehicles are fitted with an audible warning that sounds when the vehicle's reversing. This is an effective device to warn pedestrians and others of a reversing vehicle. This doesn't, however, take away the need to use effective observation all around your vehicle before and while you're reversing.

Don't use the device in built-up areas at night. Have some consideration for the residents, and don't disturb them with excessive noise.

Q. 8.28

Mark one answer

When reversing in a 30 mph limit you must NOT use a reverse warning bleeper between

- 11.30 pm and 7.30 am
- 11 pm and 7 am
- 11.30 pm and 7 am
- 11 pm and 7.30 am

Answer

☑ **11.30 pm and 7 am**

Audible warning devices are a useful means of warning pedestrians when you need to reverse in a congested area.

An override switch should be fitted to disable the bleeper if you need to reverse in a built-up area between 11.30 pm and 7 am.

Q. 8.29

Mark one answer

Your vehicle is fitted with a reverse warning bleeper. When driving backwards you

- do not need to look round
- should only use the offside mirror
- still need to take all round observation
- should only use the nearside mirror

Answer

☑ **still need to take all round observation**

Get someone to guide you if you cannot see all around when reversing.

Q. 8.30

Mark one answer

Your vehicle is fitted with a reverse warning bleeper. You MUST switch it off between the hours of 11.30 pm and 7 am on a road with a

■ 30 mph speed limit

■ temporary speed limit

■ national speed limit

■ 40 mph speed limit

Answer

☑ **30 mph speed limit**

Try to avoid making unnecessary noise. Your vehicle will make more noise than a car, so try to consider others who may be resting.

Q. 8.31

Mark one answer

On a double-deck bus, what is the MINIMUM depth of tyre tread required over three-quarters of its width?

■ 0.8 mm

■ 1 mm

■ 1.6 mm

■ 2 mm

Answer

☑ **1 mm**

It's essential that the tyres on your vehicle are in good condition. You must never forget that you have passengers on board. Their safety must be your priority. At no time should the depth of the tread be less than 1 mm over three-quarters of the width of the tyre.

Q. 8.32

Mark one answer

What is the MINIMUM depth of tread required over three-quarters of the breadth of a lorry tyre?

■ 1 mm

■ 1.5 mm

■ 2.5 mm

■ 5 mm

Answer

☑ **1 mm**

Your tyres are your only contact with the road. It's essential that this contact gives you the grip you need to control your vehicle at all times. If the weather is wet or icy you'll be asking a lot more from your tyres.

questions   answers

Q. 8.33

Mark one answer

How much of the width of a tyre must have the legal limit of tread depth?

- One-quarter
- One-half
- Five-eighths
- Three-quarters

Answer

✓ **Three-quarters**

The condition of the tyres on your vehicle will contribute to its overall stability.

Don't leave your tyres until they're at the minimum depth. Renew them before they get into that state. Ensure that the tread is always deep enough, thus reducing the risk to road safety.

Q. 8.34

Mark one answer

You are driving a vehicle on a motorway. A front tyre bursts. You should

- loosen your grip on the steering wheel
- brake firmly to a stop
- hold the steering wheel firmly
- drive to the next service area

Answer

✓ **hold the steering wheel firmly**

A front wheel blow-out can be a heart-stopping moment. Keep calm and resist the temptation to brake hard or swerve. Allow the vehicle to slow down gradually.

Be aware of anything on your left. Try to get the vehicle onto the hard shoulder, as far to the left as possible.

Switch on your hazard warning lights.

Q. 8.35

Mark one answer

How frequently should a walk-around check be done?

- Daily
- Weekly
- Every 100 miles
- Every 1,000 miles

Answer

✓ **Daily**

Check your vehicle daily, as a routine. Your vehicle should be in a good condition at all times. A badly maintained vehicle could be illegal, as well as a danger to your passengers and other road users. Get into the habit of making a visual check before you move off after rest stops, as well as before your journey.

questions   answers

Q. 8.36

Mark one answer

After recoupling a trailer, which of the following should you do LAST?

- Connect the brake lines
- Release the trailer parking brake
- Connect the electrical lines
- Raise the trailer legs

Answer

✓ **Release the trailer parking brake**

Working methodically is important when uncoupling or recoupling a tractor unit and trailer. Make a final check of all connections, systems and lights before releasing the trailer brake.

Q. 8.37

Mark four answers

After recoupling your trailer it is important to check

- lights
- indicators
- brakes
- fuel
- water
- landing legs

Answers

✓ **lights**

✓ **indicators**

✓ **brakes**

✓ **landing legs**

Do not forget to stow the handle after raising the landing legs. Finally, release the trailer brake.

Q. 8.38

Mark one answer

You are waiting to turn right in this box van. Just before turning you should

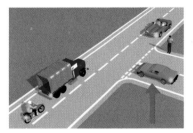

- wave the pedestrian across
- check your left mirror and blind spot
- wave out the green car (arrowed)
- check your right mirror and blind spot

Answer

✓ **check your right mirror and blind spot**

Always make a final check in your mirrors and blind spots before you turn. Another driver or motorcyclist may have committed themselves to overtaking traffic behind you before they realised you intended to turn.

questions answers

Q. 8.39

Mark one answer

High-intensity rear fog lights should be used when visibility is less than

- 100 metres (328 feet)
- 200 metres (656 feet)
- 300 metres (984 feet)
- 400 metres (1312 feet)

Answer

☑ **100 metres (328 feet)**

Large vehicles are no more visible than other vehicles in dense fog. If visibility is seriously reduced, use your fog lights to help other drivers see you.

Q. 8.40

Mark one answer

You should switch off fog lights when visibility is more than

- 10 metres (32 feet)
- your stopping distance
- your separation distance
- 100 metres (328 feet)

Answer

☑ **100 metres (328 feet)**

Do not drive with front or rear fog lights switched on unnecessarily. It is annoying for other drivers.

Q. 8.41

Mark one answer

During your journey you notice that your coach's right rear indicator is not working. You should

- continue your journey using arm signals
- get it repaired before continuing
- get it repaired on your return to the depot
- get your passengers to their destination then repair it

Answer

☑ **get it repaired before continuing**

All lights must be in working order, even in daylight. A faulty right rear indicator could cause a serious accident if another motorist attempted to overtake as you changed lanes or turned right.

Q. 8.42

Mark two answers

As a professional driver of large vehicles, why should you carry spare bulbs?

- To fix any fault for the safety of yourself
- Because bulbs are more likely to blow when your vehicle is loaded
- To repair the lights for the sake of other road users
- Because bulbs are more likely to blow when your vehicle is empty

Answers

- ☑ **To fix any fault for the safety of yourself**
- ☑ **To repair the lights for the sake of other road users**

Keep a stock of all the various bulbs used on your vehicle. This could save you wasting time trying to locate a spare bulb.

Q. 8.43

Mark one answer

It is an offence to use headlights or spot lights whose centres are less than 0.6 metres (2 feet) from the ground in

- fog
- falling snow
- mist
- daylight

Answer

- ☑ **daylight**

Drivers must conform to regulations governing the use and fitting of any additional lights.

Q. 8.44

Mark one answer

Before each journey you should check all warning lights. What should you do if a warning light remains lit?

- Report the fault when you return
- Have the fault checked before setting off
- Have the fault checked at the next service
- Ignore it until the fault shows up

Answer

- ☑ **Have the fault checked before setting off**

Many buses and coaches have a large panel of warning lights on the dashboard. A system check built into the ignition system will allow you to check that all the warning light bulbs are working before starting your journey. Familiarise yourself with the layout so you know which system is faulty if a warning light becomes illuminated during a journey. Always seek professional help and advice. Do not rely on it being an electrical malfunction.

questions   answers

Q. 8.45

Mark one answer

NI EXEMPT

The Vehicle Inspectorate and Police carry out spot checks of vehicle condition. If serious defects are found the vehicle is

- impounded until a new driver is found
- restricted to 30 mph for the remainder of the journey
- prohibited from further use until the defects are rectified
- ordered back to the depot to unload goods or passengers

Answer

☑ **prohibited from further use until the defects are rectified**

The Vehicle Inspectorate or Police can order an immediate prohibition. Details are always notified to the traffic commissioners. Drivers must NOT use vehicles which they know to be faulty.

Q. 8.46

Mark one answer

Seat belts are fitted to your lorry. The wearing of them is

- not advisable
- advisable
- required by law
- not required by law

Answer

☑ **required by law**

If seat belts are fitted in your lorry you must wear them unless you are exempt.

Q. 8.47

Mark one answer

You are driving a bus carrying passengers at night. Why should you always put the interior lights on?

- It will help you see the road ahead
- So that passengers can see to move around
- It will help passengers to see outside
- So that you can see your controls

Answer

☑ **So that passengers can see to move around**

Passengers need a properly lit area to move around safely.

Q. 8.48

Mark one answer

Why do some buses have marker lights along their sides?

- [ ] To make them easier to overtake
- [ ] To help the driver when reversing
- [ ] To help any passenger getting on or off
- [ ] To make them easier to see at junctions

Answer

✓ **To make them easier to see at junctions**

Newer buses and coaches have marker lights along the side to ensure that they are visible as they emerge from junctions etc.

Q. 8.49

Mark one answer

NI EXEMPT

A vehicle is found to have serious defects at a Vehicle Inspectorate spot-check. It is prohibited from further use. Who will be notified of the details?

- [ ] The Driver and Vehicle Licencing Agency
- [ ] The Traffic Commissioner
- [ ] The Road Transport Industry Training Body
- [ ] The bus, coach and commercial vehicle council

Answer

✓ **The Traffic Commissioner**

The Vehicle Inspectorate and Police carries out frequent spot checks of vehicle condition. Where serious defects are found the vehicle is prohibited from further use until the defects are rectified. Details of the prohibition are notified to the Traffic Commisioner.

Q. 8.50

Mark one answer

A vehicle 'reverse warning bleeper' must NOT be used

- [ ] in parking bays
- [ ] between 11.30 pm and 7.30 am in 30 mph limits
- [ ] between 11.30 pm and 7 am in 30 mph limits
- [ ] near hospitals

Answer

✓ **between 11.30 pm and 7 am in 30 mph limits**

Transport now operates around the clock, 24 hours a day.

If you are working the 'night-shift', show consideration between the hours of 11.30 pm and 7 am, when others are at rest.

Switch off reverse bleepers and try to avoid making unnecessary noise.

questions answers

Q. 8.51

Mark three answers

What extra problems will you have when driving at night?

- Increased overtaking distances
- An increase in traffic
- Reduced visibility
- Reduced braking distances
- Dazzle from other vehicles
- Becoming tired

Answers

- ☑ **Reduced visibility**
- ☑ **Dazzle from other vehicles**
- ☑ **Becoming tired**

Make sure that you drive within the speed limit, even if the roads appear to be empty. You must be able to stop safely in the distance that you can see clear ahead, which will be the distance illuminated by your headlights or by street lights.

Q. 8.52

Mark one answer

You are driving at night in a built up area. To ensure that you can be seen you should use

- dipped beam headlights
- main beam headlights
- side lights only
- front fog lights only

Answer

- ☑ **dipped beam headlights**

Using dipped headlights will help others see you and also aids your visibility if the street lighting changes or isn't working.

Q. 8.53

Mark one answer

You should switch off rear fog lights when visibility is more than

- 10 metres (32 feet)
- 50 metres (164 feet)
- 75 metres (246 feet)
- 100 metres (328 feet)

Answer

- ☑ **100 metres (328 feet)**

Be professional; switch off your fog lights when visibility improves. Don't cause unnecessary glare or distraction to other drivers.

Q. 8.54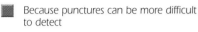

Mark one answer

Why should you check your tyres more frequently on a coach with three axles?

- ▓ Because punctures can be more difficult to detect
- ▓ Because air pressure is more easily lost
- ▓ The wheels will need balancing more often
- ▓ You have no room for a spare wheel

Answer

☑ **Because punctures can be more difficult to detect**

Tyre checks should be made as a matter of routine. Inspect both the inside and the outside walls and the treads for sign of wear, damage, bulges, separation and exposed cords.

Leaving the vehicle

This section looks at safety when leaving your vehicle.

The questions will ask you about

- **Mirrors and signals**

  using your mirrors and giving correct signals to ensure that other road users and passengers know your intentions

- **Passengers**

  choosing the correct place to stop to help your passengers leave the vehicle safely

- **The driver's cab**

  your own safety, and that of others, when you leave the vehicle's cab.

questions

answers

Mark one answer

As a bus driver your main aim should be

▪ to keep strictly to the timetable

▪ the safety of your passengers

▪ service to your colleagues

▪ to keep accurate details of ticket sales

Answer

☑ **the safety of your passengers**

You should remember that, as a driver, you are there to provide a service. Your passengers rely on you to make sure that the journey is a safe and comfortable one.

Q. 9.2

Mark one answer

As the driver of a bus your FIRST priority is

▪ the safety and comfort of your passengers

▪ making sure that you are always on time

▪ making sure that your log book and tachograph are correctly completed

▪ making sure that your destination is clearly marked

Answer

☑ **the safety and comfort of your passengers**

As a driver of a PCV you have responsibilities beyond those of other drivers. Your passengers have paid for a service, and should arrive at their chosen destination safely. By providing a courteous and comfortable service your customers will travel with you again.

Q. 9.3

Mark one answer

You are driving a one-person-operated bus. You are at a bus stop issuing tickets. You should

▪ be in gear without any signal

▪ be in gear and signalling

▪ signal only when ready to move away

▪ be in neutral but signalling to move off

Answer

☑ **signal only when ready to move away**

Giving wrong signals causes uncertainty and confusion to other road users. Only give reliable signals which are relevant to your intended actions.

questions answers

Q. 9.4

Mark one answer

As the driver of a one-person-operated double-deck bus you should be constantly aware of passengers on the top deck. How should you do this?

- By counting passengers up and down the staircase
- By frequent checks upstairs while stopped at bus stops
- By listening to passengers in the upstairs gangway when approaching bus stops
- By making full use of the internal mirror system

Answer

☑ **By making full use of the internal mirror system**

If you're driving a one-person-operated double-deck bus you must ensure that you're able to see passengers who are about to descend the stairs. Make sure that you can see them in the internal mirrors. Always consider their safety, and avoid harsh braking and steering.

Q. 9.5

Mark one answer

When driving a double-deck bus, the internal mirror system is used to

- watch for traffic on your right-hand side
- keep a look out for any overtaking vehicles
- keep a look out for passengers using the stairs
- watch for cyclists on your left-hand side

Answer

☑ **keep a look out for passengers using the stairs**

You must always be aware of anyone using the stairs. Be particularly careful to avoid any sudden movement, such as when braking or cornering, that could cause them to stumble.

Q. 9.6

Mark two answers

As a driver you should use your mirrors

- as you signal
- to check the blind spot
- when driving along
- before opening your door

Answers

☑ **when driving along**

☑ **before opening your door**

To be a safe driver, you must always be aware of where other road users are. That way you can plan your driving according to what is going on around you.

Before opening your door it's important to check the mirrors as well as looking round, to make sure that no passing or approaching vehicles are endangered.

questions answers

Q. 9.7

Mark one answer

The nearside mirror is used for checking

- if the driver's door is closed properly
- for any vehicles moving up on the left
- if passengers are seated
- for any vehicles parking in front of you

Answer

✓ **for any vehicles moving up on the left**

Always be aware of any vehicles on your nearside, particularly on dual carriageways or motorways where, because of the limits on your vehicle, it can take some distance to overtake safely. When you think you are far enough ahead to move back to the left safely, check again – car drivers have been known to accelerate up on the nearside.

Q. 9.8

Mark one answer

When you intend to open your right-hand door you should check

- the mirror
- that all other doors are closed
- the air pressure
- that the interior is clear of passengers

Answer

✓ **the mirror**

When you pull in, other vehicles may be passing on your right-hand side. It's very important to check your mirror, as well as looking round to cover the blind spot, to make sure that it's safe before opening your door.

Q. 9.9

Mark one answer

When pulling up on the left in busy places you should be careful that

- there is good access to unload
- you have disconnected all air lines
- your nearside mirror does not strike the head of a pedestrian
- you change your tachograph mode

Answer

✓ **your nearside mirror does not strike the head of a pedestrian**

When pulling up on the left you should always be aware of pedestrians, particularly if they are close to the edge of the road. The height of your nearside mirror can vary depending on the size and type of vehicle you are driving. If in doubt, approach these situations with caution, and stop if necessary.

questions
answers

Q. 9.10

Mark one answer

You are stopping to collect passengers from a bus stop. Where should you pull up?

 Close to the kerb

Away from the kerb

After the bus stop

Before the bus stop

Answer

☑ **Close to the kerb**

Too often you see a bus pull half-way into a bus stop lay-by with the rear sticking well out into the road. Pulling up where the passengers are waiting may save them walking a few paces, but is it safe? You know the answer has got to be NO! Be professional; pull up in the correct position.

Q. 9.11

Mark one answer

You should stop your bus to allow passengers to get on or off near

 soft grass

guard rails

parked cars

the kerb

Answer

☑ **the kerb**

You should stop as close to the kerb as you can, so that passengers can reach the safety of the pavement without any difficulty.

Q. 9.12

Mark one answer

A bus stop is blocked and you cannot pull into it. Before opening the exit door what is the most important action to take?

 Try to get the bus stop cleared

Carry on to the next bus stop

Check for traffic on the left

Check for traffic on the right

Answer

☑ **Check for traffic on the left**

You must take care of your passengers at all times. Ensure that you allow your passengers to get on or off the vehicle safely. If you're unable to stop close to the kerb, don't open the doors until you're sure it's safe. Always check the nearside mirror first.

Q. 9.13

Mark one answer

Several cars have parked blocking your bus stop. Before allowing passengers to get off you should

- ▊ move on to the next bus stop
- ▊ check it is clear of traffic on the left
- ▊ try and find the car owners
- ▊ check it is clear of traffic on the right

Answer

✔ **check it is clear of traffic on the left**

Always check your nearside mirror before opening the door to allow passengers to alight. When away from the kerb it is important to tell the passengers to

- look out for cyclists
- expect a long step down onto the road.

Be ready to offer assistance if required.

Q. 9.14

Mark one answer

What should you do before allowing passengers off your bus?

- ▊ Collect their used tickets
- ▊ Activate an audible warning system
- ▊ Check mirrors before opening doors
- ▊ Ask if they have luggage to collect

Answer

✔ **Check mirrors before opening doors**

The safety of passengers is your main responsibility. Before you allow them to step down from the bus you should always check mirrors to make sure that there's nothing approaching that could endanger them.

Q. 9.15

Mark one answer

Passengers may be in a hurry to get off the bus as you approach a bus stop. What should you do to reduce any dangers?

- ▊ Insist that passengers stay seated until the bus stops
- ▊ Pull up just before the stop and let passengers get off
- ▊ Let passengers on the bus before letting passengers off
- ▊ Not open the passenger doors until the bus stops

Answer

✔ **Not open the passenger doors until the bus stops**

Passengers may be in a hurry to get off at their stop. Don't

- brake harshly
- open the doors until the vehicle has come to a stop

as passengers might have left their seats early and be standing up, waiting to get off. Due to the necessary fittings on board, such as handrails, poles and luggage racks, there's a substantial risk of injury. Consider your passengers' safety first.

questions

answers

Q. 9.16

Mark one answer

You are driving a half-cab bus and carrying passengers. You must have

- a chain or strap across the doorway
- electrically operated doors
- school children only on board
- a responsible person in charge of them

Answer

✓ **a responsible person in charge of them**

When you have no direct contact with your passengers, you must have a designated person in charge of the passenger saloon.

Q. 9.17

Mark three answers

As a driver, when getting out of your bus you must make sure that

- the parking brake is on
- the vehicle is stopped in a safe place
- the engine is switched off
- the air pressure gauges read full
- you are parked at a bus stop
- you always change the destination board

Answers

✓ **the parking brake is on**

✓ **the vehicle is stopped in a safe place**

✓ **the engine is switched off**

Don't park where you will cause obstruction or inconvenience to other road users.

It's an offence to leave your bus

- with the engine running
- without applying the parking brake.

Q. 9.18 🚌

Mark three answers

Many buses have a separate door on the offside for the driver. When leaving the bus by this door you should always

- ▪ jump down from the cab
- ▪ check for traffic which may be passing
- ▪ apply the parking brake
- ▪ climb down facing the bus using the footholds
- ▪ climb down facing away from the bus using the footholds

Answers

- ☑ **check for traffic which may be passing**
- ☑ **apply the parking brake**
- ☑ **climb down facing the bus using the footholds**

Having found a safe place to park your bus, make a final offside check before opening your door. Never jump down from the cab into the road. It's particularly dangerous as you risk injury from landing badly, or falling into the path of passing traffic.

Q. 9.19 🚌

Mark two answers

When getting out of the driver's door on this bus you should

- ▪ look out for overtaking vehicles before opening the door
- ▪ climb down facing away from the bus
- ▪ climb down facing the bus
- ▪ signal your intentions to other traffic
- ▪ open the door to get a good view of approaching traffic

Answers

- ☑ **look out for overtaking vehicles before opening the door**
- ☑ **climb down facing the bus**

For your own safety, as well as that of others, you should make sure that it's safe by checking for other vehicles before getting out of the cab.

Climbing down facing the bus means that you can make proper use of the footholds to lessen the risk of slipping.

questions

answers

Q. 9.20

Mark two answers

This bus has a separate door for the driver, opening onto the offside. What should you do when getting out of such a vehicle?

◻ Climb down facing away from the vehicle

◻ Check for passing traffic

◻ Climb down facing towards the vehicle

◻ Jump down carefully, flexing the knees on landing

◻ Climb down holding the steering wheel rim tightly

Answers

☑ **Check for passing traffic**

☑ **Climb down facing towards the vehicle**

If your vehicle has a separate offside driver's door, you must take the precaution of good observation before leaving the vehicle. Don't jump down out of the cab. Leave by climbing down facing towards the vehicle. Consider your own safety as well as that of others. Always check for close passing traffic before getting out of your vehicle.

Q. 9.21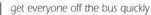

Mark two answers

You are driving a loaded school bus. Looking in your mirror you see smoke from the engine compartment at the rear. You must

◻ stop as quickly and safely as possible

◻ open the engine covers to investigate

◻ drive to the bus station for a replacement vehicle

◻ get everyone off the bus quickly

◻ move the passengers to the front away from danger

Answers

☑ **stop as quickly and safely as possible**

☑ **get everyone off the bus quickly**

Smoke from the engine compartment is very serious, as fire within a vehicle can spread very quickly. Your first priority is to make sure that all passengers get off the bus as quickly and safely as possible.

Q. 9.22

Mark one answer

You can drive a bus at night without having the interior lights on if

- the passengers want to sleep
- most passengers request it
- there are no standing passengers
- there are no passengers

Answer

☑ **there are no passengers**

Whenever passengers are aboard the lighting must be left on, but it may be turned off when the bus is empty.

Q. 9.23

Mark two answers

You are parking your coach at a coastal resort. Your passengers will still have access. You should make sure

- the cab area is isolated
- the gear lever is in neutral
- the storage lockers are open
- a responsible person is on the coach

Answers

☑ **the cab area is isolated**

☑ **a responsible person is on the coach**

Your coach must never be left unattended if passengers still have access to it. In particular, they must not be able to get into the cab area of the vehicle. You or another responsible person must always be there to supervise the coach.

Q. 9.24

Mark two answers

You have parked and left your bus. The public will still have access to it. You should make sure that

- the door key is different to the ignition key
- the cab area is shut off
- a responsible person is on board
- all interior lights are on

Answers

☑ **the cab area is shut off**

☑ **a responsible person is on board**

Your bus must never be left unsupervised when passengers are still able to get back on board. The cab area must be protected, and either yourself or another responsible person must remain on board to ensure everyone's safety.

questions

answers

Q. 9.25

Mark one answer

Before you get out of your cab, you must

- empty the air tanks
- adjust your mirrors
- apply the parking brake
- check if the warning lights are working

Answer

 apply the parking brake

The parking brake must always be set whenever you leave the vehicle, it would be an offence not to leave it properly secured.

Q. 9.26

Mark one answer

Before you leave your vehicle you must always

- empty the air tanks
- apply the parking brake
- adjust your mirrors
- switch on your hazard warning lights

Answer

 apply the parking brake

Whenever you leave the driving seat you must always make sure that your vehicle is secured by applying the parking brake. Make sure the engine is stopped. It is an offence to leave your vehicle with the engine running.

Q. 9.27

Mark one answer

Long vehicles need to straddle lanes

- to avoid mounting the kerb
- to avoid braking sharply
- when driving on motorways
- when coming to contraflow systems

Answer

 **to avoid mounting the kerb**

When driving a long vehicle it's sometimes necessary to adopt a different road position to avoid mounting the kerb or colliding with street furniture such as lamp posts, traffic signs, etc.

Other road users may not understand what you intend to do next. Watch them carefully and always signal in good time.

Q. 9.28

Mark three answers

Before leaving the cab you should make sure that

- you remove your tachograph chart
- the engine has stopped
- all warning lights are operating
- the parking brake is on
- all documents are safely stowed
- you will not endanger people when opening the door

Answers

- ☑ **the engine has stopped**
- ☑ **the parking brake is on**
- ☑ **you will not endanger people when opening the door**

Always make a systematic check of the above before leaving your vehicle. It is your responsibility to make sure your vehicle and load are safe at all times. It is an offence to leave a vehicle with the engine running on a public road. Don't leave your engine idle for long periods of time unnecessarily, as it is environmentally unfriendly.

Q. 9.29

Mark one answer

Before opening your cab door you should be aware of

- vehicles passing close by
- the height of your cab from the ground
- loose grab rails near the door
- people crossing the road behind you

Answer

- ☑ **vehicles passing close by**

Vehicles passing close by could easily be endangered if you open the door carelessly. Always look properly to make sure that it's safe, using the mirror as well as checking blindspots before you get out of the cab.

Q. 9.30

Mark three answers

Before leaving your vehicle cab you should make sure that

- the engine is running smoothly
- the engine is stopped
- the parking brake is on
- you have removed your personal things
- the ignition system is switched off

Answers

- ☑ **the engine is stopped**
- ☑ **the parking brake is on**
- ☑ **the ignition system is switched off**

The vehicle must always be left safe and secure when you leave the cab.

questions   answers

Q. 9.31

Mark two answers

Before leaving your vehicle cab you should make sure that

- your seat is correctly adjusted
- the ignition system is switched on
- the engine is stopped
- the keys are in the starter switch
- the parking brake is on

Answers

☑ **the engine is stopped**

☑ **the parking brake is on**

The law requires that the parking brake be set and the engine switched off before leaving the cab of your vehicle.

Q. 9.32

Mark one answer

You have just parked a lorry at a roadside in very heavy traffic. Before dismounting from the cab you should be particularly careful to do which one of the following?

- Make sure the radio is turned down
- Check the rear view mirrors
- Make sure the hazard warning lights are on
- Check that all windows are closed

Answer

☑ **Check the rear view mirrors**

Getting out of the cab from the offside of a vehicle directly into the road can be hazardous, especially if traffic is travelling at speed. Use your mirrors to check behind and all around the vehicle. Ensure that you use all proper footholds and hand grips. Be responsible for your own health and safety.

Q. 9.33

Mark one answer

Which ONE of the following is NOT important when getting out of a lorry cab?

- Watching for approaching traffic
- Using the mirrors
- Applying the parking brake
- Disconnecting the air lines

Answer

☑ **Disconnecting the air lines**

After getting out of your vehicle it's a good idea to walk round and check your

- tyres
- load
- lights
- brake line and electrical connections, etc.

When you return to your vehicle, or take over a different vehicle, all the safety checks should be carried out.

Q. 9.34

Mark three answers

You are the driver of a tanker vehicle. When opening the tank hatches, what dangers should you be aware of?

- Low air pressure
- Speed limiters
- Slippery walkways
- Emergency air lines
- Overhead cables
- Overhead pipeways

Answers

- ☑ **Slippery walkways**
- ☑ **Overhead cables**
- ☑ **Overhead pipeways**

Take your time if you're using walkways at high levels. Fuel can make the surface slippery and, therefore, increase the safety risk.

Q. 9.35

Mark two answers

Hazard warning lights may be used in which TWO of these situations?

- To thank a driver who has let you pull in after overtaking
- As a warning to drivers that you are towing another vehicle
- To show your intention to go ahead at a junction when your position might suggest otherwise
- When driving on motorways or dual carriageways to warn following drivers of a hazard ahead
- When your vehicle is stopped to warn others of an obstruction

Answers

- ☑ **When driving on motorways or dual carriageways to warn following drivers of a hazard ahead**

- ☑ **When your vehicle is stopped to warn others of an obstruction**

Use the hazard warning lights if you're approaching a queue of traffic on the motorway. This will alert traffic behind, which might not be able to see the hazard due to the bulk of your vehicle.

Don't use your hazard warning lights as an excuse for illegal parking. They should only be used for warning other road users of a hazard ahead, not one created by your thoughtless parking.

questions   answers

Q. 9.36

Mark one answer

When should you use hazard warning lights?

- To warn other drivers that you are towing
- Approaching queuing traffic on a motorway
- When parked illegally on a busy road
- To thank a driver for giving way to you

Answer

☑ **Approaching queuing traffic on a motorway**

You may only use hazard warning lights whilst driving if you are on unrestricted dual carriageways and motorways to warn drivers behind you of a hazard or obstruction ahead. Only use them for just long enough to ensure that your warning has been observed.

Q. 9.37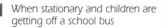

Mark four answers

As a bus driver, on which FOUR occasions should you use your hazard warning lights?

- When you are temporarily obstructing traffic
- To thank a driver who has let you pull in
- To warn of an obstruction when driving on the motorway
- When parking in a restricted area
- When you have broken down
- When stationary and children are getting off a school bus

Answers

☑ **When you are temporarily obstructing traffic**

☑ **To warn of an obstruction when driving on the motorway**

☑ **When you have broken down**

☑ **When stationary and children are getting off a school bus**

As a bus driver you may use your hazard warning lights to alert other drivers to danger on specific occasions, such as listed above.

Q. 9.38

Mark one answer

You are driving a bus in hot weather. May the passenger door be left open to let fresh air in?

- Yes, this is normal practice
- No, unless all passengers are seated
- Yes, unless carrying school children
- No, this is not allowed

Answer

☑ **No, this is not allowed**

Under no circumstances should you drive with your passenger door open. Many vehicles have air-operated doors which close automatically when the clutch is released. Do not override this set-up. An open door invites people to make rash decisions to enter or leave the vehicle as you are about to move away, which can be extremely dangerous.

questions

answers

Q. 9.39

Mark two answers

You are approaching a bus stop. A passenger is waiting there holding a white stick with a red band. This means they will NOT be able to

- ■ hear the bus approaching
- ■ see the bus approaching
- ■ climb aboard the bus
- ■ speak to you

Answers

- ☑ **hear the bus approaching**
- ☑ **see the bus approaching**

As a bus driver you need to be aware of difficulties experienced by people who can't see or hear properly. Try to be patient and considerate, be prepared to offer assistance if required, but allow them to be independent.

Some disabilities are obvious, but remember that many people suffer from invisible pain caused through arthritis and other conditions.

Q. 9.40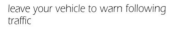

Mark one answer

When leaving the cab of your bus which of the following is NOT important?

- ■ Applying the parking brake
- ■ Switching off the engine
- ■ Watching for approaching traffic
- ■ Operating the fuel cut-off switch

Answer

- ☑ **Operating the fuel cut-off switch**

This is not normally necessary unless the vehicle has been involved in an accident and there is a risk of fire.

Q. 9.41

Mark one answer

A horse is running loose on the motorway. You should

- ■ use the size of your vehicle to block the lanes
- ■ stop and try to catch the animal
- ■ leave your vehicle to warn following traffic
- ■ call the police from the next emergency telephone

Answer

- ☑ **call the police from the next emergency telephone**

In a situation like this it's vital that the police are alerted as soon as possible. They will be able to contact the best people to deal with the emergency, and will take control themselves, to keep things as safe as possible. On no account should you walk onto the carriageway yourself; this would be dangerous and against the law.

questions answers

Q. 9.42

Mark one answer

When driving through a bus station you should

- ensure that your destination boards are correct
- drive only in first gear
- look out for people leaving the buses
- use your mirrors more than usual

Answer

✓ **look out for people leaving the buses**

If people are in a rush they may not always look properly before getting off a bus. Stations can be busy places, and you must always keep your speed down and be aware that danger may suddenly arise when you least expect it.

Q. 9.43

Mark two answers

Air suspension systems give

- increased fuel consumption
- uneven tyre wear
- increased speed
- even height
- a comfortable ride to passengers

Answers

✓ **even height**

✓ **a comfortable ride to passengers**

Air suspension can also help reduce wear on road surfaces, hence the term which is sometimes used: 'road-friendly suspension'.

Vehicle loading

This section looks at vehicle loading.

The questions will ask you about

- **Passenger safety**

  your passengers' safety and comfort, which are your responsibility

- **Legal requirements**

  the legal restrictions on your vehicle.

questions answers

Q. 10.1

Mark two answers

When driving, on which TWO occasions would you be most likely to experience weight transfer?

- Reversing
- Braking
- Overtaking
- Unloading
- Cornering
- Loading

Answers

☑ **Braking**

☑ **Cornering**

You must take extra care when your vehicle is carrying a load. When braking or cornering the vehicle's weight will transfer.

- When cornering, weight will be transferred away from the direction in which you're turning.

- When braking, weight can be transferred in several different directions.

Q. 10.2

Mark one answer

Why is it important to distribute the weight evenly over the axles when loading a lorry?

- To ensure easy unloading
- To make it easier to sheet up
- To ensure maximum ground clearance
- To ensure maximum stability

Answer

☑ **To ensure maximum stability**

A vehicle should be loaded so that the weight of a load is evenly distributed over the axles. This will increase the stability of the load.

In addition, when driving, you should brake

- in good time
- in a straight line wherever possible.

Look well ahead so that you can avoid harsh braking. Always reduce your speed before you make a turn, so that you aren't braking and steering at the same time.

Q. 10.3

Mark one answer

Which of the following is most important when loading a vehicle?

- Spreading the load evenly
- Loading it towards the rear
- Loading it towards the front
- Easy access for unloading

Answer

☑ **Spreading the load evenly**

It is your responsibility as the driver to make sure that your vehicle load is spread evenly to avoid overloading individual axles.

Overloading carries severe penalties for the driver and operator.

questions   answers

Q. 10.4

Mark one answer

You are driving a lorry with an ISO container on a trailer. You must make sure that

- the container is secured by ropes
- all locking levers are secured
- the trailer has a flat-bed platform
- the container is sealed

Answer

✓ **all locking levers are secured**

ISO (International Standards Organisation) cargo containers should only be carried on lorries or trailers with the appropriate securing points, which are designed to lock into the container body.

Q. 10.5

Mark one answer

You are loading a steel ISO container. Which statement is true?

- Its own weight will hold it in place
- It can be loaded onto any flat-bed lorry
- The locking levers must be secured
- The container should be roped in place

Answer

✓ **The locking levers must be secured**

Container loads use a different type of restraint to secure them to the vehicle.

Make sure that you are familiar with all the different kinds of load restraint. The security of the load is your responsibility; don't take chances.

Q. 10.6

Mark one answer

A lorry is found to be overloaded. Who is liable to be prosecuted for this offence?

- The people who loaded the vehicle
- Both the driver and the operator
- The operator only
- The driver only

Answer

✓ **Both the driver and the operator**

If a roadside check reveals contravention of vehicle weight limits, the police can escort the vehicle to the nearest official weigh bridge.

Q. 10.7

Mark one answer

Who is responsible for making sure that a lorry's load is secure during a journey?

- The warehouse loader
- The driver's mate
- The driver
- The transport police

Answer

☑ **The driver**

Before you leave on a journey always check that your load is secure. When you stop for a break, always walk round your vehicle and check your load.

Q. 10.8

Mark one answer

You are using three sheets to cover your load. Which of the following shows the correct overlap?

-

-

-

Answer

☑

Keep a check in your mirrors as you're driving to ensure that the sheets are secure. Air can force itself under the sheets and work them loose.

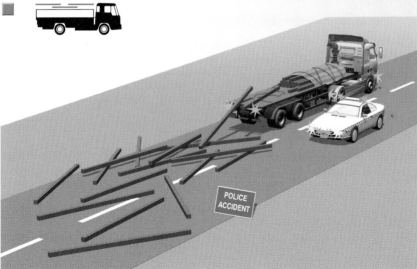

questions answers

Q. 10.9

Mark one answer

You are covering a load using more than one sheet. You should start with the rearmost sheet first, then work forwards. This will

 stop you tripping over when walking on the load

 stop wind and rain getting under the sheets

 make it much easier to fold up the sheets

make it easier to carry longer loads

Answer

☑ **stop wind and rain getting under the sheets**

If the load is sheeted incorrectly, when the wind gets underneath the sheet it will lift and flap about. This is dangerous, as it can catch unsuspecting pedestrians or cyclists and also seriously reduce the driver's view of what's happening to the rear.

Q. 10.10

Mark one answer

When roping down a load on your lorry what is the best knot to use?

A dolly knot

A reef knot

A slip knot

A bow-line knot

Answer

☑ **A dolly knot**

If a load is being secured by ropes you must ensure that they're tied securely to the body of the unit. The most effective method of tying is by 'dolly knots'. These are non-slip knots that hold firmly. You should practise tying these and use them appropriately.

Q. 10.11

Mark one answer

Ropes are unsuitable to tie down a load of scrap metal because they

are hard to tie

will loosen in rain

are hard to untie

wear and snap

Answer

☑ **wear and snap**

When securing a load, the driver must decide which is the most suitable type of restraint to use. A few extra minutes to make sure that the load is secure gives you peace of mind. It also reduces the risk of the load moving should an emergency situation arise.

Q. 10.12

Mark one answer

You are driving a tipper lorry carrying loose dry sand. Why should you sheet this load?

- To stop handling being affected
- To stop the load from shifting
- To stop the load from blowing away
- To aid your rearward vision

Answer

✓ **To stop the load from blowing away**

If you're carrying a load that consists of loose materials, it must be securely roped and sheeted. You must not risk the chance of losing any part of your load. This could cause damage to other road users, and you'll be held responsible.

Q. 10.13

Mark one answer

The load on a lorry becomes insecure on a journey. The driver should

- continue at a slower speed to ensure the load does not fall off
- attach 'hazard' boards to warn other road users
- park and resecure the load before continuing
- inform base at the earliest opportunity

Answer

✓ **park and resecure the load before continuing**

If you become aware that any part of your load is insecure you must stop as soon as it's safe to do so. Resecure the load before continuing on your journey. If this isn't possible, then you must seek assistance. Don't take risks.

Q. 10.14

Mark one answer

An articulated car-transporter will be least stable when

- only the lower deck is loaded
- only the top deck is loaded
- it is fully laden
- it is unladen

Answer

✓ **only the top deck is loaded**

Keeping the centre of gravity as low as possible will improve the handling of your lorry. Top heavy loads are more unstable and require more care when turning and cornering.

questions

answers

Q. 10.15

Mark three answers

When driving a double-deck bus on a steep camber you should be especially aware of

- ☐ lamp posts
- ☐ parking meters
- ☐ parked cars
- ☐ shop awnings
- ☐ litter bins
- ☐ traffic signs

Answers

- ☑ **lamp posts**
- ☑ **shop awnings**
- ☑ **traffic signs**

When driving high-sided vehicles, such as double-deck buses, you must be aware of how road camber changes can affect the way your vehicle handles.

Street furniture, such as lamp posts, not normally a problem, can get frighteningly close to passengers sitting on the top deck as the bus leans on an adverse camber.

Many shop awnings come out to the very edge of the footpath, and if the road drops away sharply near the kerb, this can also be a danger to watch out for.

Q. 10.16

Mark one answer

When driving high-sided coaches, you should always be aware of the

- ☐ quickest route
- ☐ nearest weighbridge
- ☐ operators licence number
- ☐ safe angle of tilt

Answer

- ☑ **safe angle of tilt**

All vehicles have safe limitations which are generally never reached in normal driving. If you enter a corner too fast on a road with an adverse camber your vehicle handling will be impaired. You will also alarm your passengers, as centrifugal forces will throw them to the outside of the bend.

questions   answers

Q. 10.17

Mark three answers

A bus driver MUST not drive whilst

- ☐ issuing tickets
- ☐ the doors are open
- ☐ wearing sunglasses
- ☐ giving change
- ☐ passengers are standing
- ☐ luggage is being carried

Answers

- ☑ **issuing tickets**
- ☑ **the doors are open**
- ☑ **giving change**

On regular services traffic congestion can soon put you behind schedule. Nevertheless, you have a responsibility to your passengers at all times not to take shortcuts or jeopardise their safety. They are paying you for a service which must always deliver them safely to their destination.

Q. 10.18

Mark one answer

What is the likely weight difference between an empty bus and a bus with 75 passengers on board?

- ☐ 5 tonnes
- ☐ 10 tonnes
- ☐ 15 tonnes
- ☐ 20 tonnes

Answer

- ☑ **5 tonnes**

The way that your vehicle handles will differ greatly when it's full compared with when it's empty. A bus with 75 passengers on board could increase the weight by up to about 5 tonnes. The passengers may also be carrying luggage, either with them or in a luggage compartment. The extra weight will have an effect on inertia and momentum.

It will take longer to build up speed, but the vehicle will maintain forward momentum, requiring controlled braking.

questions answers

Q. 10.19

Mark one answer

It is important to be able to work out the weight difference between a full bus and an empty one. About how many passengers will equal 1 tonne in weight?

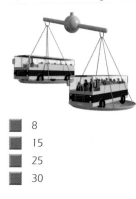

- 8
- 15
- 25
- 30

Answer

✓ **15**

You should also make allowances for any luggage your passengers may bring on board.

An average of two cases per passenger on a fifty seat coach will add approximately another 1.5 tonnes to the overall weight of your bus or coach.

Q. 10.20

Mark one answer

It is only legal to drive an empty, half-cab bus when the passenger access has

- a vertical pole
- no high steps
- no obstructions
- a chain or strap

Answer

✓ **a chain or strap**

You should never drive a half-cab bus in which you have no contact with the passengers unless a responsible person is in charge of the passenger saloon(s).

Always keep an eye on your nearside mirror when you are travelling slowly or are stationary in areas where pedestrians may attempt to jump aboard.

Q. 10.21

Mark one answer

You are driving a double-deck half-cab bus. Passengers can only be carried if

- no-one uses the upper deck
- you can see them in your mirror
- a responsible person is in charge of them
- they are all travelling to the same destination

Answer

✓ **a responsible person is in charge of them**

Under no circumstances should you drive a half-cab bus with passengers on board unless there is a responsible person in charge of them.

Q. 10.22

Mark one answer

While driving your half-cab bus you hear the three-bell signal from the conductor. This means

◼ stop when safe

◼ bus empty

◼ bus full

◼ move off when safe

Answer

☑ **bus full**

One bell means stop, two means move off when safe, and three bells are used to announce when the bus is full.

Q. 10.23

Mark one answer

You are driving a half-cab bus. The correct signal to move off when safe is

◼ one bell

◼ two bells

◼ three bells

◼ four bells

Answer

☑ **two bells**

This is the correct signal to move off when safe.

Q. 10.24

Mark one answer

It is legal to drive an empty, half-cab double-deck bus, but the passenger access must have

◼ a hand rail

◼ a vertical pole

◼ a chain or strap

◼ a warning notice

Answer

☑ **a chain or strap**

The chain or strap will prevent any passengers jumping on board while you're stationary or waiting in traffic queues.

You must not carry any passengers unless there's a responsible person on board to supervise.

questions   answers

Q. 10.25

Mark one answer

Your vehicle leaks diesel fuel on a roundabout. This will MOST affect

 three-wheel vehicle drivers

 motorcyclists

 towed vehicles

car drivers

Answer

✓ **motorcyclists**

When diesel fuel makes contact with most types of road surface it becomes extremely slippery. This can cause danger for all types of vehicle, but particularly those on two wheels, because it reduces the grip between tyres and the road surface.

Q. 10.26

Mark one answer

You have lost the filler cap to your diesel tank. You should

 get a replacement before driving

push a rag into the filler pipe

drive slowly back to your depot

only fill the tank half full

Answer

✓ **get a replacement before driving**

You shouldn't drive without a fuel filler cap in place as fuel could spill out onto the carriageway when cornering or turning at roundabouts.

Diesel fuel, in particular, will make the road surface extremely slippery, and any spillage should be reported so that the emergency services can make the road safe.

Q. 10.27

Mark one answer

Vehicles are fitted with air suspension to

reduce wear to roads

reduce tyre wear

improve fuel consumption

help the driver stay awake

Answer

✓ **reduce wear to roads**

Air suspension causes less damage to the road surface than conventional suspension systems.

Vehicles transporting glass and fragile loads also use it.

It is considered environmentally friendly.

Q. 10.28

Mark one answer

Damage can be caused when parking close to another vehicle if your coach is fitted with

 air brakes

 hydraulic suspension

air suspension

hydraulic brakes

Answer

✓ **air suspension**

Vehicles fitted with air suspension can sometimes move a considerable amount when first started, as the air bags are injected with gas.

If you're too close to another vehicle or obstruction this could result in collision damage.

Q. 10.29

Mark one answer

Buses and coaches used for school contract work MUST have

- ▉ yellow reflective signs
- ▉ only one door
- ▉ a conductor
- ▉ a 'no overtaking' sign

Answer

✓ **yellow reflective signs**

Vehicles carrying school children display this sign to alert other drivers to the possible danger of young children crossing the road.

As the bus driver, you must make every effort to ensure their safety at all times.

Q. 10.30

Mark one answer

Baffle plates are fitted to tankers to help

- ▉ reduce wind resistance
- ▉ reduce the wave effect
- ▉ stop the brakes from locking
- ▉ make the steering lighter

Answer

✓ **reduce the wave effect**

Fluids carried in tanks can move in 'waves' as the vehicle's speed changes, particularly when braking and then easing off the pedal. This shift of weight could cause the vehicle to surge forward. Baffle plates are designed to reduce the wave effect in the liquid.

Q. 10.31

Mark three answers

Which THREE of these vehicles are most likely to be affected by strong winds?

- ▉ Flat-bed lorries
- ▉ Double-deck buses
- ▉ Motorcycles
- ▉ Horse boxes
- ▉ Tractors
- ▉ Estate cars

Answers

✓ **Double-deck buses**

✓ **Motorcycles**

✓ **Horse boxes**

Strong winds can force other vehicles into your path. You should be aware of the vehicles which are most likely to be affected. Adjust your speed so that you can stop or take avoiding action safely if necessary. Be vigilant for the more vulnerable road users in these conditions.

questions   answers

Q. 10.32

Mark one answer

Which of the following would reduce the 'wave effect' when driving tankers?

- Spray guards
- Harsh braking
- Baffle plates
- Wind deflectors

Answer

☑ **Baffle plates**

Modern tankers are fitted with baffle plates inside the tank compartment. This helps to minimise the movement of liquids and therefore reduce the 'wave effect'.

Q. 10.33

Mark one answer

You are driving an articulated tanker vehicle on a straight road. When braking to a stop the liquid load will tend to

- push the vehicle forward
- push the vehicle to the side
- make the trailer wheels bounce
- make the trailer wheels skid

Answer

☑ **push the vehicle forward**

When braking with a vehicle carrying a liquid load it's important to apply even pressure on the brake pedal. Do not relax the pedal pressure until the vehicle has stopped. Secure the vehicle with the parking brake before releasing the footbrake. This will minimise the risk of unintentional movement of the vehicle caused by 'surge' from the liquid load.

Q. 10.34

Mark one answer

You are driving a tanker that is half full. The inside of the tank is not divided into compartments. When braking to a stop you should

- avoid relaxing the footbrake
- relax the footbrake
- pump the footbrake rapidly
- use the footbrake and parking brake together

Answer

☑ **avoid relaxing the footbrake**

Baffle plates help prevent liquids 'surging' around, but extra care is still necessary when driving a tanker vehicle.

When braking, always maintain steady pressure on the brake pedal until after the vehicle has stopped. This helps reduce the 'wave' effect which can build up as the liquid load surges back and forth when the vehicle changes speed.

questions answers

Q. 10.35

Mark one answer

What shape are hazardous cargo labels?

- Diamond
- Triangle
- Circle
- Oval

Answer

✓ **Diamond**

Hazardous substances in transit are readily identified by a diamond shaped warning label. This label carries other information to identify more specifically the type of hazard, such as

- flammable gas
- toxic gas
- corrosive agents
- oxidising agents.

These are some of the types of hazard encountered. Strict regulations apply to the storage and carriage of these goods. All drivers of this type of load must receive specific certificated training.

Q. 10.36

Mark one answer

Which type of load would most benefit from being carried on a lorry fitted with road-friendly suspension?

- Steel
- Timber
- Glass
- Cables

Answer

✓ **Glass**

Fragile loads need extra care in loading and handling. The load must be secured using the most appropriate form of restraint. Air suspension reduces the vibration caused by the impact of the lorry wheels on road surfaces. This also reduces damage to the road, bridges and adjacent structures.

Q. 10.37

Mark one answer

An attendant must accompany you when your load is wider than

- 2.6 metres (8 feet 5 inches)
- 3.0 metres (9 feet 9 inches)
- 3.3 metres (10 feet 9 inches)
- 3.5 metres (11 feet 5 inches)

Answer

✓ **3.5 metres (11 feet 5 inches)**

Wide loads are a hazard to other road users. In addition to having an attendant with you, you must also notify the police.

Side markers must also be used to help others be aware that your load overhangs the limits of your vehicle.

Q. 10.38

Mark one answer

Which of these vehicles will be most at risk of 'roll-over' when laden?

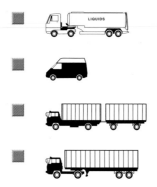

Answer

✓

Roll-over usually occurs as a result of the inside rear wheels of an articulated vehicle starting to lift when negotiating a curve, such as exiting a roundabout.

Changes of direction can create a situation where the vehicle is unstable due to movement of the load. The problem frequently involves vehicles carrying fluids in bulk.

Q. 10.39

Mark three answers

When driving a laden vehicle downhill, the effect of gravity will tend to

- make the vehicle use more fuel
- make the vehicle's speed increase
- require more braking effort
- require less braking effort
- increase stopping distances
- reduce stopping distances

Answers

✓ **make the vehicle's speed increase**

✓ **require more braking effort**

✓ **increase stopping distances**

Always plan ahead; take note of warning signs informing you of the gradient of the hill. Make sure you reduce your speed and select an appropriate lower gear in good time.

Q. 10.40

Mark one answer

Jack-knifing of an articulated lorry is more likely to occur when the trailer is

- loaded at the front
- loaded at the rear
- unloaded
- fully loaded

Answer

✓ **unloaded**

Severe braking can result in jack-knifing as the tractor unit is pushed by the semi-trailer pivoting around the coupling (fifth wheel).

This is more likely to occur when the brakes are applied on a bend.

Q. 10.41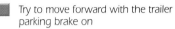

Mark one answer

After recoupling, how should you make sure that the tractor and trailer are secure?

- Try to move forward with the trailer parking brake on
- Reverse with the trailer parking brake on
- Try to move forward with the trailer parking brake off
- Reverse with the trailer parking brake off

Answer

✓ **Try to move forward with the trailer parking brake on**

Ensure the locking mechanism is secure by selecting a low gear and attempting to move forward.

Apply the parking brake before leaving the the cab.

Connect the 'dog-clip' to secure the kingpin release handle.

Q. 10.42

Mark one answer

When uncoupling or recoupling your trailer, what must you check first?

- The lights are working
- The tilt cab mechanism is secure
- The trailer brake is applied
- The air lines are safely stowed

Answer

✓ **The trailer brake is applied**

If the trailer begins moving while you're working on it, you could put yourself and others into great danger.

You must make sure that it's properly secured with the brake before you start work.

Q. 10.43

Mark one answer

You are uncoupling a lorry and trailer. After disconnecting the electric line you should

- stow it away safely
- drive forward slowly
- lower the landing gear
- apply the trailer brake

Answer

✓ **stow it away safely**

It's important to stow away all your electric cables and air lines safely to avoid causing injury to others. If left lying around, connectors can get damaged if run over by another vehicle.

It's your responsibility as the driver to make sure that this does not occur.

questions   answers

Q. 10.44

Mark one answer

Your lorry has a demountable body. Before demounting the body you should ensure that

- the rear doors are open
- the legs are up
- the body is unloaded and empty
- the surface is firm and level

Answer

☑ **the surface is firm and level**

If you demount the body on a poor or soft surface there is a danger of it sinking and becoming difficult to handle. Always think carefully before you demount the body and be sure that the site is suitable.

Q. 10.45

Mark one answer

After recoupling your trailer you should adjust your mirrors to enable you to see

- the full view of your load
- both pairs of rear wheels
- down each side of the trailer
- the road on the other side

Answer

☑ **down each side of the trailer**

The view you get in your mirrors may vary depending on the size of the trailer and the load it carries. Always adjust them to make sure that you have the best possible view down each side of the trailer before you drive away.

Q. 10.46

Mark one answer

When uncoupling a trailer the very FIRST thing you must do is

- lower the trailer legs to the ground
- apply the parking brake
- release the brake air lines
- uncouple the electrical lines

Answer

☑ **apply the parking brake**

Before leaving the cab it is very important to secure the vehicle by applying the vehicle parking brake.

After leaving the cab apply the trailer parking brake.

Q. 10.47

Mark one answer

You are uncoupling a trailer. Before disconnecting any of the airlines, you MUST

- drain the air tanks
- apply the trailer parking brake
- lower the landing gear
- disconnect the electrical line

Answer

☑ **apply the trailer parking brake**

Whenever you drop or pick up a trailer you must always work through the process methodically to avoid causing danger to yourself or other people.

Q. 10.48

Mark one answer

Who is responsible for ensuring that a lorry's load does not move whilst in transit?

- The factory manager
- The lorry driver
- The driver's mate
- The loaders at the factory

Answer

✓ **The lorry driver**

You should check your load carefully before starting a journey. Every time you stop for a break, walk around the vehicle and check that your load is still secure. If the load causes danger to other road users you, as the driver, are responsible. Take time to check it properly.

Q. 10.49

Mark one answer

Which one of the following vehicles is most likely to be affected by 'vehicle bounce'?

- A long wheel-base empty vehicle
- A short wheel-base laden vehicle
- A short wheel-base empty vehicle
- A long wheel-base laden vehicle

Answer

✓ **A short wheel-base empty vehicle**

A short wheel-base empty vehicle will bounce more noticeably than some long wheel-base vehicles. This can affect braking efficiency and all-round control.

Don't be tempted to push this type of vehicle into bends or corners simply because the vehicle appears to be easier to drive.

Q. 10.50

Mark one answer

Your engine catches fire. Before attempting to put the fire out you should

- shut off the fuel supply
- open the engine housing wide
- drive to the nearest fire station
- empty the air tanks

Answer

✓ **shut off the fuel supply**

An engine fire is serious enough, but were this to reach the fuel tank the results would be disastrous. You should ensure that the fuel supply is cut off as your first priority.

questions answers

Q. 10.51

Mark one answer

Before reversing you MUST always

- remove your seatbelt
- look all around
- use an audible warning device
- change the tachograph setting

Answer

 look all around

Large or long vehicles can have many blindspots when reversing. It's very important to check all angles before starting to reverse, as well as keeping all-round observation going while completing the manoeuvre.

Q. 10.52

Mark one answer

You have parked your vehicle on a two-way road at night. You should

- leave the lights on
- switch off all lights
- leave your lights on if you have parked on the right-hand side
- switch off your lights if you have parked underneath a street lamp

Answer

 leave the lights on

Large vehicles, buses and coaches, are required by law to leave lights on when parked at night, unless in a designated off-road parking area. Also, unless you're in a one-way street, you must only park on the left-hand side.

It's generally much better to park off-road if you can, particularly if you're going to be stationary for a long period of time.

Q. 10.53

Mark one answer

When a red route is in operation you must not

- stop and park
- overtake
- change lanes
- straddle the lines

Answer

 stop and park

The hours of operation of red routes vary from one area to another. As a rule you must not stop in these areas, but there may be special marked boxes where loading and unloading can be carried out at certain times. Look out for signs giving information regarding the restrictions in place.

questions

answers

Q. 10.54

Mark one answer

Ropes should NOT be used to tie down a load of

- ■ timber planks
- ■ hay bales
- ■ steel plates
- ■ canvas sacks

Answer

☑ **steel plates**

Ropes are totally unsuitable for loads such as steel plates. If there is danger of sharp edges shearing ropes then chains must be used with a suitable tensioning device.

Q. 10.55

Mark one answer

Which of the following loads is most likely to move forward with some force if you brake sharply?

- ■ Heavy material in canvas sacks
- ■ Loose sand
- ■ Timber secured with dolly knots
- ■ Tubular metal

Answer

☑ **Tubular metal**

When deciding which type of restraint to use consider what may happen if you have to brake sharply. Tubular loads may move forward with some force if emergency braking occurs. In such cases the headboard of the vehicle can be demolished with fatal results.

Q. 10.56

Mark one answer

When part loading a lorry with an empty ISO container you should position it

- ■ close to the fifth wheel
- ■ over the front axle
- ■ close to the trailer edge
- ■ over the rear axles

Answer

☑ **over the rear axles**

To increase stability and reduce the risk of the trailer wheels lifting when turning, it is preferable to locate part loads over the rear axle.

questions   answers

Q. 10.57

Mark two answers

NI EXEMPT

The load on your trailer hits a railway bridge. You must report it to

- The Police
- The Transport Police
- The Highways Agency
- Railtrack
- The Local Council

Answers

☑ **The Police**

☑ **Railtrack**

If your vehicle hits a bridge you must report it to the Police. If a railway bridge is involved you must also report it to Railtrack on 0345 114 141.

Q. 10.58

Mark one answer

When carrying spare sheets and ropes on your trailer you MUST make sure that they are

- laid out flat
- visible from the cab
- tied down securely
- stacked loosely

Answer

☑ **tied down securely**

All spare sheets and ropes must be tied down securely to prevent them falling into the path of following vehicles.

Q. 10.59

Mark one answer

Jack-knifing is more likely to occur when driving

- a flat-bed lorry
- a laden lorry
- a high-sided lorry
- an unladen lorry

Answer

☑ **an unladen lorry**

Jack-knifing occurs when the tractor unit is pushed by the semi trailer pivoting around the coupling (fifth wheel). This is more likely to occur with an unladen vehicle.

questions answers

Q. 10.60

Mark one answer

Short wheel-base vehicles will bounce more noticeably than some long wheel-base vehicles particularly when

- ⬛ laden
- ⬛ turning
- ⬛ empty
- ⬛ unloading

Answer

✓ **empty**

Short wheel-base vehicles will bounce more noticeably than some long wheel-base vehicles when empty. This can affect braking efficiency and all round control.

Q. 10.61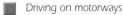

Mark four answers

What are the main causes of a lorry shedding its load?

- ⬛ Driving on motorways
- ⬛ Sudden change of direction
- ⬛ Driving over a level crossing
- ⬛ Harsh use of brakes
- ⬛ Driving too fast
- ⬛ Sudden change of speed

Answers

✓ **Sudden change of direction**

✓ **Harsh use of brakes**

✓ **Driving too fast**

✓ **Sudden change of speed**

The main causes of shed loads are

- driver errors
- sudden change of speed or direction
- too high a speed
- skidding.

Q. 10.62

Mark one answer

How many people can you have standing on the upper deck of a double deck bus?

- ⬛ None
- ⬛ Two
- ⬛ Five
- ⬛ Ten

Answer

✓ **None**

Double deck buses are provided with internal mirrors so that the driver can see the passengers at the top of the stairs. You should be aware that passengers may get up from their seats and descend the stairs some distance from their stop. Standing passengers are less stable, and for this reason they aren't allowed to travel on the top deck without a seat.

questions

answers

Q. 10.63

Mark one answer

You become stuck in snow. What might help you to move off?

- [ ] Trolley jack
- [ ] Can of de-icer
- [ ] Flask of drink
- [ ] Shovel

Answer

 Shovel

A shovel can be used to clear away deep snow, and to make a clear path for the vehicle to pull away in.

Cloth sacks can be placed under the wheels in order for them to have something to grip on while the vehicle pulls clear.

Q. 10.64

Mark one answer

What might help you to move off when you are stuck in snow?

- [ ] Trolley jack
- [ ] Cloth sacks
- [ ] Windscreen scraper
- [ ] Can of de-icer

Answer

 Cloth sacks

Cloth sacks placed under the wheels will provide extra grip. It will also be useful to carry a shovel in your vehicle.

Restricted view

This section looks at the subject of restricted views when driving a large vehicle.

The questions will ask you about

● **Mirrors**

use your mirrors effectively to help spot hazards around you

● **Signals**

give clear and well-timed signals to help other road users understand your intentions

● **Parking**

understand that thoughtless parking or unloading might cause a hazard on the road

● **Moving off**

take effective all-round observation to ensure safety

● **Blind spots**

understand that parts of your vehicle might restrict your vision. Extra effort should be taken to observe all around your vehicle

● **Observation at junctions**

understand that effective observation is essential to reduce the risk of an accident.

questions   answers

Q. 11.1

Mark one answer

What should you first check before moving to the LEFT?

- The nearside mirror
- The offside mirror
- Behind, over your right shoulder
- Behind, over your left shoulder

Answer
☑ **The nearside mirror**

The left side of the vehicle, as you face forwards, is often referred to as the nearside; the right side of the vehicle as the offside. Before you make a turn or a change of direction, however slight, you should always check the mirrors. If you intend to turn left, check your left-hand (nearside) mirror first, then your right-hand (offside) mirror, and then your left-hand mirror again as you turn.

Q. 11.2

Mark one answer

What should you first check before moving to the RIGHT?

- The nearside mirror
- Behind, over your left shoulder
- Behind, over your right shoulder
- The offside mirror

Answer
☑ **The offside mirror**

If you intend to turn right, check your right-hand (offside) mirror first, then your left-hand (nearside) mirror, then check your right-hand mirror again before you turn.

You must ensure that all your mirrors are properly adjusted to give a clear view around and behind. They should be free from dirt and grime and not be broken.

Q. 11.3

Mark two answers

Some lorries have an extra mirror angled down towards the nearside front wheel. This mirror is ESPECIALLY useful when

- moving off
- parking
- checking your trailer
- turning right
- overtaking

Answers
☑ **moving off**

☑ **parking**

Sitting in a high cab doesn't always give you all-round visibility. Other road users might assume that you can see them and position themselves out of sight close to your vehicle. Making good use of any extra mirrors can help prevent dangerous incidents with less experienced road users, especially when turning left.

questions

answers

Q. 11.4

Mark two answers

Some coaches have a mirror on their nearside angled down to show the front nearside wheel. This should be used when you are

- pulling in after overtaking
- pulling up to park at the kerb
- moving close to the left in normal driving
- changing lanes on a motorway

Answers

☑ **pulling up to park at the kerb**

☑ **moving close to the left in normal driving**

This mirror offers the most benefit when manoeuvring in confined spaces.

Q. 11.5

Mark one answer

You are about to move off. You should always

- extend your right arm as far as you can out of the window
- use only the offside mirror and move away quickly
- signal right with indicator and arm together
- use your mirrors and look behind

Answer

☑ **use your mirrors and look behind**

You must use the mirrors well before you signal your intention to make any manoeuvre. Use them before

- moving away
- changing direction
- turning left or right
- overtaking
- changing lanes
- slowing or stopping
- speeding up
- opening the cab door.

Q. 11.6

Mark three answers

In which THREE of the following situations would you FIRST need to check your nearside mirror?

- Before moving out to pass a car parked on your left
- After passing cars on your left
- Before moving to the left
- After passing pedestrians standing on the nearside kerb
- Before moving out to the right

Answers

- ☑ **After passing cars on your left**
- ☑ **Before moving to the left**
- ☑ **After passing pedestrians standing on the nearside kerb**

On a large vehicle the nearside mirror is very important and it's essential to use it before moving off. You must check for pedestrians and cyclists along the nearside of your vehicle. Cyclists might ride up along your nearside while you're stationary.

If you're driving a bus passengers might be running for your bus or waiting very close to the kerbside. As you pass pedestrians or vehicles on your left you should use your nearside mirror and check that you are passing them safely. Leave a safety margin before you move back to the left. This applies whether the vehicles are stationary or moving.

Q. 11.7

Mark one answer

The MSM routine is used to negotiate a hazard. What do the initials MSM stand for?

- Mirror, signal, manoeuvre
- Manoeuvre, speed, mirror
- Mirror, speed, manoeuvre
- Manoeuvre, signal, mirror

Answer

- ☑ **Mirror, signal, manoeuvre**

A 'hazard' is any situation that could involve adjusting speed or altering course. Look well ahead so that you're ready to deal with them in good time. Always use the MSM routine when you're approaching a hazard.

M – Mirror – Check the position of the traffic behind you.

S – Signal – Signal your intention to slow down or change course in good time.

M – Manoeuvre – A manoeuvre is any change in position, from slowing or stopping the vehicle to turning off a busy road.

questions   answers

Q. 11.8

Mark one answer

You want to park a semi-trailer and leave it unattended. Where should you NOT do this?

- In a lorry park
- On level ground
- In a factory
- In a lay-by

Answer

☑ **In a lay-by**

If you need to park the semi-trailer of your vehicle, find a safe place. Don't park it in a lay-by. Leave these available for drivers who wish to stop and rest. Find a place off the road, preferably a lorry park or somewhere safe which will decrease the risk of theft.

Q. 11.9

Mark three answers

You wish to park your trailer. The site you choose should be

- firm
- downhill
- uphill
- legal
- grassed
- level

Answers

☑ **firm**

☑ **legal**

☑ **level**

Check that the ground is firm and level before you uncouple the trailer. If you need to, place a heavy plank under the legs to distribute the weight and stop the legs sinking into the ground.

Don't park illegally. Make sure that your untended trailer is not blocking access for others.

Q. 11.10

Mark one answer

When parking a lorry at night, where must you have lights on?

- On the road
- In a motorway service area
- In a factory entrance
- In dock authority areas

Answer

☑ **On the road**

If you have to stop for a short while in a lay-by you should always leave the side lights on. The lay-by might be away from street lighting, and other vehicles entering the lay-by must be able to see your vehicle. You must always leave your side lights on when parked on the road.

questions

answers

Q. 11.11

Mark three answers

You are driving a lorry. You are about to move off from behind a stationary car. What should you do?

- Start to signal when moving
- Signal before moving, if necessary
- Check the blind spot before moving
- Use both mirrors before moving
- Use both mirrors only after moving

Answers

☑ **Signal before moving, if necessary**

☑ **Check the blind spot before moving**

☑ **Use both mirrors before moving**

Because the body of your vehicle is designed to take loads, your view around it will be restricted. Take extra care to look well out of the window to check the blind spots. Don't forget to check all the mirrors. Check ahead and signal, if necessary, before moving off.

Q. 11.12

Mark one answer

What does this sign mean?

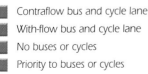

- Contraflow bus and cycle lane
- With-flow bus and cycle lane
- No buses or cycles
- Priority to buses or cycles

Answer

☑ **With-flow bus and cycle lane**

In some towns there are special lanes set aside for certain types of vehicle. These lanes show a picture of, or state, the authorised road users, and there's usually a sign showing the time that the lane is in operation. Some lanes might only be in operation for a short time. Check the sign and use the lane only if it's permitted.

questions answers

Q. 11.13

Mark one answer

You are driving in fast-moving traffic along a motorway. There is a stationary queue of traffic ahead. What should you do?

- Move to the hard shoulder
- Change lanes
- Switch on your rear foglights
- Switch on your hazard warning lights

Answer

☑ **Switch on your hazard warning lights**

Traffic queues on the motorway are becoming more common, whether due to the sheer volume of traffic at peak times or to incidents. Keep well back from the vehicle in front so you'll be able to see the problems ahead on the road. If you see a queue of stationary traffic ahead, switching on your hazard warning lights will warn those behind you of the hazard ahead.

Q. 11.14

Mark one answer

You are driving a long articulated vehicle. Your view is restricted by buildings and parked cars. How should you turn right out of a T-junction?

- Look both ways at the same time as emerging
- Ease forward slowly until you have a clear view
- Sound your horn while emerging to warn other vehicles
- Emerge quickly to clear the junction

Answer

☑ **Ease forward slowly until you have a clear view**

If your view at a junction is restricted by parked vehicles you should ease forward slowly until you can see.

IF YOU DON'T KNOW, DON'T GO.

Your vehicle takes longer than a car to gather speed, so you won't be able to accelerate out of trouble. Don't impede the progress of the traffic in the road that you're turning into.

Q. 11.15

Mark one answer

You are turning right onto a dual carriageway from a side road. Your vehicle is too long for the central gap. How should you proceed?

- Move forward and wait in the middle
- Wait until it is clear from both directions
- Move out blocking traffic from the right
- Edge out slowly so other traffic will see you

Answer

✓ **Wait until it is clear from both directions**

If you wish to turn right onto a dual carriageway, don't stop in the middle unless the gap is big enough for your vehicle to do so without impeding the moving traffic. Consider turning left and using a roundabout further on up the road to avoid crossing the central reservation.

Q. 11.16

Mark three answers

You want to turn left at a road junction. What is most important when deciding your position?

- The length of the vehicle
- The width of the roads
- The camber of the road
- The type of road surface
- The angle of the corner

Answers

✓ **The length of the vehicle**

✓ **The width of the roads**

✓ **The angle of the corner**

Where you position your vehicle on approach to a left turn will depend on several factors. You should be considering and deciding on the best position as you approach. If you need to take up part of any other lane, be extra cautious. Other road users might not understand your reasons for doing this. They might try to pass on the left in the gap that you need to make the turn. Always check the left-hand mirror as you approach and just before you turn. It's better to take extra road space on the road that you're leaving than to expect there to be extra room on the road that you're entering. There might not be any.

questions answers

Q. 11.17

Mark one answer

You wish to turn left into a side road. In front of you is a cyclist. You should

- overtake the cyclist before the turning
- wait until the cyclist has passed the turning
- sound your horn, the cyclist will give way to you
- drive alongside and check for the cyclist in the mirrors

Answer

✓ **wait until the cyclist has passed the turning**

Stay back and allow the cyclist to proceed. You must not cut across their front. Beware of the cyclist who tries to ride into any blind spot on your nearside.

Q. 11.18

Mark one answer

You are waiting to turn left at a junction. In your mirror you can see a cyclist moving up between the kerb and nearside of your vehicle. You should

- allow them to move in front of you
- move off and make them wait for you
- steer to the left to make them dismount
- tell them to move out of your way

Answer

✓ **allow them to move in front of you**

You need to be aware of the limited vision you have around your vehicle due to its size and shape. Never move off without checking along the nearside of your vehicle.

You should always be aware of the possibility of cyclists between your vehicle and the kerb.

Q. 11.19

Mark one answer

You are approaching a roundabout. You see a cyclist signal right. Why is the cyclist keeping to the left?

- It is a quicker route for the cyclist
- The cyclist is going to turn left
- The cyclist is more vulnerable
- The Highway Code does not apply to cyclists

Answer

✓ **The cyclist is more vulnerable**

The cyclist may not be able to get into a right-hand lane due to heavy traffic. Give the cyclist room. They may not be taking the exit you expect.

questions   answers

Q. 11.20

Mark one answer

You are entering a roundabout. A cyclist in front of you is signalling to turn right. What should you do?

- ▪ Overtake on the right
- ▪ Sound the horn
- ▪ Overtake on the left
- ▪ Allow plenty of room

Answer
☑ **Allow plenty of room**

Allow the cyclist plenty of room. Give them space to get into the correct lane. Always be prepared for them to change direction without looking or signalling their intentions.

Q. 11.21

Mark one answer

You are driving this lorry. Emerging at this junction needs extra care because of the

- ▪ bollards in the middle of the road
- ▪ traffic from the right
- ▪ motorcycle on the left
- ▪ grass verge on the left

Answer
☑ **motorcycle on the left**

Make sure that you signal in good time so that the following motorcyclist knows your intention. You may have to position yourself wide in order to negotiate the junction. Be aware that the motorcyclist may see this as an opportunity to filter through on your nearside. Check your left-hand mirror carefully before you start to turn.

questions answers

Q. 11.22

Mark two answers

You are turning right in this lorry (arrowed). The main dangers to be aware of are

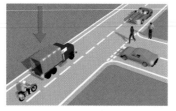

- the pedestrian stepping out
- the following motorcyclist
- the oncoming car
- the give way lines

Answers

- ☑ **the pedestrian stepping out**
- ☑ **the following motorcyclist**

Make sure that you indicate in good time to ensure other road users know your intentions. Always check your mirrors and blind spots before turning. Make sure the following motorcyclist is not about to overtake you. Keep an eye on the pedestrian who may step out unexpectedly.

Q. 11.23

Mark one answer

You are driving this lorry (arrowed). An emergency vehicle is trying to emerge from the side road. You should

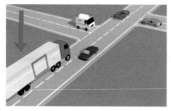

- brake hard to a stop and wave it out
- brake smoothly and allow it to emerge
- drive on, you are on the major road
- turn left quickly to give it a clear view

Answer

- ☑ **brake smoothly and allow it to emerge**

Good forward planning will allow you to deal safely with this situation. Good intentions are only 'good' if they are achieved safely. Reacting late to this situation may cause danger to other road users. How often have you seen other drivers' 'good intentions' cause problems and danger to other road users because they acted without thinking?

Good forward planning to deal with any situation involves having an all-round awareness of other road users. You need to assess how your actions will affect these other road users.

Acting on impulse can have disastrous consequences. Be professional, and be safe at all times.

Q. 11.24

Mark two answers

You are waiting to turn right in this lorry (arrowed). What dangers should you be most aware of?

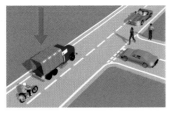

- [ ] The oncoming car
- [ ] The pedestrians
- [ ] The hazard line
- [ ] The motorcycle
- [ ] The car waiting to emerge
- [ ] The give way lines

Answers

☑ **The pedestrians**

☑ **The motorcycle**

Indicate your intentions in good time so that both the motorcyclist and pedestrians know your intention is to turn right. You should note all potential hazards and keep checking as you turn.

Q. 11.25

Mark one answer

You are turning right at a T-junction. Your view to the right and left is blocked due to parked vehicles. You should

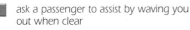

- [ ] lean forward to get a better view without crossing the give way lines
- [ ] edge out until you are about 1 metre (3 feet 3 inches) over the give way lines
- [ ] ease forward until you can see clearly past the vehicles
- [ ] ask a passenger to assist by waving you out when clear

Answer

☑ **ease forward until you can see clearly past the vehicles**

When emerging, if you don't know, then don't go. There could be an approaching cyclist or motorcyclist hidden by parked vehicles.

questions answers

Q. 11.26

Mark one answer

You are driving a bus in a built up area. You should NOT

- block side road junctions
- leave a safe stopping distance
- anticipate traffic ahead
- use the MSM routine

Answer

☑ **block side road junctions**

This is inconsiderate to other road users. You should look at the flow of traffic and be aware of side junctions when you are slowing down or stopping.

Q. 11.27

Mark two answers

Which of the following are most likely to share a bus lane?

- Cyclists
- Lorries
- Orange badge holders
- Cars towing caravans
- Taxis

Answers

☑ **Cyclists**

☑ **Taxis**

Cyclists can be safer travelling in the bus lane. Taxis are allowed to use these lanes as they provide a clearer route and can be quicker, thereby, encouraging people to use public transport and so reduce the amount of traffic congestion.

Q. 11.28

Mark one answer

You are driving a bus. What is the 'swept path'?

- The space between parked vehicles
- The way the bus overhangs kerbs and verges
- A clean and empty passenger saloon
- The ground needed to park overnight

Answer

☑ **The way the bus overhangs kerbs and verges**

You need to visualise in your mind's eye a footprint of the space your vehicle requires when you turn. Be aware of the front and rear overhang on the vehicle you're driving. This could be a danger to pedestrians when moving away from the kerb or turning right. Be aware that your vehicle may be damaged if it overhangs raised kerbs or verges when turning.

Q. 11.29

Mark one answer

As you are driving a group of horse riders comes towards you. The leading rider's horse suddenly becomes nervous of your presence. What should you do?

- Brake gently to a stop until they have passed
- Brake quickly to a stop, applying the parking brake
- Continue driving, keeping well in to the nearside
- Increase speed to pass the riders quickly

Answer

✓ **Brake gently to a stop until they have passed**

If you have to pass a group of riders on horseback you must give them plenty of room. Try not to startle the animals – the riders might be learners and have limited control. If any of the animals do become unsettled, you should brake gently and come to a stop. A nervous animal is unpredictable; you should wait until the animal is settled or has passed by.

Other road users behind you might have limited vision of the hazard, so good mirror work and early signalling will be required.

Q. 11.30

Mark one answer

To have good all-round vision you should make sure that

- windows are open
- a sun visor is fitted
- your seat is properly adjusted
- all lights are clean

Answer

✓ **your seat is properly adjusted**

Large vehicles are designed for their specific function, and this often means the shape and size can impair all-round visibility for the driver. You must make sure that you adjust the seat so that you're able to reach all the controls and see in all the mirrors. You should be seated in such a way that you're able to lean out of the window and check all offside blind spots.

questions · answers

Q. 11.31

Mark one answer

You are emerging from a side road into a queue of traffic. Which of these vehicles are especially hard to see?

- ■ Cycles
- ■ Tractors
- ■ Milk floats
- ■ Cars

Answer

✓ **Cycles**

Cyclists are much narrower than any other vehicle. Bear in mind that you may not see them easily. Although they take up less road space, they are just as important as the largest vehicle on the road.

Q. 11.32

Mark two answers

Some high vehicles have a high windscreen line. This can make it difficult for you to see

- ■ cyclists directly in front of you
- ■ pedestrians directly in front of you
- ■ motorcyclists directly behind you
- ■ cars turning right in the distance
- ■ traffic emerging from side roads

Answers

✓ **cyclists directly in front of you**

✓ **pedestrians directly in front of you**

If you drive too close to the cyclist in front they can be lost in a blind spot caused by a high windscreen line.

Keep your distance so that you are fully aware of the position of all road users.

Q. 11.33 🚌

Mark three answers

Cyclists and pedestrians can be out of sight below the windscreen line of your bus. You should check for them

- ■ before moving off
- ■ when reversing
- ■ when driving on narrow roads
- ■ in slow moving congested traffic
- ■ when turning to park
- ■ when passengers are getting on or off the bus

Answers

✓ **before moving off**

✓ **in slow moving congested traffic**

✓ **when turning to park**

Always make all-round observations before manoeuvring. Whether you're moving away or parking, cyclists and pedestrians can enter your blindspot. Always check all around your vehicle.

questions answers

Q. 11.34

Mark one answer

Motorcycle riders are more at risk from other road users. This is because they

- are easier for other road users to see
- are more likely to break down
- cannot give arm signals
- are more difficult for other road users to see

Answer

☑ **are more difficult for other road users to see**

Always look out for the more vulnerable users on our roads, such as

- motorcyclists
- children
- the elderly

All need extra consideration. Motorcyclists, in particular, can appear very quickly.

Q. 11.35

Mark one answer

In a bus with a high driving position you may have to look out for

- cyclists close in front
- cyclists close behind
- large vehicles close in front
- large vehicles close behind

Answer

☑ **cyclists close in front**

It's essential that you're constantly aware of other road users and pedestrians around you. A routine of effective mirror checking should be established. You must also know when it's essential to make checks in the blind spots, such as just below the nearside front of the vehicle. A cyclist in that space could be out of your normal vision. Constant awareness will ensure that you've seen any riders getting into that position.

questions answers

Q. 11.36

Mark one answer

What is the MAIN cause of motorcycle collisions?

 Other drivers

Other motorcyclists

Wet roads

Icy roads

Answer

☑ **Other drivers**

Motorcyclists are more difficult to see, particularly when the light is poor or it's raining. Look for the bright jacket or single headlight that will help you identify an approaching motorcyclist.

Q. 11.37

Mark two answers

Motorcyclists often filter between lines of slow-moving vehicles. Which of the following will cause them particular danger?

The queuing vehicles

Vehicles changing lanes

Vehicles emerging from junctions

Traffic lights

Zebra crossings

Answers

☑ **Vehicles changing lanes**

☑ **Vehicles emerging from junctions**

In slow moving traffic, particularly on dual carriageways or motorways, always be on the lookout for motorcyclists who approach from behind and filter through narrow gaps between vehicles.

Q. 11.38

Mark one answer

Motorcyclists ride in daylight with their headlights switched on because

it helps the motorcyclist to see

there is a speed trap ahead

they can be seen more easily

there are speed humps ahead

Answer

☑ **they can be seen more easily**

Using a dipped headlight makes motorcyclists more visible to other road users.

Motorcyclists don't ride with their headlight on to claim right of way, it is to alert you and other road users to their presence.

Q. 11.39

Mark three answers

At road junctions, which of the following are most at risk?

- Motorcyclists
- Pedestrians
- Car drivers
- Cyclists
- Lorry drivers

Answers

- ✓ **Motorcyclists**
- ✓ **Pedestrians**
- ✓ **Cyclists**

At busy junctions scan near, middle and far distances to identify all the hazards before emerging with a long vehicle.

Be alert for other road users hidden by parked vehicles.

Q. 11.40

Mark one answer

Some large vehicles with restricted vision to the rear may be fitted with an audible warning device for reversing. In areas with a 30 mph restriction the device may be used

- between 7 am and 11.30 pm only
- between 11.30 pm and 7 am only
- during hours of daylight only
- at any time

Answer

- ✓ **between 7 am and 11.30 pm only**

Some vehicles are fitted with an audible warning device that sounds when the vehicle is being reversed. This is an effective safety feature, but doesn't take away the need to use good, effective observation around the vehicle before and while reversing. As these devices make a loud noise they shouldn't be used between 11.30 pm and 7 am.

questions

answers

Q. 11.41 🚛

Mark one answer

You are unable to see clearly when reversing into a loading bay. You should

- get someone to guide you
- use an audible warning signal
- back into the bay until your bumper touches
- open your door and lean well out.

Answer

☑ **get someone to guide you**

Don't take chances when reversing in a confined space. It is too easy to crush or kill someone without knowing they are in danger. Always double check, and if in doubt get help from a reliable person.

Q. 11.42

Mark one answer

Driving too close to the vehicle in front will

- decrease your view ahead
- increase your view ahead
- increase the view of following drivers
- decrease the view of following drivers

Answer

☑ **decrease your view ahead**

Don't get into a position where you reduce your vision unnecessarily, such as driving too close to the vehicle in front.

At all times you must be aware that, as a driver of a large vehicle, you won't be able to see all around the vehicle. This is why you must have an excellent mirror routine and be constantly updating your information on what's going on around you.

Q. 11.43 🚌

Mark one answer

The 'turning circle' is the

- number of turns of the steering wheel between locks
- amount of space needed for the vehicle to turn
- amount by which the vehicle overhangs kerbs
- amount by which a vehicle cuts corners

Answer

☑ **amount of space needed for the vehicle to turn**

You should be familiar with the room that your vehicle requires to make turns or carry out a manoeuvre. You'll need to consider this as you approach junctions and road layouts. If you're driving a new or temporary vehicle, familiarise yourself with its characteristics before you drive on public roads.

Q. 11.44

Mark one answer

TV and video equipment fitted to a coach must ONLY be used when

- ☐ the coach is moving slowly
- ☐ it cannot be seen by the driver
- ☐ on long motorway journeys
- ☐ the coach is on tour

Answer

☑ **it cannot be seen by the driver**

Make sure that you are not distracted by any TV or video equipment fitted to your vehicle. Your main responsibility at all times is the safety and comfort of your passengers.

Q. 11.45

Mark one answer

You have a sleeper cab fitted to your lorry. This could make your driving more difficult because it

- ☐ increases your blind spots
- ☐ increases your view of the road ahead
- ☐ reduces your view in the right-hand mirror
- ☐ reduces your view in the left-hand mirror

Answer

☑ **increases your blind spots**

A sleeper cab can cause extra blind spots. Make sure that you are aware of all your blind spot areas. Be alert for vehicles just to the rear offside and nearside of your cab – they could soon become 'invisible', hidden in your blind spot.

questions   answers

Q. 11.46

Mark one answer

You are driving this lorry and turning right from this minor road. What should you be ESPECIALLY aware of?

- Motorcyclist from the right passing the parked van
- Vehicles coming from the left along the main road
- Pedestrians on the footpath on the main road
- Vehicles coming from the rear on the minor road

Answer

- ✓ **Motorcyclist from the right passing the parked van**

Parked vehicles near junctions can hide smaller road users such as cyclists and motorcyclists. Double check before emerging with a large vehicle. If in doubt, move forward slowly into a position where you can safely have another look.

Q. 11.47

Mark two answers

At junctions it is difficult to see motorcyclists because they

- are easily hidden in blind spots
- always ride in the gutter
- always wear black leathers
- are smaller than other vehicles

Answers

- ✓ **are easily hidden in blind spots**
- ✓ **are smaller than other vehicles**

When driving large vehicles, windscreen pillars and large mirrors can easily create large blind spots as you look left and right at junctions.

Altering your body position slightly while taking observation can give you a much improved view of the traffic.

If in doubt, look again. Re-assess the situation.

DON'T TAKE CHANCES.

Q. 11.48

Mark three answers

Drivers should be aware that motorcyclists are more vulnerable ESPECIALLY

 to emerging vehicles

in gusting winds

on poor road surfaces

at traffic lights

near zebra crossings

when exiting motorways

Answers

☑ **to emerging vehicles**

☑ **in gusting winds**

☑ **on poor road surfaces**

Always be concerned for the safety of yourself and other road users. Be aware of the various factors that create situations where you will sometimes have to take action to keep more vulnerable road users safe.

Q. 11.49

Mark one answer

The most common cause of accidents involving motorcyclists is

the motorcycle being poorly maintained

 the other driver not seeing them

a slippery road surface

the inexperience of the rider

Answer

☑ **the other driver not seeing them**

Emerging at junctions with a large vehicle requires consideration, sound judgement and good observation.

Some road users are more difficult to see than others. Cyclists generally keep close to the kerb.

Motorcyclists are usually travelling faster and can be more difficult to see.

Don't emerge until you know it is clear.

Q. 11.50

Mark one answer

Just before turning right from a main road to a side road, you should check your right-hand mirror. This is because

there may be pedestrians stepping off the kerb

you need to check your position

a motorcyclist may be overtaking you

your rear view to the left is blocked

Answer

☑ **a motorcyclist may be overtaking you**

Looking and acting sensibly on what you see in your mirrors before you change speed or direction are essential. Driving a large vehicle will sometimes require you to position your vehicle well to the left before making a tight right turn. Inexperienced drivers or riders may not realise your intentions. Make sure you signal in good time.

Make a final mirror check before committing yourself to the turn.

questions · answers

Q. 11.51

Mark one answer

Before turning left you should have a final look into the

- left-hand mirror
- interior mirror
- right-hand mirror
- overtaking mirror

Answer

☑ **left-hand mirror**

When making a left turn with a long vehicle you may have to adopt an unusual position well over to the centre of the road. Always signal your intentions in good time, and make good use of the nearside mirror. Be alert for less experienced road users putting themselves in danger by coming up along your nearside.

Q. 11.52

Mark one answer

On a coach with high side windows it can be difficult to see either side. Before you pull away from a bus stop you should

- get out of your vehicle and stop the traffic
- ask a passenger to make sure it is safe
- indicate before checking your mirrors
- look down and round to the right

Answer

☑ **look down and round to the right**

You should be aware that high sided coaches can create extra blind spots.

Q. 11.53

Mark two answers

You are driving a long vehicle. Before turning left onto a main road you should be ESPECIALLY careful of

- cyclists alongside you on the left
- motorcyclists alongside you on the left
- motorcyclists coming from your left
- cyclists coming from your left

Answers

☑ **cyclists alongside you on the left**

☑ **motorcyclists alongside you on the left**

You should always check your nearside mirror before any change of direction. Be alert for cyclists and motorcyclists who don't realise the potential danger involved in trying to squeeze through on your nearside when you are waiting at a junction. Always check for pedestrians and cyclists on the nearside of your vehicle before moving away.

Q. 11.54

Mark one answer

You want to turn right at a roundabout marked with two right-turn lanes. There is ample room for your vehicle in either lane. You should

- use the right-hand of the two lanes
- use the left-hand of the two lanes
- use the left-hand lane then move to the right as you enter the roundabout
- use the right-hand lane then move to the left as you enter the roundabout

Answer

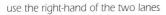 **use the left-hand of the two lanes**

By doing this it will make it easier for you when you leave the roundabout. If you use the right lane there could be traffic on your left and in your blind spot when you exit and try to move back to the left.

Q. 11.55

Mark one answer

What would you do if smoke started coming from the exhaust system, making it difficult for others to see?

- Carry on driving
- Drive back to your depot
- Stop and get the fault fixed immediately
- Let the engine cool down

Answer

☑ **Stop and get the fault fixed immediately**

You should respect the environment and try to keep excessive noise and exhaust fumes to a minimum. Smoke from the exhaust is unpleasant and could indicate a fault with the vehicle, which should be checked as soon as possible. If smoke from the exhaust system does become a problem, do the responsible and professional thing – stop and seek assistance to get the fault repaired straight away.

Overtaking

This section looks at precautions to take when overtaking.

The questions will ask you about

- **Planning**

  making sure you have enough time to get past

- **Observation**

  taking effective all round observation before overtaking

- **Mirrors**

  checking carefully to avoid moving back to the left too soon

- **Lane discipline**

  using the correct lane.

Q. 12.1

Mark one answer

You should take extra care when overtaking at night because

- every driver will normally be tired
- large vehicles are subject to a 10% speed reduction
- speed and distance are harder to judge
- most towns are not adequately lit

Answer

 speed and distance are harder to judge

In the darkness it will be difficult to assess the road ahead, especially if there are bends or hills which may prevent you from seeing an oncoming vehicle.

Q. 12.2

Mark one answer

You are driving along a motorway in thick fog at night. The reflective studs are red on your left and white on your right. You are driving

- in the right-hand lane
- on the hard shoulder
- in the left-hand lane
- in the middle lane

Answer

 in the left-hand lane

The red studs indicate the hard shoulder. Always use more than one reference point at all times. This will help you be more certain of your position.

Q. 12.3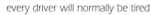

Mark one answer

You are driving an articulated lorry on a three-lane motorway. When can you drive in the right-hand lane?

- When overtaking a slow moving car in the middle lane
- When the escort vehicle of an oversized load signals you to pass
- If no speed limiter is fitted to your lorry
- If your vehicle is unladen

Answer

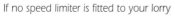 **When the escort vehicle of an oversized load signals you to pass**

Articulated lorries are prohibited from driving in the right-hand lane of motorways with three or more lanes except when an escort vehicle gives you a signal or when road signs indicate.

questions

answers

Q. 12.4

Mark one answer

You are driving on a three-lane motorway. You are about to move into the middle lane to overtake a slower vehicle. You should check

- for traffic in the right-hand lane returning to the middle lane
- for traffic which is intending to leave at the next exit
- the nearside mirror before pulling out
- for any traffic behind that is trying to pass you on the left

Answer

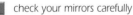 **for traffic in the right-hand lane returning to the middle lane**

Traffic returning from the right-hand lane can be a hazard to be aware of when overtaking. Always check your blind spot before changing lanes.

Q. 12.5

Mark one answer

Before overtaking or changing lanes on a motorway you should always

- check your mirrors carefully
- change to a lower gear
- look over your left shoulder
- increase your speed gently

Answer

 check your mirrors carefully

Check your mirrors to ensure that it is safe to overtake. Remember that traffic coming up behind you will probably be travelling at a faster speed.

Q. 12.6

Mark one answer

You are driving at the maximum speed limit for your vehicle on a clear motorway. You should keep to

- any one of the lanes
- the middle lane
- the right-hand lane
- the left-hand lane

Answer

 the left-hand lane

You should remain in the left-hand lane unless you are overtaking other vehicles.

Don't be inconsiderate and hog the centre lane or right-hand lane of a two-lane motorway.

Q. 12.7

Mark one answer

You are driving in the left-hand lane of a motorway. You see another large vehicle merging from a slip road. It is travelling at the same speed as you. You should

- ▪ try to race and get ahead of it
- ▪ leave the other vehicle to adjust its speed
- ▪ stay at the maximum speed allowed for your vehicle
- ▪ be ready to adjust your speed

Answer

✓ **be ready to adjust your speed**

Be alert for this type of situation developing; it is not always possible to change lanes safely. The merging driver has a responsibility to give way if necessary. Don't change lanes if it will inconvenience or endanger other road users on the main carriageway.

Q. 12.8

Mark two answers

When driving in the left-hand lane of a motorway you see merging vehicles travelling at the same speed as you. You should

- ▪ try and accelerate past them
- ▪ move to the next lane if safe
- ▪ allow the traffic to merge by adjusting your speed
- ▪ expect the traffic to let you pass

Answers

✓ **move to the next lane if safe**

✓ **allow the traffic to merge by adjusting your speed**

Only change lanes if doing so will not inconvenience other road users on the main carriageway. Merging drivers have a responsibility to give way, if necessary, and not force their way into the main carriageway.

Planning ahead will ensure you are well prepared to deal with these situations.

questions answers

Q. 12.9

Mark three answers

You should take extra care before moving into the centre lane of a three-lane motorway because

the centre lane is narrower

another vehicle might be planning to use the same lane

other drivers need time to react

car drivers might not know they must give way to large vehicles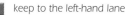

the bridge height clearance will be less in that lane

traffic from behind may be travelling much faster than you

Answers

 another vehicle might be planning to use the same lane

☑ **other drivers need time to react**

☑ **traffic from behind may be travelling much faster than you**

You should plan ahead to assess the actions of other vehicles using the road. Always indicate your intentions in good time, this will allow others to revise their course of action if necessary. Always check your blind spots before changing lanes.

Q. 12.10

Mark one answer

You are driving on a three-lane motorway. Unless overtaking slower vehicles you should

stay in the middle lane

keep to the left-hand lane

maintain a constant 56 mph

keep to the right-hand lane

Answer

 keep to the left-hand lane

If you keep to the left-hand lane this will allow faster moving vehicles to overtake you safely. Don't hog the middle lane unnecessarily.

Q. 12.11

Mark one answer

You are in the left hand lane on a three lane motorway. Before you overtake you should check for any vehicles in the right-hand lane that might be about to

move to the right

move back to the left

cut in sharply behind you

accelerate briskly in front of you

Answer

 move back to the left

Vehicles overtaking in the right hand lane may return to the centre lane when they have finished their manoeuvre. You should look for this before starting to pull out. Don't rely on the size of your vehicle to claim right of way.

Q. 12.12

Mark one answer

Normally, vehicles over 7.5 tonnes maximum authorised mass may use the right-hand lane of a motorway only when

 it is a three-lane motorway

it is three-lane motorway

there are vehicles on the hard shoulder

 it is a two-lane motorway

other vehicles are turning right

Answer

☑ **it is a two-lane motorway**

On two lane motorways, vehicles over 7.5 tonnes maximum authorised mass can only use the right-hand lane to overtake. When you have completed your manoeuvre, return to the left as soon as it is safe to do so.

Q. 12.13

Mark one answer

You have just overtaken another vehicle on a motorway. When moving back to the left you should avoid

cutting in

increasing your speed

changing gear

signalling

Answer

☑ **cutting in**

Always check your nearside mirror carefully before moving back to the left after overtaking. Don't rely on the other drivers flashing headlights. Remember, The Highway Code explains that the correct interpretation simply means 'I am here'.

Q. 12.14

Mark one answer

What is a crawler lane for?

To enable other traffic to overtake on the nearside

To enable large vehicles to pull over and park out of the way

To enable slow-moving traffic to move further over to the left on uphill gradients

To enable emergency vehicles to get to the scene of an accident quicker

Answer

☑ **To enable slow-moving traffic to move further over to the left on uphill gradients**

On a motorway where there's long uphill gradients there may be a crawler lane. This type of lane helps the traffic to flow by diverting the slower, heavy vehicles into an extra lane on the left.

questions

answers

Q. 12.15

Mark one answer

You see this sign on a motorway. It means you are coming to a

◼ long downhill slope

◼ long uphill slope

◼ 'lorries only' lane

◼ service area

Answer
✓ **long uphill slope**

The term 'crawler lane' doesn't mean the lane is only for extremely slow vehicles. It is advising you of an extra lane on the left.

Crawler lanes are usually built on sections of road where the length of the gradient is such that some large vehicles will be slowed to the point where they become a hazard for other road users.

Q. 12.16

Mark one answer

You should use a crawler lane

◼ to let faster traffic overtake you

◼ when turning right from major roads

◼ for parking when having a break

◼ when slowing down for a motorway exit

Answer
✓ **to let faster traffic overtake you**

Many vehicles are very powerful and can maintain speed even when climbing a gradient. Even if your vehicle is capable of maintaining speed, you can still use the crawler lane to allow other road users to overtake safely.

Q. 12.17

Mark one answer

Before overtaking you should

◼ flash your headlights to oncoming traffic

◼ look ahead for right-turn lane markings

◼ drive very close to the vehicle in front

◼ make a final check in your left mirror

Answer
✓ **look ahead for right-turn lane markings**

Consider

- the power limitations of your vehicle
- oncoming traffic
- bends
- junctions
- road markings
- traffic signs
- gradients
- other traffic.

questions answers

Q. 12.18

Mark three answers

You should not overtake when

- there are signs and road markings that allow you to
- you are unable to see clearly ahead
- you would have to break the speed limit
- your view of the road ahead is clear
- approaching motorway exits or slip roads
- other road users would have to slow down

Answers

✓ **you are unable to see clearly ahead**

✓ **you would have to break the speed limit**

✓ **other road users would have to slow down**

Never commit yourself to an overtaking manoeuvre with a large vehicle unless you are absolutely certain you have the time and space to see it through safely. Don't take unnecessary risks which endanger other road users.

Q. 12.19

Mark one answer

You are driving a fully-laden vehicle. You are approaching an uphill gradient as you are overtaking another vehicle. Which of the following is INCORRECT?

- You will be able to get past quicker
- The extra weight will make you slower
- It will take you longer to get past
- You will need more power from the engine

Answer

✓ **You will be able to get past quicker**

Always plan well ahead before overtaking. Take into consideration the size of your vehicle. The load on your vehicle will influence its handling and speed characteristics.

Q. 12.20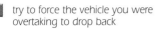

Mark one answer

You are overtaking another lorry. Due to an uphill gradient you start to lose speed. You should

- continue at the same speed and position
- try to force the vehicle you were overtaking to drop back
- try to force the vehicle you were overtaking to speed up
- ease off and drop behind the vehicle you were trying to overtake

Answer

✓ **ease off and drop behind the vehicle you were trying to overtake**

If you try to overtake another vehicle and you realise that you're unable to complete the manoeuvre, ease off the accelerator and drop back behind the vehicle. If the vehicle you're trying to overtake is large then it will take longer to pass. You should assess whether you have the time and the power to complete the manoeuvre before you try to overtake.

questions

answers

Q. 12.21

Mark one answer

After overtaking another large vehicle how would you know when it was safe to move back to the nearside lane?

- By waiting for the driver you have just overtaken to flash the headlights
- By checking your nearside mirror
- By using your hazard warning lights as a signal
- By moving over to the nearside in the hope that the other vehicle will slow down

Answer

☑ **By checking your nearside mirror**

If you're driving a long vehicle you'll have to judge carefully when to pull back into the nearside lane after overtaking. Don't cut in on the vehicle you've overtaken – leave a safety margin. Check your left-hand (nearside) mirror to see whether the rear of your vehicle is well clear of the vehicle you've just passed. You should allow for the length of your vehicle and judge the manoeuvre accordingly.

Don't rely on signals from other drivers. They may be signalling to someone else.

Q. 12.22

Mark one answer

Because of its size and design a large vehicle will have

- less blind spots than smaller vehicles
- more blind spots than smaller vehicles
- the same blind spots as smaller vehicles
- no blind spots at all

Answer

☑ **more blind spots than smaller vehicles**

Always take the time to check where your blind spots are at the earliest opportunity when driving a different vehicle. If you are aware of the point when a vehicle disappears from view in your mirrors, then you can take steps to prevent an accident by checking that blind spot area before changes of direction. Good use of the mirrors when driving will help eliminate the possibility of being unaware of a vehicle in your blind spot areas.

Q. 12.23

Mark one answer

You are driving on a dual carriageway and intend to overtake the vehicle ahead. Behind there is a car approaching quickly in the right-hand lane. You should

 keep behind the slower vehicle

■ signal and move out

■ move up closer to the slower vehicle

■ stay on the left, large vehicles cannot use the right-hand lane

Answer

 keep behind the slower vehicle

This will allow the faster moving vehicle to overtake safely. If you pull out to overtake at this time, you will cause the car behind to brake sharply. Don't use the size of your vehicle to intimidate. Be professional and show consideration to other road users.

Q. 12.24

Mark one answer

What should you do AFTER overtaking on a dual carriageway?

■ Move back to the left as soon as possible

■ Indicate left then right

■ Wait until the other driver flashes their headlights

■ Switch your rear lights on and off

Answer

 Move back to the left as soon as possible

When you are sure it is safe, signal if necessary and move back to the left.

Don't drive for long distances in the centre or right-hand lane unnecessarily.

Q. 12.25

Mark one answer

You are turning right at a roundabout driving a long vehicle. You need to occupy the left-hand lane. You should check mirrors and

■ signal left on approach

■ signal right on approach

■ avoid giving a signal on approach

■ signal right after entering the roundabout

Answer

■ **signal right on approach**

There are times when, due to the size of your vehicle, you'll have to take up part of another lane. If you need to do this, make sure that you use effective observation all around.

Be aware that other road users might not understand the reasons for your position on the road. You should signal your intentions and take up your position in good time.

questions

answers

Q. 12.26

Mark one answer

With a long bus, under normal driving conditions, when is it acceptable to straddle lanes?

- Only when joining a bus lane
- On all bends and corners
- On the approach to all roundabouts
- To avoid mounting the kerb

Answer

☑ **To avoid mounting the kerb**

There are times when you might have to take up part of another lane in order to make a turn or manoeuvre. Be on your guard for other road users by using your mirrors to check all around your vehicle.

Other traffic might try to move up alongside in the gap you've left to make your turn. Good planning and anticipation will allow you to signal your intentions to other road users and take up your position in good time.

Q. 12.27

Mark one answer

Long vehicles need to straddle lanes

- to avoid braking sharply
- when driving on motorways
- to avoid mounting the kerb
- when coming to contraflow systems

Answer

☑ **to avoid mounting the kerb**

When you have to straddle the lanes at small roundabouts or junctions, always signal in good time. Be alert for inexperienced road users who may attempt to put themselves into a dangerous position.

questions

answers

Q. 12.28

Mark two answers

You are about to pass this car. What are the main hazards you should be aware of?

- Bright sunshine reflecting off the car windscreen
- The driver's side door may suddenly open
- The parked car may move off with no warning
- The narrow pavement on the right

Answers

 **The drivers side door may suddenly open**

 **The parked car may move off with no warning**

You do not know what the driver of this car will do. Be prepared for any hazard. The driver may not have seen you. Planning ahead will allow you to be in the correct gear and at the correct speed to be able to deal safely with this hazard.

Q. 12.29

Mark two answers

When approaching these roadworks, you should NOT

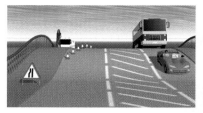

- start to overtake
- increase speed
- flash your headlights
- give any signals

Answers

 start to overtake

 increase speed

Slow down and look out for warning signs. Always obey speed limits at roadworks. Look for workmen stepping into the road.

Be aware that the footpath may be blocked and pedestrians will step into the road. Don't use the size of your vehicle to force your way through. If the obstruction is on your side of the road, give way to oncoming traffic.

Look for and act according to signals given by the person in charge of a 'Stop–Go' board or temporary traffic lights.

questions

answers

Q. 12.30

Mark one answer

It is very windy. You are about to overtake a motorcyclist. You should

 allow extra room

overtake slowly

sound your horn as you pass

keep close as you pass

Answer

☑ **allow extra room**

Cyclists and motorcyclists may become unbalanced by your vehicle passing too close. Plan ahead and give them plenty of room. Remember that your large vehicle can cause a vacuum which will suck the rider towards it. The noise and close proximity of your vehicle can also startle them, which could cause them to swerve suddenly.

Q. 12.31

Mark one answer

You are driving behind two cyclists. They are approaching a roundabout in the left-hand lane. What should you expect them to do?

 Go in any direction

Turn left

Turn right

Go straight ahead

Answer

☑ **Go in any direction**

When following cyclists into a roundabout be aware that they might not take the exit you expect them to. Cyclists approaching in the left hand lane may be turning right. They may not have been able to get into the correct lane due to busy traffic. Be courteous and give them room.

Q. 12.32

Mark one answer

You should never attempt to overtake a cyclist

on a roundabout

before you turn left

before you turn right

on a one-way street

Answer

☑ **before you turn left**

Always make good use of your nearside mirror before you turn left with a large vehicle. Cyclists don't always understand the reasons why a large vehicle will adopt a position away from the kerb before turning left. Wait for them to pass the junction before you turn left.

Q. 12.33

Mark one answer

You are about to overtake a lorry. You should

 look well ahead for uphill gradients

check your position in the left mirror

quickly change to a higher gear

close right up before pulling out

Answer

☑ **look well ahead for uphill gradients**

Plan your overtaking carefully. The weight of your vehicle combined with the restrictions imposed by a speed limiter are all factors you should take into consideration.

Q. 12.34

Mark one answer

On a motorway what do signs showing a crawler lane suggest?

- Advance warning for a steep downhill section
- Lorries and buses are limited to use of that lane
- Vehicles other than lorries and buses are banned from that lane
- There will be a long, gradual uphill gradient ahead

Answer

☑ **There will be a long, gradual uphill gradient ahead**

Before you overtake another vehicle, there are several things to consider. Due to the size and weight of your vehicle you'll need a long, clear road ahead before you attempt the manoeuvre. There are several factors to think about, but first ask yourself if overtaking is really necessary.

You'll have to use your skill and judgement to assess the situation and decide whether you can overtake safely. If you see a crawler lane sign ahead this would indicate an uphill gradient.

You shouldn't attempt any manoeuvre that would require an increase in speed, such as overtaking. The combination of a heavy load, a speed limiter and a gradient may leave you without the power to overtake safely.

Q. 12.35

Mark one answer

You are driving a lorry weighing more than 7.5 tonnes maximum authorised mass. You may only use the right-hand lane to overtake on a motorway with

- two lanes
- three lanes
- a 50 mph speed limit
- a 40 mph speed limit

Answer

☑ **two lanes**

You may only use the right hand lane to overtake on a two-lane motorway. Lorries weighing more than 7.5 tonnes maximum authorised mass are not allowed to use the far right-hand lane of a motorway with three or more lanes.

Environmental issues

This section looks at environmental issues.

The questions will ask you about

- **Vehicle vibration**

  using air suspension

- **Wind resistance**

  fitting a wind deflector to reduce fuel consumption

- **Fuel consumption**

  planning routes to reduce mileage

- **Refuelling**

  taking care when refuelling.

questions   answers

Q. 13.1

Mark one answer

The road surface is more likely to be damaged by large vehicles with

- a mixture of tyre makes
- a mixture of re-cut and new tyres
- faulty spray-suppression equipment
- faulty suspension

Answer

☑ **faulty suspension**

Suspension faults may result in road damage. Road-friendly suspension is being used and developed to lessen the impact on the environment, the road surface and under-road services.

Q. 13.2

Mark three answers

Vehicles have damaged the environment. This has resulted in

- air pollution
- reduced traffic noise
- building deterioration
- less road surface damage
- using up of natural resources

Answers

☑ **air pollution**

☑ **building deterioration**

☑ **using up of natural resources**

The increased number of vehicles on the roads has damaged the environment. Transport is an essential part of modern life, but we should not ignore its environmental consequences.

Q. 13.3

Mark one answer

Which of the following will help to reduce damage, caused by large vehicles, to buildings in town and city centres?

- Wind deflector
- Brake retarder
- Tachograph recorder
- Air suspension

Answer

☑ **Air suspension**

Air suspension can reduce the vibrations caused by large vehicles. Air suspension systems use a compressible material (usually air), contained in chambers located between the axle and vehicle body. This can help reduce vibration.

questions

answers

Q. 13.4

Mark two answers

Which of the following would be most affected by a vehicle with faulty suspension?

 Underground pipes

Road surfaces

Tyre pressures

Road tunnels

Overhead gantries

Answers

☑ **Underground pipes**

☑ **Road surfaces**

If your suspension is damaged, all the weight of the vehicle is compressing the road and anything located below it. The vibrations travel through the ground and can also damage surrounding buildings.

Q. 13.5

Mark three answers

The pictured vehicle is 'environmentally friendly' because it

reduces noise pollution

uses diesel fuel

uses electricity

uses unleaded fuel

reduces parking places

reduces town traffic

Answers

☑ **reduces noise pollution**

☑ **uses electricity**

☑ **reduces town traffic**

This is the sign for a tram. These vehicles are powered by electricity and reduce the emissions released into the environment. As they can carry many people they can contribute to the reduction in the number of other vehicles on the road.

Q. 13.6

Mark two answers

Which of the following vehicles are MOST likely to cause severe damage to road surfaces?

 Lorries

Cars

Motorcycles

Bicycles

 Buses

Answers

☑ **Lorries**

☑ **Buses**

Lorries and buses are much heavier than cars and will have a greater impact on the road surface.

questions   answers

Q. 13.7

Mark three answers

Air suspension can reduce damage to

- the fuel system
- the road surface
- passengers
- bridges
- the tachograph
- underground services

Answers

- ☑ **the road surface**
- ☑ **bridges**
- ☑ **underground services**

Air suspension reduces the pressure of the weight of the vehicle driving on an uneven surface. This in turn reduces the vibrations transmitted to buildings along the route.

Q. 13.8

Mark three answers

You are driving a vehicle fitted with 'road-friendly' suspension. This will mostly reduce damage caused to

- the driver's seat
- historical buildings
- the road surface
- overhead cables
- river banks
- bridges

Answers

- ☑ **historical buildings**
- ☑ **the road surface**
- ☑ **bridges**

Road-friendly suspension reduces the vibration caused by the impact of the wheels on the road surface.

Q. 13.9

Mark one answer

Cab mounted wind deflectors are fitted to

- increase wind buffeting
- increase engine power
- reduce exhaust emissions
- reduce fuel consumption

Answer

- ☑ **reduce fuel consumption**

Cab-mounted wind deflectors can effectively lower wind resistance created by large box bodies. Together with lower side panel skirts, this will help reduce fuel consumption.

questions   answers

Q. 13.10

Mark two answers

Your lorry has been fitted with wind deflectors. When driving in windy conditions these will help to

- increase the amount of fuel you will use
- increase the wind resistance on your vehicle
- increase the pressure in the tyres
- reduce the wind resistance on your vehicle
- reduce the amount of fuel you will use

Answers

☑ **reduce the wind resistance on your vehicle**

☑ **reduce the amount of fuel you will use**

Wind deflectors direct the wind either around or over your vehicle. Your vehicle then requires less power to make progress against the wind. As a result your vehicle will use less fuel.

Q. 13.11

Mark one answer

Cab-mounted wind deflectors can reduce

- journey times
- load capacity
- tyre wear
- fuel consumption

Answer

☑ **fuel consumption**

A wind deflector redirects the air flow around the vehicle, this reduces the amount of fuel required to propel the vehicle forward.

Q. 13.12

Mark two answers

Fuel consumption for lorries can be reduced by fitting

- single axles only
- a high-level exhaust pipe
- side skirts
- wind deflectors

Answers

☑ **side skirts**

☑ **wind deflectors**

Both of these reduce resistance to wind, which will help the vehicle to use less fuel when driving.

Q. 13.13

Mark two answers

How could you improve the fuel consumption of your lorry?

- Brake late as often as you can
- Fit a cab-mounted wind deflector
- Avoid sheeting any bulky loads
- Try to increase your overall speed
- Make regular checks on tyre pressures

Answers

☑ **Fit a cab-mounted wind deflector**

☑ **Make regular checks on tyre pressures**

As a professional driver you should consider fuel efficiency and the effect on the environment. Loads covered by sheets that are loose can flap and increase the "drag" effect. Wind deflectors can effectively lower wind resistance. Correct tyre pressures and proper maintenance also play their part in fuel efficiency.

Q. 13.14

Mark three answers

How could you save fuel when driving?

- By reducing overall speed
- By braking as late as you can
- By planning routes to avoid congestion
- By having properly inflated tyres
- By extending vehicles' service times

Answers

☑ **By reducing overall speed**

☑ **By planning routes to avoid congestion**

☑ **By having properly inflated tyres**

Your driving skills reflect on the environment. You should consider the impact your attitude will have on the environment every time you drive. By driving sensibly, maintaining your vehicle and planning ahead, you will deserve to be called a professional driver.

Q. 13.15

Mark one answer

You are a driver who is certified to carry dangerous goods. The certificate is valid for

- one year
- two years
- five years
- ten years

Answer

☑ **five years**

The operator of a UK-registered vehicle engaged in carriage of dangerous goods should ensure that the driver has a valid vocational training certificate. These certificates are valid for five years.

questions answers

Q. 13.16

Mark one answer

An ADR qualification is necessary for drivers who carry

- school children
- liquids
- oversize loads
- dangerous goods

Answer

✓ **dangerous goods**

ADR regulations govern movement of hazardous goods. The driver of any vehicle engaged in the carriage of dangerous goods should carry the vocational training certificate at all times, and produce it on request to a police constable or goods vehicle examiner.

Q. 13.17

Mark three answers

Which of the following would help to reduce the impact that your lorry has on the environment?

- Driving through town centres
- Braking in good time
- Planning routes to avoid busy times
- Racing to make up time
- Anticipating well ahead

Answers

✓ **Braking in good time**

✓ **Planning routes to avoid busy times**

✓ **Anticipating well ahead**

Avoiding town centres will lessen the vibration and pollution caused by your vehicle. Good anticipation and forward planning will always benefit you and the environment, wherever you drive.

Q. 13.18

Mark two answers

You can help to reduce the impact of road transport on the environment by

- avoiding high gears
- reducing rest periods
- braking in good time
- increasing your overall speed
- avoiding over-acceleration

Answers

✓ **braking in good time**

✓ **avoiding over-acceleration**

Good forward planning will reduce the emissions being dispersed into the air and contribute to less environmental pollution.

questions   answers

Q. 13.19

Mark one answer

The purpose of a fly sheet tightly fastened over a tipper body is to reduce the

- drag effect
- steering effort
- legal load weight
- load capacity

Answer

☑ **drag effect**

The drag effect is caused by wind entering the body of the tipper. If the cavity is covered, then the drag is reduced.

Q. 13.20

Mark one answer

You are driving a lorry with a loaded skip. The skip should be covered with a net to

- prevent rubbish from falling out of it
- protect the contents from the weather
- make it more visible to other traffic
- stop others from adding to the load

Answer

☑ **prevent rubbish from falling out of it**

If the load is not covered, rubbish can be caught by the wind and blown onto the carriageway. This will create unnecessary hazards for other road users.

Q. 13.21

Mark one answer

Drivers of large vehicles can help to reduce vibration to buildings by

- fitting wind deflectors to cab roofs
- planning routes along bypasses
- fitting spray suppressors over road wheels
- placing your load to the rear

Answer

☑ **planning routes along bypasses**

Bypasses are usually away from buildings and are often quicker. These routes are usually designed for large vehicles. You will enjoy the benefit of better journey times and avoid the frustration of queues and slow-moving traffic.

questions

answers

Q. 13.22

Mark one answer

As a driver you can help to protect the environment by

 driving faster to reduce travelling time

avoiding town centres and using bypasses

filling your fuel tank with red diesel fuel

leaving your engine running in traffic jams

Answer

 **avoiding town centres and using bypasses**

By using bypasses, you are less likely to be held up and can travel at a constant speed, thereby reducing the amount of pollution from your vehicle.

Q. 13.23

Mark one answer

As a driver you can help to ease traffic congestion by

 planning routes to avoid the busy times

 planning routes to avoid driving at quiet times

driving on motorways for all journeys

avoiding using motorways for all journeys

Answer

 **planning routes to avoid the busy times**

By planning your journey to avoid busy times you will avoid the build up of traffic that can often occur.

Q. 13.24

Mark one answer

As a professional driver you should

keep to maximum speeds for shorter journeys

 plan routes to avoid busy times and congestion

avoid route-planning because of the time it takes

drive at a faster speed through hazardous areas

Answer

plan routes to avoid busy times and congestion

If you plan routes to avoid busy times, your journey time may be improved as you can avoid congestion.

questions answers

Q. 13.25

Mark one answer

You have just refilled your fuel tank. You MUST make sure that the

 tank is completely full up to the filler neck

filler cap is vented correctly by keeping it loose

filler cap is properly closed and secure

tank is nearly full and the filler cap is slightly loose

Answer

☑ **filler cap is properly closed and secure**

Because of the extremely slippery characteristics of diesel fuel, care must be taken at all times to avoid spillages.

Q. 13.26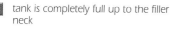

Mark one answer

After refuelling your bus, what MUST you check before driving?

 Your filler caps are securely shut

Your tank is full to the top

The position of the emergency fuel cut off switch

The low-fuel warning light is working

Answer

☑ **Your filler caps are securely shut**

It is a legal requirement that you check all filler caps are properly closed and secure before driving off.

Q. 13.27

Mark one answer

To prevent fuel spillages it is important to

stop refuelling when half full

use a filtered system

close and secure all filler caps

place the drip tray correctly

Answer

☑ **close and secure all filler caps**

Fuel spilled onto the road as you negotiate a roundabout causes a serious danger to other road users, especially motorcyclists.

questions

answers

Q. 13.28

Mark one answer

You are following a lorry with a leaking fuel tank. What should you be especially aware of?

- The road may be very slippery
- The fuel may splash your vehicle
- Your brake linings will become slippery
- Your spray reducers will not be effective

Answer

✓ **The road may be very slippery**

The leaking fuel can make the road surface extremely slippery. Look out for this, particularly on roundabouts.

Q. 13.29

Mark one answer

You may park a lorry over 7.5 tonnes on a verge for essential loading, but it must have

- a collection note
- an orange badge
- the owner's permission
- an attendant

Answer

✓ **an attendant**

Goods vehicles with a maximum laden weight of over 7.5 tonnes (including any trailer) must not be parked on a verge except where this is essential for loading, in which case the vehicle must not be left unattended.

Q. 13.30

Mark one answer

You must not park any unattended lorry over 7.5 tonnes on a verge without

- police permission
- warning lights
- the owner's permission
- a loading permit

Answer

✓ **police permission**

If your vehicle has to be left unattended on a verge for any reason, you must inform the police.

Q. 13.31

Mark one answer

The occupants of about how many cars can be carried by one double-deck bus

- [ ] 20
- [ ] 30
- [ ] 40
- [ ] 50

Answer

- [x] **20**

By being able to carry as many passengers as 20 cars, the bus is helping to reduce pollution. The bus has only one engine and, therefore, emits less fumes.

Q. 13.32

Mark one answer

You are waiting at a terminus for some time. You will reduce pollution by

- [ ] revving your engine
- [ ] switching off your engine
- [ ] leaving your engine on tickover
- [ ] keeping your engine at high revs

Answer

- [x] **switching off your engine**

If you have to wait for long periods of time you should turn your engine off as noise and exhaust fumes can cause annoyance.

Q. 13.33

Mark three answers

You are waiting for some time in a stationary traffic queue. Why should you switch your engine off?

- [ ] To reduce noise levels
- [ ] To save on vehicle air pressure
- [ ] To reduce exhaust fumes
- [ ] To reduce television interference
- [ ] To prevent local annoyance

Answers

- [x] **To reduce noise levels**
- [x] **To reduce exhaust fumes**
- [x] **To prevent local annoyance**

When you are delayed in a traffic jam or stationary by the side of a road or in a lay-by, switch your engine off to help protect the environment in which you live. By doing this you will be helping others who are not road users.

questions   answers

Q. 13.34

Mark one answer

You have been waiting in a traffic queue for several minutes. The road in front is blocked. What should you do?

- Keep your engine at tickover speed
- Rev your engine occasionally
- Switch off your engine
- Run the engine at a constant higher speed

Answer

✓ **Switch off your engine**

Switch your engine off when stationary for some time, especially when noise and exhaust fumes cause annoyance and could be harmful.

PROTECT YOUR ENVIRONMENT AND SAVE FUEL.

Q. 13.35

Mark one answer

You are parked for a short period in a town whilst you plan a route. You should

- keep the engine running on tickover
- rev the engine occasionally for air pressure
- never turn off the engine for short periods
- switch off the engine

Answer

✓ **switch off the engine**

This will be safer and emit less fumes into the environment.

When left idling for any length of time diesel engines emit excessive smoke as you drive off. This is unpleasant for any pedestrians who are nearby at the time.

Q. 13.36

Mark one answer

Your vehicle is fitted with a reverse warning bleeper. You must switch the bleeper off when reversing

- after 11.30 at night along a 30mph road
- after 11.30 at night along a 40mph road
- near a school entrance
- near a hospital entrance

Answer

✓ **after 11.30 at night along a 30mph road**

It is an offence to operate an audible warning system on a road subject to a 30 mph speed limit between 11.30 pm and 7.00 am. Always remember to reset the alarm outside these times.

questions answers

Q. 13.37

Mark three answers

Which three of the following could cause unnecessary pollution to the environment?

 Excessive exhaust fumes

Regular servicing

Vehicles driven poorly

Badly maintained vehicles

High level exhaust systems

Answers

✓ **Excessive exhaust fumes**

✓ **Vehicles driven poorly**

✓ **Badly maintained vehicles**

All drivers on the road should play their part in protecting the environment against pollution. Ensure the vehicle you drive is maintained properly. Report any defects immediately such as unusual exhaust smoke. Consider whether further training could improve your driving skills.

CARE FOR THE ENVIRONMENT AS YOU DRIVE.

Q. 13.38

Mark one answer

Diesel fuel has been spilled on the road. This will cause particular danger to

lorries

motorcycles

horses

cars

Answer

✓ **motorcycles**

Spilt diesel creates a serious risk to other road users, especially motorcyclists.

Take care when refuelling and ensure that all filler caps and tank hatches are properly closed and secure.

Q. 13.39

Mark one answer

You should only sound your horn in a built up area between 11.30 pm and 7.00 am when

you are parked

your vehicle is moving

you are stationary

another vehicle poses a danger

Answer

✓ **another vehicle poses a danger**

The horn should not be used between 11.30 pm and 7.00 am in built up areas unless another vehicle is unaware of you and poses a danger.

questions   answers

Q. 13.40

Mark one answer

Members of the public are encouraged to report any vehicle with

- excessive exhaust fumes
- an un-sheeted load
- different makes of tyres
- no contact address visible

Answer

☑ **excessive exhaust fumes**

You should ensure that maintenance schedules are strictly followed and that

- filters are changed regularly
- exhaust emissions meet current regulations
- diesel injectors are operating efficiently.

Q. 13.41

Mark one answer

You should take great care to avoid spilling diesel. It is very slippery and causes a serious risk on the road particularly to

- motorcycles
- tractors
- buses
- lorries

Answer

☑ **motorcycles**

Take care to secure caps and tank hatches - diesel is very slippery and if spilled on the road it is particularly dangerous to motorcyclists.

Q. 13.42

Mark one answer

In a diesel engine which of the following fuels would most improve vehicle emissions?

- High sulphur diesel
- Red diesel
- Low sulphur diesel
- Blue diesel

Answer

☑ **Low sulphur diesel**

This is widely available and has been formulated so that the sulphur content is very low. It makes a considerable improvement to vehicle emissions.

Q. 13.43

Mark one answer

In diesel engined vehicles low sulphur diesel can

 increase pollutants

■ reduce emissions

■ increase power

■ reduce consumption

Answer

☑ **reduce emissions**

To improve exhaust emissions low sulphur diesel can be used. Sulphur is the main cause of particulates in exhaust emissions.

Q. 13.44

Mark one answer

Using which of the following fuels in a diesel engine would most help the environment?

■ Anti-waxing diesel

■ Low sulphur diesel

■ Red diesel

■ Anti-foaming diesel

Answer

☑ **Low sulphur diesel**

Sulphur produces acid gases. Diesel fuels with lower sulphur content have been produced to lessen damage to the environment.

Q. 13.45

Mark one answer

Red diesel is

■ only used by private cars

■ for authorised purposes only

■ available at all garages

■ very environmentally friendly

Answer

☑ **for authorised purposes only**

Red diesel is subject to less excise duty so it is considerably cheaper. Any driver whose vehicle is found to be illegally using this fuel faces severe penalties, so should only be used for authorised purposes.

questions

answers

Q. 13.46

Mark one answer

Fuel consumption could be made worse by continous use of

- air suspension
- heated mirrors
- air conditioning
- electrical retarder

Answer

☑ **air conditioning**

Use air conditioning sparingly - running it continuously increases fuel consumption by about 15%.

Q. 13.47

Mark one answer

Using air conditioning systems continuously will usually increase fuel consumption by about

- 15%
- 30%
- 50%
- 75%

Answer

☑ **15%**

Avoid using air conditioning systems for long periods as this can increase fuel consumption by about 15%.

Q. 13.48

Mark two answers

What must you do after filling your fuel tanks?

- Return the pump keys to the office
- Check your tachograph
- Clean up any fuel that has spilled
- Check that the filler caps are closed
- Complete the fuel log sheets
- Check your fuel gauge

Answers

☑ **Clean up any fuel that has spilled**

☑ **Check that the filler caps are closed**

If fuel has spilled it can be hazardous for anyone stepping onto it. Take care to make certain your filler caps are closed properly.

Section 14

Windy weather

This section looks at the effect of windy weather on your vehicle.

The questions will ask you about

- **High-sided vehicles**

  the risks associated with high-sided vehicles in windy weather

- **Crosswinds**

  the increased likelihood of crosswinds being encountered on open, exposed roads

- **Air deflectors**

  the equipment available to lessen wind resistance on your vehicle.

Q. 14.1

Mark one answer

When driving in windy weather, you should

- drive in a normal manner in exposed areas
- anticipate how conditions may affect other road users
- never alter your intended route if this would lengthen a journey
- always overtake smaller or vulnerable vehicles quickly

Answer

☑ **anticipate how conditions may affect other road users**

Cyclists and motorcyclists are very vulnerable in high winds. They can be blown into your path. Plan ahead and give them a wide berth.

Q. 14.2

Mark one answer

When driving an empty curtain-sided vehicle how could you reduce crosswind problems on exposed bridges?

- Tie just one curtain side back and lock open the rear doors
- Leave both curtain sides closed
- Tie both curtain sides at one end of the vehicle
- Tie the curtain sides halfway back

Answer

☑ **Tie both curtain sides at one end of the vehicle**

If you're driving an empty vehicle that's curtain-sided, you'll help lower the resistance to side winds if you tie back the curtains. The air will be able to flow across the flat bed of the vehicle and lessen any loss of control, particularly when crossing exposed viaducts or bridges.

Q. 14.3

Mark one answer

A high-sided vehicle will be MOST affected by crosswinds when it is

- stationary
- travelling loaded
- reversing
- travelling empty

Answer

☑ **travelling empty**

Take care when driving an empty high-sided vehicle when the wind is blowing across the road you are travelling on. Watch for places where the conditions could suddenly change, such as a gap in the trees or when passing under a bridge.

questions answers

Q. 14.4

Mark one answer

You are driving an empty curtain-sided vehicle. Why might you consider tying the curtains open?

- To use less fuel
- It is a legal requirement
- To prevent the curtains tearing
- To reduce the effect of crosswinds

Answer

☑ **To reduce the effect of crosswinds**

Closed curtains on large empty vehicles can hold the wind. Strong side winds can actually lift and blow the semi-trailer off course as the vehicle is travelling along the road.

Q. 14.5

Mark one answer

A box van will be MOST affected by crosswinds when it is

- travelling empty
- stationary
- travelling loaded
- reversing

Answer

☑ **travelling empty**

High-sided vehicles such as box vans are affected by strong winds, particularly when unladen. Reduce your speed and stay alert for other road users who are also affected by weather conditions.

Q. 14.6

Mark one answer

You are driving a high-sided vehicle on a motorway. You should be ESPECIALLY aware of the effects of crosswinds on your vehicle

- when travelling in cuttings
- after passing motorway bridges
- after passing motorway signs
- when travelling in tunnels

Answer

☑ **after passing motorway bridges**

Bridges provide shelter from wind. The force of wind after passing a bridge can be stronger than expected. Be prepared for this and be ready to react.

questions   answers

Q. 14.7

Mark three answers

You are driving a high-sided vehicle on a motorway. You should be ESPECIALLY aware of the effects of crosswinds on your vehicle

- after passing motorway bridges
- when travelling in cuttings
- when travelling in tunnels
- when passing vehicles towing caravans
- after passing motorway signs
- when travelling on exposed sections

Answers

- ☑ **after passing motorway bridges**
- ☑ **when passing vehicles towing caravans**
- ☑ **when travelling on exposed sections**

Bridges, cars towing caravans or large vehicles all provide shelter from crosswinds as you overtake. When you have passed them the wind will hit your vehicle and may cause you steering difficulties. On exposed sections of the road you will have no shelter and will have to be aware of the effects of the wind on other road users too.

Q. 14.8

Mark two answers

High-sided vehicles can be affected by side winds. In which TWO situations is this most likely?

- Narrow country roads
- Open roads
- Motorway flyovers
- Motorway underpasses
- Built-up areas
- Roads with speed humps

Answers

- ☑ **Open roads**
- ☑ **Motorway flyovers**

As a driver of a large vehicle you should listen to weather forecasts, which will tell you of any severe weather conditions. Plan your route accordingly. You're most likely to be subjected to high winds where there are

- high-level bridges
- high-level roads
- exposed viaducts
- exposed stretches of motorway.

questions

answers

Q. 14.9

Mark two answers

You are driving a high-sided vehicle in very windy conditions. Which TWO of the following should you avoid if possible?

- ■ Suspension bridges
- ■ Steep hills
- ■ Country lanes
- ■ Viaducts
- ■ Road tunnels

Answers

- ☑ **Suspension bridges**
- ☑ **Viaducts**

In windy weather try to avoid routes where you would have to negotiate these. Think about other factors that might lead to changes in route or rest periods, such as ferry cancellations.

Q. 14.10

Mark two answers

What TWO effects will a strong side-wind have on a bus?

- ■ Steering will be easier
- ■ The bus will tend to go off course
- ■ Braking will be affected
- ■ Stopping distance will be increased
- ■ Steering will be more difficult
- ■ Stopping distance will be decreased

Answers

- ☑ **The bus will tend to go off course**
- ☑ **Steering will be more difficult**

Be alert for places where the road is shielded from the wind. When you are steering into the wind you may suddenly find yourself making an unintentional change of direction.

Q. 14.11

Mark two answers

You are driving a high-sided vehicle. Which of these places may cause you problems on a windy day?

- ■ Road tunnels
- ■ High-level roads
- ■ Dead ground
- ■ Ring roads
- ■ Exposed viaducts
- ■ Residential roads

Answers

- ☑ **High-level roads**
- ☑ **Exposed viaducts**

Listen to the weather forecasts and plan your route to avoid exposed roads. If you can delay your journey or take an alternative route you could save

- yourself
- your employer
- the emergency services

a lot of unnecessary work and expense.

questions answers

Q. 14.12

Mark three answers

In high winds, drivers of lorries approaching high bridges or viaducts should expect

- lower speed limits
- minimum speed limits
- no restrictions for loaded vehicles
- lane closures
- no restrictions for lorries
- diversions

Q. 14.13

Mark one answer

Lanes may be closed on high bridges in very windy weather. A reason for this is to create

- a lane for emergency vehicles
- a buffer lane for large vehicles
- a lane for motorcyclists
- a contraflow system

Q. 14.14

Mark one answer

Which of these vehicles is MOST at risk from high crosswinds?

- A laden lorry with box body
- An unladen lorry with box body
- An unladen lorry with platform body
- A laden lorry with platform body

questions

answers

Q. 14.15

Mark one answer

Which vehicle is most at risk when being driven in strong crosswinds?

- A box van carrying light goods
- An unladen lorry with platform body
- A container vehicle with a heavy load
- A low-loader carrying heavy machinery

Answer

☑ **A box van carrying light goods**

High-sided vehicles catch the wind more than flat-bed vehicles. You should be aware of the places where you are likely to be at risk.

Q. 14.16

Mark one answer

Which of the following vehicles is least likely to be affected by high winds?

Answer

☑

The car is the most stable of the vehicles shown. All vehicles are affected by crosswinds and buffeting from larger vehicles. Don't be guilty of causing unnecessary turbulence when passing smaller vehicles.

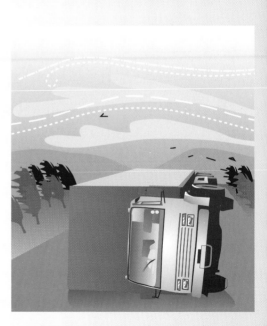

Q. 14.17

Mark one answer

What is a 'buffer' lane?

- A lane for large vehicles blown off course
- A lane for overtaking
- A lane to park in until the wind drops
- The only lane to be used in high winds

Answer

✓ **A lane for large vehicles blown off course**

During high winds one of the lanes on high bridges might be closed to traffic to create a 'buffer' lane. This lane is kept free to prevent vehicles being blown into the path of other road users in the next lane.

The closure of this lane may cause traffic congestion and delay.

Q. 14.18

Mark one answer

In high winds where would you expect to find 'buffer' lanes?

- In built-up areas
- On high bridges
- On country roads
- In roadworks

Answer

✓ **On high bridges**

If your route takes in any locations that are frequently subjected to high winds, such as

- high-level bridges
- high-level roads
- exposed viaducts
- exposed stretches of motorway

listen to the weather forecasts, which will inform you of any need to replan your route.

Q. 14.19

Mark one answer

When is a 'buffer' lane most likely to be in use?

- When windy
- When raining
- When foggy
- When icy

Answer

✓ **When windy**

A buffer lane is established when the wind begins to cause a risk to high-sided vehicles. At other times it will be a normal lane.

Don't use the buffer lane unless your vehicle has been blown off course into it, or you need to use it to avoid an accident. Leave it free, however heavy the traffic.

questions answers

Q. 14.20

Mark one answer

Your vehicle has been blown into deep snow by high winds. When trying to free the vehicle you should AVOID

 using a diff-lock

continual revving in a low gear

rocking between reverse and forward

using a high gear

Answer

✓ **continual revving in a low gear**

Too many engine revs will make the wheels spin and quickly dig you deeper into the snow.

Q. 14.21

Mark one answer

How can you best control your vehicle when driving on snow in windy conditions?

 By keeping the engine revs high and spinning the wheels

By driving in your very lowest crawler gear

By keeping the engine revs high and slipping the clutch

By driving slowly in as high a gear as possible

Answer

✓ **By driving slowly in as high a gear as possible**

Driving slowly will give you better control of your vehicle. By using a high gear you reduce the chance of your wheels spinning and skidding on the snow.

Q. 14.22

Mark one answer

Which of these vehicles is most at risk from strong crosswinds on motorways?

 A motorcycle

 An unladen lorry

A sports car

A road tanker

Answer

✓ **A motorcycle**

Motorcyclists overtaking high-sided vehicles experience a drop in pressure when they're alongside and protected from side winds. This can cause them to veer to one side.

The effect will be reversed when they complete the manoeuvre and emerge again from the shelter of the bigger vehicle.

Q. 14.23

Mark one answer

You are driving a large vehicle in gusty conditions. Which of the following is most likely to be affected when you overtake it?

 A motorcycle

A flat-bed lorry

A car

A loaded tanker

Answer

✓ **A motorcycle**

Give motorcyclists extra room in windy conditions. A combination of gusty conditions and buffeting caused by your vehicle can easily upset the motorcyclist's control and balance.

Q. 14.24

Mark one answer

In strong winds an overtaking lorry can affect other road users. Which vehicle is most at risk?

A car

A furniture van

A motorcycle

A coach

Answer

✓ **A motorcycle**

Other road users, such as cyclists, could be blown off course by high winds. You should be aware of this when you're following or planning to overtake them.

Vehicles that are towing caravans can also feel the effect of high winds, to a degree where it might blow them off course.

Q. 14.25

Mark one answer

You are driving on a motorway in high winds. You are overtaking a motorcyclist. You should be especially aware of the effects caused by

 exhaust smoke

engine noise

buffeting

tyre noise

Answer

✓ **buffeting**

Always watch motorcyclists carefully in your nearside mirror when you overtake them. Give them plenty of room as the rider might wobble or be blown off course.

questions

answers

Q. 14.26

Mark two answers

Which TWO types of vehicle are most at risk in windy conditions?

- High-sided lorries
- Saloon cars
- Unladen vans
- Single-deck buses
- Tractor units

Answers

- ✓ **High-sided lorries**
- ✓ **Unladen vans**

The higher the sides of your vehicle, the more the vehicle will be buffeted by strong winds. The large area of bodywork will present a resistance to crosswinds, and this in turn will affect the control you have on the vehicle.

The risk of loss of control will be increased if your vehicle isn't carrying a load. The vehicle will be lighter and so could be more easily pushed off course by the wind.

Q. 14.27

Mark one answer

In gusty winds on a motorway you must be aware of motorcyclists as they may

- be blown into your path
- leave at the next exit
- suddenly stop on the hard shoulder
- position to turn right

Answer

- ✓ **be blown into your path**

On motorways there may be exposed stretches of road where there are strong crosswinds. A gust of wind might blow the motorcycle across the lane, or the rider might experience buffeting when overtaking or being overtaken.

If you're following or are alongside a motorcyclist you should be aware that the weather will also affect the rider's control of the motorcycle.

Q. 14.28

Mark three answers

Which road users are in the most danger from the buffeting effects of large vehicles?

- Lorry drivers
- Coach drivers
- Tractor drivers
- Pedestrians
- Horse riders
- Cyclists

Answers

- ✓ **Pedestrians**
- ✓ **Horse riders**
- ✓ **Cyclists**

Remember that buffeting can affect other road users including

- cars towing caravans
- motorcyclists.

Q. 14.29

Mark four answers

Which road users would be most affected by turbulence caused by your vehicle?

Pedestrians
Car drivers towing caravans
Drivers of skip lorries
Cyclists
Coach drivers
Horse riders

Answers

☑ **Pedestrians**

☑ **Car drivers towing caravans**

☑ **Cyclists**

☑ **Horse riders**

Be considerate when passing more vulnerable road users. Give them plenty of room, don't use the size of your vehicle to bully other road users.

Q. 14.30

Mark four answers

Turbulence is created by large vehicles travelling at speed. This is most likely to be a danger to

low-loaders
cyclists
pedestrians
motorcyclists
tankers
caravans

Answers

☑ **cyclists**

☑ **pedestrians**

☑ **motorcyclists**

☑ **caravans**

Passing too close to any of the above will create turbulence which will affect their balance or control. Don't be guilty of putting others in danger through thoughtless or inconsiderate driving.

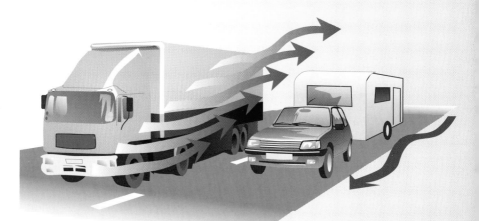

questions   answers

Q. 14.31

Mark one answer

You are overtaking a motorcycle in windy conditions. Why should you always check your nearside mirror?

- To check your road position
- To see if the rider is still in control of the motorcycle
- To see if other vehicles have been affected
- To check if it is properly adjusted

Answer

✓ **To see if the rider is still in control of the motorcycle**

You must check the nearside mirror during and after overtaking a motorcyclist. Make sure that the rider is still in control and that your vehicle hasn't caused buffeting.

Q. 14.32

Mark three answers

Which THREE of the following are most likely to be affected by high winds?

- Slow-moving vehicles
- Cyclists
- Vehicles towing caravans
- Curtain-sided vehicles
- Track-laying vehicles
- Front-wheel-drive vehicles

Answers

✓ **Cyclists**

✓ **Vehicles towing caravans**

✓ **Curtain-sided vehicles**

If you're driving a curtain-sided vehicle in very windy weather it's safer to secure both curtain sides at one end of the vehicle. This cuts down the wind resistance and lessens the risk of being blown off course.

Q. 14.33

Mark one answer

When are air deflectors most effective?

- When there is a crosswind
- When there is a headwind
- When reversing
- When there is a strong tailwind

Answer

✓ **When there is a headwind**

Cab-mounted air deflectors and lower panels will streamline the vehicle and it will, therefore, offer less resistance to the air around it. This will decrease its fuel consumption, and we should all be concerned with the conservation of fuel. This aim is linked not only to financial issues, although these are important, but to environmental conservation as well.

Conserving energy and resources should be a concern for all drivers on the road.

Q. 14.34

Mark one answer

Double-deck buses are more likely than single-deck buses to be affected by

- strong winds
- heavy rain
- thick fog
- dense spray

Answer

✓ **strong winds**

If you're driving a double-deck bus you'll feel the effect of the wind to a greater degree, due to the vehicle's extra height.

Q. 14.35

Mark two answers

As a bus driver, which TWO of the following should you do when overtaking a motorcyclist in strong winds?

- Sound the horn
- Pass close
- Use the nearside mirror
- Move back in early
- Pass wide

Answers

✓ **Use the nearside mirror**

✓ **Pass wide**

You should always check your nearside mirror as you overtake. If you're overtaking a motorcyclist and the weather is windy, pass them leaving plenty of room, as the rider might wobble or swerve.

Q. 14.36

Mark three answers

What are the extra hazards when driving through a contraflow system?

- Less traffic
- No street lights
- Narrow lanes
- No permanent barriers
- Oncoming traffic

Answers

✓ **Narrow lanes**

✓ **No permanent barriers**

✓ **Oncoming traffic**

Reduced lane widths may cause problems when negotiating the changes of direction associated with contraflow systems. Always maintain all round awareness of the position of other road users, particularly motorcyclists who may try and overtake in unsuitable places.

questions

answers

Q. 14.37

Mark one answer

As a bus driver what should you do when overtaking a motorcycle in strong winds?

 Pass close

Move back early

Pass wide

Signal left

Answer

☑ **Pass wide**

Motorcycles can be blown into your path in strong winds. Allow them plenty of room when you are overtaking.

Q. 14.38

Mark one answer

You are driving a high sided vehicle on a motorway. You should be especially aware of the effects of crosswinds on your vehicle when

travelling in cuttings

travelling through tunnels

driving across viaducts

passing motorway signs

Answer

☑ **driving across viaducts**

On motorways you should be especially aware during high winds when you are driving over bridges and viaducts which are frequently subjected to high winds. Be prepared to reduce your speed.

Q. 14.39

Mark one answer

You are following a scooter on an uneven road. You should

allow extra room, they may swerve to avoid pot holes

leave less room so they can see you in their mirrors

drive closely behind and get ready to overtake

drive close to shield them

Answer

☑ **allow extra room, they may swerve to avoid pot holes**

Never follow any road user too close. This is particularly important if there is a possibility of them braking or swerving suddenly due to poor road surface conditions.

Don't use the size of your vehicle to intimidate the more vulnerable road users. Be professional and set an example to others.

questions   answers

Q. 14.40

Mark one answer

Before driving your lorry in high winds, you should always

- check your wind deflector
- check your spray suppression equipment
- plan your journey well in advance
- only half load your vehicle

Answer

☑ **plan your journey well in advance**

Plan your route with care. Take into account whether the road will be exposed and if there will be bridges or viaducts to cross. Be sensible and avoid these areas if possible in high winds.

Heavy rain

This section looks at the effects of heavy rain.

The questions will ask you about

- **Spray**

  excessive spray from your vehicle affecting other road users

- **Saturated roads**

  the grip of your tyres being reduced on very wet roads.

questions answers

Q. 15.1

Mark one answer

On a motorway the surface is still wet after rain. You should take extra care when overtaking because

 wet roads may create more buffeting

other vehicles will have their lights on

vehicles may be parked on the hard shoulder

the road may still be slippery

Answer

 the road may still be slippery

Rain reacts with oil, dirt and debris on the surface, reducing grip between the tyres and the road.

Q. 15.2

Mark one answer

The road is wet. Why might a motorcyclist steer around drain covers on a bend?

 To prevent the motorcycle skidding

To avoid puncturing the tyres

To help steer around the bend

To avoid splashing pedestrians

Answer

 To prevent the motorcycle skidding

Drain covers usually have a metal surface. When wet they can cause the motorcycle to skid.

Q. 15.3

Mark one answer

In heavy rain what is the least amount of space you should allow for braking?

 The normal distance

Twice the normal distance

Three times the normal distance

Five times the normal distance

Answer

 Twice the normal distance

Your tyres could lose their grip in wet conditions. If you're travelling in heavy rain you should be aware that it could take twice as long for you to stop as in dry weather. Therefore increase your distance from the vehicle in front.

Q. 15.4

Mark three answers

You are driving on a motorway. Your view ahead is poor due to heavy spray. Which THREE of the following should you do?

- Move into the lane on the right
- Use the four-second rule
- Switch on your dipped headlights
- Switch on your full-beam headlights
- Reduce your speed

Answers

- ☑ **Use the four-second rule**
- ☑ **Switch on your dipped headlights**
- ☑ **Reduce your speed**

If you're travelling on a motorway and your view ahead is poor then you should reduce your speed.

Leave about four seconds between you and the vehicle in front, and make sure that others can see you by using your dipped headlights.

Q. 15.5

Mark one answer

When overtaking on motorways in very wet weather, what is the main danger that can affect your vehicle?

- Your engine may get flooded
- Your braking distance may be reduced
- Your steering may become heavy
- Your tyres may lose grip

Answer

- ☑ **Your tyres may lose grip**

Water can form a layer between the road and the tyre resulting in a loss of contact with the road. This is known as aquaplaning.

Q. 15.6

Mark one answer

Overtaking on a motorway in heavy rain needs extra care because of

- slippery manhole covers
- spray from traffic
- reduced braking distances
- bright reflections

Answer

- ☑ **spray from traffic**

Other vehicles can be affected by the spray created by your vehicle causing them to be temporarily blinded. Always take care when you need to change lanes, give a signal in good time and watch your mirrors carefully before pulling out in these conditions.

questions

answers

Q. 15.7

Mark one answer

Visibility can be worse when driving at
higher speeds in wet weather because

- drivers always bunch together
- headlights will dazzle you more easily
- of people driving at different speeds
- more spray is thrown up

Answer

✓ **more spray is thrown up**

The faster a wheel turns, the more spray
is thrown up from the road to the side and
rear of the vehicle. Always use dipped
headlights in poor visibility caused by
rain and spray.

Q. 15.8

Mark two answers

You are driving your lorry on the motorway.
Visibility is reduced by heavy rain and spray.
You should

- maintain a constant speed
- use main beam headlights
- double your dry weather separation
  distance
- stay in the left-hand lane
- obey advisory speed limit signs

Answers

✓ **double your dry weather
separation distance**

✓ **obey advisory speed limit signs**

Wet roads reduce tyre grip and can make
the surface even more slippery. Give
yourself plenty of time and room for slowing
down and stopping. Keep well back from
other vehicles.

Advisory signs are set by the police and
should be adhered to when they are shown.

Q. 15.9

Mark one answer

You intend to overtake a large vehicle that is
throwing up spray. You should

- get much closer before moving out
- wait until the other driver gives a left
  signal
- move out earlier than normal
- wait for the other vehicle to slow down
  on a hill

Answer

✓ **move out earlier than normal**

If you wish to overtake a vehicle that's
throwing up spray, move out to overtake
earlier than normal. This will prevent you
being affected by the rear spray as well as
the side spray as you pass.

questions answers

Q. 15.10

Mark one answer

You are driving a bus in heavy rain. When overtaking a cyclist extra care has to be taken because of

- spray from your vehicle
- exhaust fumes from your vehicle
- noise from your vehicle
- the size of your vehicle

Answer

☑ **spray from your vehicle**

When passing other road users, especially motorcyclists and cyclists, the spray from your vehicle could affect their control. Pass them leaving plenty of room, and check in your left-hand mirror as you pass to see whether they're still in control.

Q. 15.11

Mark one answer

Spray suppression equipment fitted to buses is particularly useful when it is

- raining
- icy
- foggy
- windy

Answer

☑ **raining**

If there's heavy rain the spray suppression equipment fitted on your vehicle will protect other road users from loss of vision when following or passing your vehicle. Check the wheel arches to ensure that the fitments haven't worked loose and that no parts have broken off. Well-maintained equipment will force the spray back down onto the road instead of to the rear and the sides of the vehicle.

Q. 15.12

Mark one answer

Your vehicle is fitted with spray suppression equipment. What effect will this have on other drivers if it is NOT in good working order?

- Their vision will be increased
- Their vision will be reduced
- They will be able to overtake quickly
- They will be able to follow closely

Answer

☑ **Their vision will be reduced**

Spray suppression equipment reduces the amount of spray thrown up to other road users. Check the equipment regularly to make sure it is secure.

Q. 15.13

Mark one answer

The purpose of the brushes fitted to this vehicle is to

- clear mud from the tyres on building sites
- remove objects from the tyre tread
- stop snow building up behind the wheel
- reduce spray and increase visibility

Answer

☑ **reduce spray and increase visibility**

The brushes are part of a spray suppression system which stops water from being thrown up at the sides and to the rear of the vehicle. Check them regularly for security, and if they become worn make sure they are replaced.

Q. 15.14

Mark one answer

You should check your vehicle's spray suppression equipment

- only when you will be using a motorway
- before setting out on a journey
- only at the start of winter as a pre-winter check
- yearly before the MOT test

Answer

☑ **before setting out on a journey**

You should check all your spray suppression equipment before setting out. Bear in mind that weather may change during the course of the journey.

questions   answers

Q. 15.15

Mark one answer

In wet weather, following drivers will be able to see better if your vehicle is fitted with

 spray reducers

side-panel skirts

wind deflectors

a catalytic converter

Answer

☑ **spray reducers**

Spray reducers or spray suppression equipment are attachments fitted around the wheel arch area of large vehicles. They effectively trap the water thrown up from the wheels when driving on wet roads. This improves visibility for you and other drivers who wish to overtake.

Q. 15.16

Mark one answer

This vehicle is fitted with spray suppression equipment. This will be most useful when it is

 raining

snowing

windy

foggy

Answer

☑ **raining**

The spray suppression equipment helps prevent water being thrown up and causing reduced visibility. Driving at a reduced speed in wet weather conditions will also help to reduce the amount of water thrown into the atmosphere by your vehicle.

Q. 15.17

Mark one answer

When driving through deep water you should drive

 slowly in a low gear with engine speed high

slowly in a high gear with engine speed low

as quickly as possible to cause less delay

at normal speed if you have spray reducers fitted

Answer

☑ **slowly in a low gear with engine speed high**

It is important to keep the engine speed high to prevent water entering the engine through the exhaust system.

It may be necessary to slip the clutch in these circumstances to keep the road speed as low as possible.

questions answers

Q. 15.18

Mark two answers

Your bus breaks down on the motorway. You have several passengers on board. You should

- move the passengers to the rear
- place a warning triangle in front of the bus
- stop on the hard shoulder
- move the passengers to the front

Answers

☑ **stop on the hard shoulder**

☑ **move the passengers to the front**

Stop as far to the left as possible on the hard shoulder. Make sure all your passengers have moved as far as possible to the front of the vehicle. Send a responsible person to the nearest telephone, which will be marked by small arrows on marker posts.

Q. 15.19

Mark one answer

Before driving your lorry from a wet construction site at the side of a motorway, you should

- inform the local council
- hose down the road
- hose down the wheels
- inform the lorry operator

Answer

☑ **hose down the wheels**

It is important that you prevent any mud or debris from being deposited on the road. This can cause danger to other road users. If possible, hose the mud off your vehicle before driving on the public road.

Q. 15.20

Mark one answer

You are driving a lorry from a wet construction site onto a motorway. You must take extra precautions before driving because

- your lorry will be unladen and liable to 'bounce'
- it is an offence to emerge from a works site straight onto a motorway
- your lorry's spray suppression equipment will be inoperative
- it is an offence to deposit mud on a road

Answer

☑ **it is an offence to deposit mud on a road**

You should take all possible precautions to prevent any mud being deposited on the road as this is a hazard to other road users. It is also an offence for which you could be prosecuted.

questions answers

Q. 15.21

Mark one answer

You are approaching a working snow plough on a motorway. You should not overtake because

☐ it is illegal to overtake snow ploughs

☐ snow ploughs are left hand drive only

☐ your speed could cause snow to drift behind

☐ there may be deep snow ahead

Answer

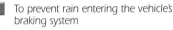 **there may be deep snow ahead**

There is no way of knowing how deep the snow could be ahead. If you overtake and then become stuck in the snow you may cause problems for the snow plough, particularly if you block the road.

Q. 15.22

Mark three answers

You are driving in heavy rain. Why is there a need to increase your distance from the vehicle in front?

☐ To prevent rain entering the vehicle's braking system

☐ The tyres will have less grip on the road surface

☐ Spray from traffic will make it difficult to see ahead

☐ To reduce the risk of water spraying into filters

☐ Normal stopping distances could be doubled

Answers

✓ **The tyres will have less grip on the road surface**

✓ **Spray from traffic will make it difficult to see ahead**

✓ **Normal stopping distances could be doubled**

Extra care is needed when driving in adverse weather conditions. Reduce your speed and switch on your lights.

Tyres will have less grip on a wet road so it will take longer to stop. Spray from large vehicles will be an added hazard especially on motorways.

Q. 15.23

Mark one answer

You are driving a large vehicle on a motorway. Why should you slow down when the roads are very wet?

  To force other drivers to act properly and slow down

☐ To reduce the amount of spray thrown up

☐ To prevent water entering the braking system

☐ To stop the electrics getting wet

Answer

✓ **To reduce the amount of spray thrown up**

Driving at high speed on a wet motorway can seriously reduce vision. Spray thrown up by large, fast moving vehicles can make it very difficult for other drivers to see ahead.

questions

answers

Q. 15.24

Mark one answer

You are driving on a motorway in heavy rain. When would you be allowed to use high-intensity rear fog lights?

- When visibility is more than 100 metres (328 feet)
- Only when the national speed limit applies
- Only when you are being followed closely by other traffic
- When visibility is reduced to 100 metres (328 feet) or less

Answer

 When visibility is reduced to 100 metres (328 feet) or less

Heavy rain and the resulting spray from higher speeds and large vehicles can seriously affect visibility on the motorway.

Reduce your speed and use your headlights. Do not use high-intensity rear lights UNLESS visibility is reduced to 100 metres (328 feet) or less.

Q. 15.25

Mark one answer

You are driving on a motorway in heavy rain. What could cause your steering to be less responsive?

- Water reducing the tyre grip on the road
- Tyres becoming hotter in the bad weather
- Braking gently and in good time
- Water entering the braking system

Answer

 Water reducing the tyre grip on the road

Be careful when driving in any bad weather and adopt an appropriate attitude.

Steering can be less responsive when the roads are wet because water prevents the tyres from gripping the road. Ease off the accelerator and slow down gradually.

Q. 15.26

Mark one answer

You are driving on a motorway after heavy rain. Visibility is low because of spray being thrown up by other lorries. You should

- use dipped headlights
- use sidelights only
- remove spray suppression equipment
- use the two second rule

Answer

☑ **use dipped headlights**

If visibility is reduced use dipped headlights to make yourself seen. During and after heavy rain you should also reduce speed and increase your distance from the vehicle in front.

questions answers

Q. 15.27

Mark one answer

You are on a motorway just after heavy rain. Spray is being thrown up causing poor visibility. What should you do?

- Use the two second rule
- Use sidelights only
- Remove spray suppression equipment
- Leave a greater separation distance

Answer

☑ **Leave a greater separation distance**

When visibility is poor and the road is wet leave a greater separation distance. You should leave at least a four second time gap from the vehicle in front. You should also reduce speed and use dipped headlights.

Q. 15.28

Mark one answer

Spray is causing poor visibility on the motorway. What should you do?

- Use the two second rule
- Use sidelights only
- Slow to a safe speed
- Remove spray suppression equipment

Answer

☑ **Slow to a safe speed**

Spray from other vehicles, particularly lorries, will reduce visibility. Slow down and leave a greater separation distance from the vehicle in front. You should also use dipped headlights.

Q. 15.29

Mark one answer

Before braking in wet conditions you should make sure, as far as possible, that

- the gear lever is in neutral
- all spray suppression equipment is working
- there is no mist on your rear view mirrors
- your vehicle is travelling in a straight line

Answer

☑ **your vehicle is travelling in a straight line**

If you need to brake when the road surface is wet, do so while your vehicle is travelling in a straight line. This will lessen the risk of skidding. As a professional driver you should be in the routine of braking in good time, so that you aren't braking and steering at the same time.

Q. 15.30

Mark one answer

What causes extra danger when overtaking in rain?

- Other vehicles driving slowly
- Vehicles wandering across lanes
- Increase in vehicle noise
- Spray from large vehicles

Answer

☑ **Spray from large vehicles**

Other vehicles might create heavy spray, so you must be cautious when you're overtaking. Severe spray can result in a complete loss of vision as you overtake. Be aware of this and anticipate it happening.

Spray from your vehicle could cause the driver of an overtaking vehicle to lose visibility. You should be aware of this as smaller vehicles overtake you.

Section 16

Traffic signs

This section looks at road traffic signs.

The questions will ask you about

- **Road signs**

  these tell you about the road ahead

- **Speed limits**

  recognise signs showing speed limits

- **Regulations**

  these can be shown by means of a road sign.

questions   answers

Q. 16.1

Mark one answer

Which sign means no overtaking?

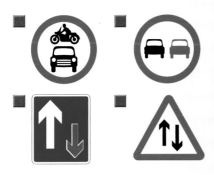

Answer

✓

This sign indicates that overtaking here would be dangerous. Don't take risks.

Q. 16.2

Mark one answer

What does this sign mean?

■ End of restricted speed area
■ End of restricted parking area
■ End of clearway
■ End of cycle route

Answer

✓ **End of restricted parking area**

Even though there are no restrictions make sure that you park where you won't cause an obstruction or endanger other road users.

questions answers

Q. 16.3

Mark one answer

Which sign means 'No stopping'?

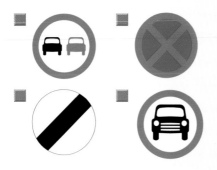

Answer

☑

Stopping where you see this sign is likely to cause congestion. Allow the traffic to flow by obeying the signs.

Q. 16.4

Mark one answer

What is the meaning of this traffic sign?

- End of two-way road
- Give priority to vehicles coming towards you
- You have priority over vehicles coming towards you
- Bus lane ahead

Answer

☑ **You have priority over vehicles coming towards you**

Although you have priority make sure oncoming traffic is going to give way.

Q. 16.5

Mark one answer

What does this sign mean?

▪ No overtaking

▪ You are entering a one-way street

▪ Two-way traffic ahead

▪ You have priority over vehicles from the opposite direction

Answer

☑ **You have priority over vehicles from the opposite direction**

Don't force the issue. Slow down and give way to avoid confrontation or an accident.

Q. 16.6

Mark one answer

At a junction you see this sign partly covered by snow. What does it mean?

▪ Crossroads

▪ Give way

▪ Stop

▪ Turn right

Answer

☑ **Stop**

The 'Stop' sign is the only sign this shape. This is to give it greater prominence. Although the snow has covered the wording, you must still be able to recognise and obey this sign.

questions

answers

Q. 16.7

Mark one answer

What does this sign mean?

■ Service area 30 miles ahead

■ Maximum speed 30 mph

■ Minimum speed 30 mph

■ Lay-by 30 miles ahead

Answer

☑ **Minimum speed 30 mph**

This sign is shown where slow-moving vehicles would impede the flow of traffic. However, if you need to slow down to avoid a potential accident you should do so.

Q. 16.8

Mark one answer

Which of these signs means turn left ahead?

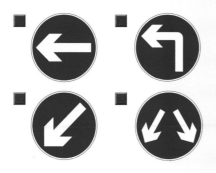

Answer

This sign gives a clear instruction. You should be looking out for signs as you drive. Prepare to negotiate a left-hand turn.

Q. 16.9

Mark one answer

What does this sign mean?

- Route for trams
- Give way to trams
- Route for buses
- Give way to buses

Answer

☑ **Route for trams**

Take extra care when you first encounter trams. Look out for road markings and signs that alert you to them. Modern trams are very quiet and you may not hear them approaching.

Q. 16.10

Mark one answer

Which of these signs means that you are entering a one-way street?

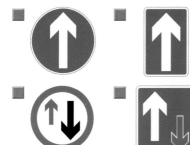

Answer

☑

If the road has two lanes you can use either lane and overtake on either side. Use the lane that's more convenient for your destination.

questions

answers

Q. 16.11

Mark one answer

What does this sign mean?

 Bus station on the right

Contraflow bus lane

With-flow bus lane

Give way to buses

Answer

☑ **Contraflow bus lane**

There will also be markings on the road surface to indicate the bus lane. Don't use this lane for parking or overtaking.

Q. 16.12

Mark one answer

What does a sign with a brown background show?

Tourist directions

Primary roads

Motorway routes

Minor routes

Answer

☑ **Tourist directions**

Signs with a brown background give directions to places of interest.

Q. 16.13

Mark four answers

Which FOUR of these would be indicated by a triangular road sign?

- Road narrows
- Ahead only
- Low bridge
- Minimum speed
- Children crossing
- T-junction

Answers

- ☑ **Road narrows**
- ☑ **Low bridge**
- ☑ **Children crossing**
- ☑ **T-junction**

Make use of the warning sign and be prepared for the hazard ahead.

Q. 16.14

Mark one answer

Which sign means that pedestrians may be walking along the road?

Answer

Be extra cautious, especially if there is a bend in the road and you're unable to see well ahead. When you pass, leave plenty of room. Consider that you might have to use the right-hand side of the road, so look well ahead down the road, as well as in your mirrors, before you pull out.

questions

answers

Q. 16.15

Mark one answer

What does this sign mean?

- Crosswinds
- Road noise
- Airport
- Adverse camber

Answer

☑ **Crosswinds**

Where weather conditions are often bad, signs will give you a warning. A sign with a picture of a wind-sock will indicate there may be strong crosswinds. This sign is often found on exposed roads.

Q. 16.16

Mark one answer

What does this traffic sign mean?

- Slippery road ahead
- Tyres liable to punctures ahead
- Danger ahead
- Service area ahead

Answer

☑ **Danger ahead**

A sign showing an exclamation mark (!) will alert you to the likelihood of danger ahead. Be ready for any situation that requires you to reduce your speed.

Q. 16.17

Mark one answer

You are about to overtake when you see this sign. You should

Hidden dip

- overtake the other driver as quickly as possible
- move to the right to get a better view
- switch your headlights on before overtaking
- hold back until you can see clearly ahead

Answer

☑ **hold back until you can see clearly ahead**

You won't be able to see any hazards that might be out of sight in the dip. Imagine there might be

- cyclists
- horse riders
- parked vehicles
- pedestrians.

There might be oncoming traffic to deal with, too.

Q. 16.18

Mark one answer

What does this sign mean?

Ford

- Uneven road surface
- Bridge over the road
- Road ahead ends
- Water across the road

Answer

☑ **Water across the road**

This sign is found where a shallow stream crosses the road. Heavy rainfall could increase the flow of water. If the water looks too deep or the stream has swelled over a large distance, stop and find another route.

questions answers

Q. 16.19

Mark one answer

You see this traffic light ahead. Which light(s) will come on next?

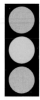

| Red alone
| Red and amber together
| Green and amber together
| Green alone

Answer

☑ **Red alone**

At junctions controlled by traffic lights you must stop behind the white line until the lights change to green. Don't

- move forward when the red and amber lights are showing together
- proceed when the light is green if your exit road is blocked.

If you're approaching traffic lights that are visible from a distance and the light has been green for some time, it's likely to change. Try to anticipate this. Be ready to slow down and stop.

Q. 16.20

Mark three answers

These flashing red lights mean STOP. In which THREE of the following places could you find them?

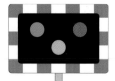

| Pelican crossings
| Lifting bridges
| Zebra crossings
| Level crossings
| Motorway exits
| Fire stations

Answers

☑ **Lifting bridges**

☑ **Level crossings**

☑ **Fire stations**

Don't take risks by trying to beat the lights, even if it's clear. You must stop.

Q. 16.21

Mark one answer

You are driving a 38 tonnes lorry on a single carriageway road. You see this sign. You may drive at up to

- 40 mph
- 50 mph
- 60 mph
- 70 mph

Answer

☑ **40 mph**

The national speed limit for a goods vehicle exceeding 7.5 tonnes on a single carriageway road is 40 mph. A speed limit does not mean it is safe to drive at that speed. Drive according to the road conditions.

Q. 16.22

Mark one answer

You are driving a 38 tonnes lorry and trailer on a dual carriageway. This sign means you may drive at up to

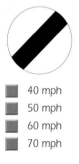

- 40 mph
- 50 mph
- 60 mph
- 70 mph

Answer

☑ **50 mph**

This may be the legal limit but it does not mean that it is safe to drive at that speed in all conditions. You should always take into account the road and weather conditions and drive accordingly.

questions

answers

Q. 16.23

Mark one answer

As a lorry driver, when MUST you use these two signs?

	When the load overhangs the front or rear of the vehicle by more than one metre (3 feet 3 inches)
	Every time your vehicle is being towed
	Every time a police escort is required
	When the load overhangs the front or rear of the vehicle by more than two metres (6 feet 6 inches)

Answer

☑ **When the load overhangs the front or rear of the vehicle by more than two metres (6 feet 6 inches)**

The law requires you to use projection markers for long or wide loads. It is also the driver's responsibility to ensure the markers are clean and secure.

Q. 16.24

Mark one answer

You see this sign when driving through roadworks. What does it tell you?

	Large vehicles must go straight ahead
	Traffic is joining from the left
	All traffic must leave at the next exit
	The distance to the next exit

Answer

☑ **The distance to the next exit**

Advance warning of a junction where the permanent sign is obscured by roadworks.

Q. 16.25

Mark one answer

What does this sign mean on a motorway?

◼ Right hand lane closed ahead

◼ One ton weight limit ahead

◼ Left hand lane closed ahead

◼ T- junction one mile ahead

Answer

☑ **Right hand lane closed ahead**

Four amber lights flash in alternate horizontal pairs to provide a warning and to draw the driver's attention to the message displayed.

Q. 16.26

Mark one answer

What does this sign mean?

◼ Stop only to pick up passengers

◼ No stopping at any time

◼ Stop only to set down passengers

◼ No stopping at peak times

Answer

☑ **No stopping at any time**

This traffic sign means no stopping on the main carriageway at any time - not even to set down passengers unless in a lay-by.

Q. 16.27

Mark one answer

You are driving on a motorway and there is no traffic ahead. You see this sign. Where should you be driving?

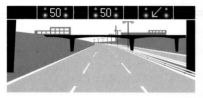

- In the right-hand lane
- Along the hard shoulder
- In the left-hand lane
- Along the middle lane

Answer
☑ **In the left-hand lane**

Signals on gantries over the motorway are normally blank. But in abnormal conditions they are switched on by the Police to warn drivers of an emergency ahead. There may have been a serious accident, so don't take chances – OBEY THE SIGNALS.

Q. 16.28

Mark one answer

What does this sign mean?

- Accident black spot ahead
- Ancient monument ahead
- Humpback bridge ahead
- Tunnel ahead

Answer
☑ **Tunnel ahead**

Check any height limits that may accompany this sign.

Q. 16.29
Mark one answer
What does this sign mean?

- No U-turns
- Two way traffic
- One way system
- End of one way system

Answer
✓ **No U-turns**

Where changes of direction are prohibited a red bar across the face of the sign is used in addition to the red circle.

Q. 16.30
Mark one answer
Which of these signs shows an uphill gradient?

Answer
✓

You will need to identify the sign in time so that you can select an appropriate gear.

questions

answers

Q. 16.31

Mark one answer

Which of these signs means uneven road?

Answer

Many signs can look similar but each one has a different meaning. You should learn the meaning of every sign.

Q. 16.32

Mark one answer

Some junctions are marked with advanced stop lines. What are these for?

■ To allow room for pedestrians to cross the road

■ To allow space for large vehicles to turn

■ To allow cyclists to position in front of other traffic

■ To allow you to select where to stop

Answer

✓ **To allow cyclists to position in front of other traffic**

Advanced stop lines are to allow cyclists and buses to be positioned ahead of other traffic. It allows them time and space to move off when the green signal shows in front of the following traffic.

Q. 16.33

Mark one answer

The driver of the car in front is giving this arm signal. This means the driver

- [ ] intends to turn left
- [ ] is slowing down
- [ ] wants you to keep back
- [ ] wants you to go past

Answer

✓ **intends to turn left**

Sometimes it may be necessary to reinforce direction indicator signals and stop lights with an arm signal e.g. in bright sunshine.

Q. 16.34

Mark one answer

This motorway sign means

- [ ] use the hard shoulder
- [ ] contraflow system ahead
- [ ] overhead bridge repairs
- [ ] all lanes ahead closed

Answer

✓ **all lanes ahead closed**

Signals on motorways are located on the central reservation, at the back of the hard shoulder or on gantries over the road.

Q. 16.35

Mark one answer

This sign warns of

- a slippery road
- a double bend
- an overhead electric cable
- a series of bends

Answer

✓ **an overhead electric cable**

This sign is used to warn of overhead electric cables and is usually accompanied by a plate indicating the safe height limit.

Q. 16.36

Mark one answer

You are approaching this sign. Who has priority?

- Larger vehicles
- Oncoming traffic
- Smaller vehicles
- You have right of way

Answer

✓ **Oncoming traffic**

When you see this sign you must give way to traffic from the opposite direction regardless of the size of your lorry or bus.

questions
answers

Q. 16.37
Mark one answer

What does this sign mean?

■ Car lane only

■ Single file only

■ Queues likely

■ Keep your distance

Answer

✓ Queues likely

When you see this sign beware of traffic queues ahead, check your mirrors and reduce your speed.

Exercise patience when you are delayed. Understand that annoyance and frustration lead to a poor attitude on the road and ultimately, an accident.

Q. 16.38
Mark one answer

What does this sign mean?

■ Road flooded

■ Risk of punctures

■ Loose chippings

■ Uneven surface

Answer

✓ Loose chippings

This is a warning sign to indicate loose chippings ahead. The sign is usually accompanied by an advisory speed limit. Vehicles travelling too fast for the conditions can throw up chippings or stones. Paintwork and windscreens can be easily damaged through lack of consideration.

Q. 16.39

Mark one answer

What does this sign mean?

 You are allowed to carry on but only with a police escort

You should continue very slowly if your weight is above the limit

Do not cross unless the bridge is clear of other vehicles

Do not cross the bridge if your weight exceeds the limit

Answer

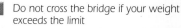 **Do not cross the bridge if your weight exceeds the limit**

Vehicles over the weight advised are prohibited from using the bridge ahead. An alternative route must be found. Plan your route in advance to avoid delays and congestion.

This will save time, fuel and frustration.

Q. 16.40

Mark one answer

What does this sign mean?

Low bridge

Tunnel ahead

Accident black spot

Speed camera

Answer

✓ **Tunnel ahead**

Remember the height of your vehicle. Reduce speed, your eyes may need to adjust to sudden darkness.

Be ready to turn on your headlights.

questions

answers

Q. 16.41

Mark one answer

What does this sign mean?

⬛ Rumble strips

⬛ Road humps

⬛ Uneven road

⬛ Double humpback bridge

Answer

☑ **Uneven road**

Prepare to slow down especially if carrying passengers, livestock or fragile items.

Q. 16.42

Mark one answer

This is the first countdown marker to a

⬛ motorway slip road

⬛ primary road junction

⬛ concealed level crossing

⬛ roadside rest area

Answer

☑ **concealed level crossing**

Reduce your speed, you may well have to stop. Be sure that you can stop within the distance you can see to be clear.

questions

answers

Q. 16.43

Mark one answer

This sign means

- buses only
- bus lane
- no buses
- bus stop

Answer

☑ **no buses**

Order signs must be obeyed.

No buses over 8 passenger seats are permitted past this sign.

Q. 16.44

Mark one answer

You are driving a 12m, fully loaded coach. What should you do when you approach this sign?

- Do not proceed past the sign but find another route
- Set down all your passengers at a safe place before the sign
- Stop and check the legal lettering on the side panel
- Proceed as normal, the sign does not apply to you

Answer

☑ **Proceed as normal, the sign does not apply to you**

The sign shows the maximum authorised mass allowed for goods vehicles. This sign may be used to restrict heavy lorries in residential areas and does not apply to buses and coaches.

Q. 16.45

Mark one answer

You are driving an articulated lorry. What should you do when you see this sign ahead?

- [ ] Turn round and find an alternative route
- [ ] Park safely and arrange alternative transport for the goods
- [ ] Inform your vehicle operator and await further instructions
- [ ] Proceed as normal, the sign does not apply to you

Answer

- [✓] **Proceed as normal, the sign does not apply to you**

The sign prohibits buses and coaches with more than eight passenger seats.

Q. 16.46

Mark one answer

You are driving a 14 tonne lorry on a dual carriageway. What does this sign mean?

- [ ] Maximum speed 40 mph
- [ ] Maximum speed 50 mph
- [ ] Maximum speed 60 mph
- [ ] Maximum speed 70 mph

Answer

- [✓] **Maximum speed 50 mph**

Be aware of the speed limits applying to different types of vehicles on particular roads. These are the maximum speeds allowed but it may not always be safe to drive at this speed.

questions

answers

Q. 16.47

Mark one answer

You are driving a 14 tonne lorry on a motorway. What does this sign mean ?

- Maximum Speed 40 mph
- Maximum speed 50 mph
- Maximum speed 60 mph
- Maximum speed 70 mph

Answer

☑ **Maximum speed 60 mph**

The maximum speed for lorries over 7.5 tonnes on a motorway is 60 mph. It may not always be appropriate or possible to drive at this speed.

Q. 16.48

Mark one answer

You are driving a 14 tonne lorry on a single carriageway road. What does this sign mean?

- Maximum speed 30 mph
- Maximum speed 40 mph
- Maximum speed 50 mph
- Maximum speed 60 mph

Answer

☑ **Maximum speed 40 mph**

The national speed limit for lorries over 7.5 tonnes on a single carriageway road is 40 mph.

questions

Q. 16.49

Mark one answer

Which sign must you NOT drive your lorry past?

answers

Answer

☑

This sign means no motor vehicles. Although a motorcycle and car are shown it applies to all classes of motor vehicle.

Q. 16.50

Mark one answer

You are driving a lorry 30 feet long and towing a trailer 15 feet long. You see this sign ahead. What should you do?

- Find an alternative route to your destination
- Stop and wait for a police escort
- Continue past the sign but reduce your speed
- Carry on, as the sign applies to the towing vehicle only

Answer

☑ **Find an alternative route to your destination**

The maximum permitted length of vehicle includes any trailer being towed. Ensure you know the total length of your vehicle.

questions answers

Q. 16.51

Mark one answer

What do DOUBLE red lines at the edge of a road mean?

- Limited loading
- No stopping
- Bus route
- Short term parking

Answer

✓ **No stopping**

Red route signs and red road markings have replaced some yellow line resrictions.

Q. 16.52

Mark one answer

Where would you expect to see these road markings?

- At the entrance to a car park
- On the approach to an arched bridge
- At the start of a cycle lane
- On the approach to a lifting barrier

Answer

✓ **On the approach to an arched bridge**

High vehicles are often directed to the centre of the road to go under an arched bridge. Check that your vehicle does not exceed the posted height restriction.

Q. 16.53

Mark one answer

You are approaching a red traffic light. What signal or signals will show next?

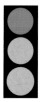

- red and amber, then green
- green, then amber
- amber, then green
- green and amber, then green

Answer

☑ **red and amber, then green**

If you know which light is going to show next you can plan your approach. This will prevent excessive braking or hesitation at the junction.

Q. 16.54

Mark two answers

The double white line along the centre of the road is continuous on your side. You may cross the line to

- overtake any slower moving vehicle
- pass a stationary vehicle
- see if it is safe to overtake
- overtake a learner driver travelling at 20 mph or less
- pass a pedal cycle travelling at 10 mph or less

Answers

☑ **pass a stationary vehicle**

☑ **pass a pedal cycle travelling at 10 mph or less**

You may only cross over the solid side of a double white line to enter premises on the right. You may also cross the solid line to overtake a stationary vehicle, pedal cycle or road maintenance vehicle provided they are travelling at 10 mph or less.

This book is intended to help you to prepare for the lorry or bus theory test. If you've prepared properly and fully you won't find your questions difficult.

Sitting your theory test means that you've taken the first step towards driving as a career. Passing the theory test, however, is only one stage in becoming a safe and competent professional driver. The knowledge you've learned should be put into practice on the road. By passing a stringent, two-part test and continuing to apply the knowledge that you've gained on the way, you can make an important contribution to safety on our roads.

You'll never know all the answers. Throughout your driving career there will always be more to learn. Remember, the passengers or goods you carry are your responsibility. By being reliable, efficient and safe you'll be on your way to becoming a good professional driver.

Cancelling your test

If you wish to cancel your theory test appointment, you must give us at least three whole working days notice, or you will forfeit your theory test fee. In Great Britain telephone 0870 01 01 372; in Northern Ireland telephone 0845 600 6700.

Service standards for theory test candidates

DSA and DVTA are committed to providing the following standards of service for test candidates.

1   Following routing by our call handling systems, ninety percent of telephone calls will be answered within twenty seconds.

2   Theory tests will be available during weekdays, evenings and on Saturdays. A test appointment should be available for 95% of test candidates within two weeks.

3   99% of test notifications will be issued within five working days of receipt of a correctly completed application form and appropriate fee.

4   More time may be needed to make arrangements for candidates with special needs, but a test should be available for 95% of such candidates within four weeks.

5   99.8% of all candidates should be able to obtain a test booking within two months of their preferred date at the centre of their choice.

6   A refund of test fees will be issued within three weeks of a valid claim with the supporting information.

7   No more than 0.5% of tests will be cancelled by contractors (acting on behalf of DSA and DVTA).

8   All letters, including complaints, will be answered within 15 working days.

9   98% of all candidates should receive their test result within 30 minutes of completing their test.

Complaints guide for theory test candidates

DSA and DVTA aim to give their customers the best possible service. Please tell us

- when we've done well
- when you aren't satisfied.

Your comments can help us to improve the service we offer. If you have any questions about your theory test please contact DSA.

Tel: 0870 01 01 372

Fax: 0870 01 04 372.

Candidates with comments or queries about tests in Northern Ireland please contact DVTA.

Tel: 0845 6006700

Fax: 0870 01 04 372.

If you have any complaints about how your theory test was carried out, or any part of our customer service, please take up the matter with a member of staff if the circumstances allow. Alternatively you can write to the Customer Services Manager at the following address

Customer Services
Driving Theory Test
PO Box 148
Salford
M5 3SY

If you're dissatisfied with the reply you can write to the Managing Director at the same address.

If you're still not satisfied, you can take up your complaint with

The Chief Executive
Driving Standards Agency
56 Stanley House
Talbot Street
Nottingham NG1 5GU.

In Northern Ireland

The Chief Executive
Driver & Vehicle Testing Agency
Balmoral Road
Belfast BT12 6QL.

None of this removes your right to take your complaint to your Member of Parliament, who may decide to raise your case personally with the DSA or DVTA Chief Executive, the Minister or the Parliamentary Commissioner for Administration (the Ombudsman). Please refer to our leaflet 'If things go wrong.'

DSA is a Trading Fund, we are required to cover our costs from the driving test fee. We do not have a quota for test passes or fails and if you demonstrate the standard required, you will pass your test.

Compensation code for theory test candidates

DSA will normally refund the test fee, or give a free re-booking, in the following cases

- if we cancel your test
- if you cancel and give us at least three clear working days notice
- if you keep the test appointment but the test doesn't take place, or isn't finished, for a reason that isn't your fault.

We'll also repay you the expenses that you incurred on the day of the test because we cancelled your test at short notice. We'll consider reasonable claims for

- travelling to and from the test centre
- any pay or earnings you lost after tax (usually for half a day).

Please write to the address below and send a receipt showing travel costs and/or an employer's letter, which shows what earnings you lost.

DVTA has a different compensation code. If you think you're entitled to compensation write to

Customer Services
Driving Theory Test
PO Box 148
Salford
M5 3SY

This compensation code doesn't affect your existing legal rights.

Theory Test Centres in Great Britain and Northern Ireland

England

Aldershot
Barnstaple
Barrow
Basildon
Basingstoke
Bath
Berwick-Upon-Tweed
Birkenhead
Birmingham
Blackpool
Bolton
Boston
Bournemouth
Bradford
Brighton
Bristol
Bury St Edmunds
Cambridge
Canterbury
Carlisle
Chelmsford
Cheltenham
Chester
Chesterfield
Colchester
Coventry
Crawley
Derby
Doncaster
Dudley
Durham
Eastbourne
Exeter
Fareham
Gillingham
Gloucester

Grantham
Grimsby
Guildford
Harlow
Harrogate
Hastings
Hereford
Huddersfield
Hull
Ipswich
Isle of Wight
Isles of Scilly*
Kings Lynn
Leeds
Leicester
Lincoln
Liverpool

London
– Croydon
– Ilford
– Kingston
– Palmers Green
– Southwark
– Staines
– Uxbridge

Lowestoft
Luton
Manchester
Mansfield
Middlesbrough
Milton Keynes
Morpeth
Newcastle
Northampton

Norwich
Nottingham
Oldham
Oxford
Penzance
Peterborough
Plymouth
Portsmouth
Preston
Reading
Redditch
Runcorn
Salford
Salisbury
Scarborough
Scunthorpe
Sheffield
Shrewsbury
Sidcup
Slough
Solihull
Southampton
Southend on Sea
Southport
St Helens
Stevenage
Stockport
Stoke-on-Trent
Stratford Upon Avon
Sunderland
Sutton Coldfield
Swindon
Taunton
Torquay
Truro
Watford
Weymouth

Wigan
Wolverhampton
Worcester
Workington
Worthing
Yeovil
York

Scotland

Aberdeen
Ayr
Dumfries
Dundee
Dunfermline
Edinburgh
Elgin
Fort William
Gairloch
Galashiels
Glasgow N West
Glasgow Central
Greenock
Helmsdale
Huntly
Inverness
Isle of Arran
Isle of Barra
Isle of Benbecula
Isle of Islay, Bowmore
Isle of Mull Salen
Isle of Tiree
Kirkwall
Kyle of Lochalsh
Lerwick
Motherwell
Oban

Pitlochry
Portree
Stirling
Stornoway
Stranraer
Tarbert, Argyllshire
Tongue
Ullapool
Wick

Wales

Aberystwyth
Bangor
Builth Wells
Cardiff
Haverfordwest
Merthyr Tydfil
Newport
Rhyl
Swansea

Northern Ireland

Ballymena
Belfast
Londonderry
Newry
Omagh
Portadown

Essential reading from the Driving Standards Agency

Prepare for the professional tests and a new career with the official guidance ...

Driving LGVs – the Official DSA Syllabus

This book is a useful aid for new or established drivers. It is the only official manual covering this category. It contains clear, easy to understand instructions. It has been written by the Driving Standards Agency – the people who set the tests – and set out the syllabus. Information is given on applying for a licence, medical requirements, handling techniques, driving skills, environmental impact, hazard labels and regulations.

ISBN 0 11 552255 7 £14.99

Publishing June 2001

The Official Goods Vehicle Driving Video

Safe driving practice and defensive driving techniques for both new and established drivers. Covering all classes of goods vehicle above 3.5 tonnes, this video stresses how good, all round observation and sound planning can reduce accident risk. It adopts a realistic approach to meeting tight schedules whilst taking maximum care of other road users, drivers and vehicles.

ISBN 0 11 551971 8 £29.99 (INCL VAT)

Printed in The United Kingdom for The Stationery Office TJ004263 05/01 C30 63789

Driving PCVs – the Official DSA Syllabus

A companion volume to *The Official Theory Test for Drivers of Large Vehicles*, covering every aspect of driving a passenger carrying vehicle (PCV). Definitive information on the PCV practical test: everything from initial applications and the latest legislation, through to general road safety, driving attitude, First Aid and, of course, the officially recommended syllabus.

ISBN 0 11 552256 5   £14.99

Publishing June 2001

The Highway Code

The Highway Code is essential reading for everyone. It explains road traffic law and gives guidance as to best driving practice, with particular reference to vulnerable road users such as horse riders, cyclists and the elderly. The current version was prepared to reflect the changes in lifestyle and technology, giving rules for dealing with driver fatigue and recommendations about the use of mobile phones.

ISBN 0 11 552290 5   £1.49

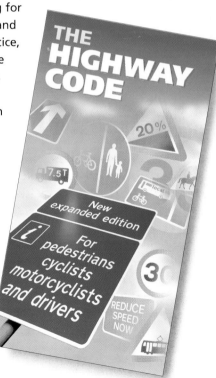

Order Form

5 easy ways to order:

- **Online:** Visit www.**clicktso**.com
- **Tel:** Please call **0870 600 5522** *quoting ref BCH*
- **Fax:** Fax this form to **0870 600 5533**
- **Post:** **The Stationery Office, PO Box 29, Norwich NR3 1GN**
- **TSO Bookshops:** Visit your local The Stationery Office Bookshop

---

Please send me the following publications:

Title	ISBN	Price	Quantity
Driving LGVs – the Official DSA Syllabus	0 11 552255 7	£14.99	....
Official Goods Vehicle Driving Video	0 11 551971 8	£29.99 (incl VAT)	....
Driving PCVs – the Official DSA Syllabus	0 11 552256 5	£14.99	....
The Highway Code	0 11 552290 5	£1.49	....

Handling charge per order: £3.00
for orders including VAT: £3.53
Total enclosed: £.................

PLEASE COMPLETE IN BLOCK CAPITALS

Name..

Address ....

....

....

.... Postcode .... ⎡ BCH ⎤

☐ I enclose a cheque for £.................. payable to: *'The Stationery Office'*

☐ Please charge to my account with The Stationery Office, No:

....

☐ Please debit my Mastercard/Visa/Amex/Diners/Connect Card Account No.

Signature.. Expiry date..................................

☐ Please send me information about relevant products and services from The Stationery Office

We can now also send you updates on your specific area of interest by e-mail. To register, visit **clicktso.com**

the **Stationery Office**

DSA DRIVING STANDARDS AGENCY SAFE DRIVING FOR LIFE